Annual Editions: Criminal Justice, 39/e

Edited by Joanne Naughton

http://create.mheducation.com

ISBN-10: 1259343677   ISBN-13: 9781259343674

Contents

Preface

In publishing *Annual Editions,* we recognize the enormous role played by the public press in providing current, first-rate information about a broad spectrum of criminal justice issues. Many of the articles in various magazines, newspapers, and journals are appropriate for students, researchers, and professionals seeking accurate, current material to help bridge the gap between principles and theories, and the real world. These articles, however, become more useful for study when those of lasting value are carefully collected, organized, indexed, and reproduced in a low-cost format, providing easy, and permanent access when the material is needed. That is the role played by *Annual Editions.*

During the 1970s, criminal justice emerged as an appealing, vital, and unique academic discipline. It emphasizes the professional development of students who plan careers in the field, and attracts those who want to know more about a complex social problem and how the United States deals with it. Criminal justice incorporates a vast range of knowledge from a number of different specialties, including law, history, and the behavioral and social sciences. Each specialty contributes to our fuller understanding of criminal behavior and of society's attitudes toward deviance.

In view of the fact that the criminal justice system is in a constant state of flux, and because the study of criminal justice covers such a broad spectrum, today's students must be aware of a variety of subjects and disciplines. Standard textbooks and traditional anthologies cannot keep pace with the changes as quickly as they occur. In fact, many such sources are already out of date the day they are published. *Annual Editions: Criminal Justice 39th Edition* strives to maintain currency in matters of concern by providing up-to-date information from the most recent literature in the criminal justice field.

This volume contains six units that treat Crime and Justice in America, Victimology, The Police, The Judicial System, Juvenile Justice, and Punishment and Corrections. The articles in these units were selected because they are informative as well as provocative. The selections are timely and useful in their treatment of ethics, punishment, juveniles, courts, police, prosecutors, and other related topics.

Also incorporated are a number of features designed to be useful to students, researchers, and professionals in the criminal justice field. They include the *Table of Contents,* setting out the titles of the articles and the units in which they can be found; *Learning Outcomes* related to the topics and issues in each article; *Critical Thinking* questions designed to spur thoughtful consideration of the ideas raised in the article; and a list of relevant *Internet References* for further investigation of the topics for each article. Finally, each unit is preceded by an overview that provides a background for informed reading of the articles.

Editor

Joanne Naughton is a former member of the NYPD, where she encountered most aspects of police work as a police officer, detective, sergeant, and lieutenant. She is also a former staff attorney with the Legal Aid Society, where she represented indigent criminal defendants. In addition to her hands-on experience in criminal justice, she was an adjunct professor at John Jay College of Criminal Justice and has retired from Mercy College where she was an assistant professor. She received her BA and JD at Fordham University.

Academic Advisory Board

Members of the Academic Advisory Board are instrumental in the final selection of articles for *Annual Editions* books. Their review of the articles for content, level, and appropriateness provides critical direction to the editor and staff. We think that you will find their careful consideration reflected here.

Kelli Callahan
Park University

Terry Campbell
Kaplan University

James Cunningham
State Fair Community College

Michael T. Eskey
Park University

Bonnie Fisher
University of Cincinnati

Barry Goodson
Columbia Southern University

Ken Haas
University of Delaware

Unit 1

UNIT

Prepared by: Joanne Naughton

Crime and Justice in America

The American justice system comprises three traditional components: police, courts, and corrections. In addition, special attention is also given to crime victims and juveniles. Crime continues to be a major problem in the United States. Court dockets are full, our prisons are overcrowded, probation, and parole caseloads are overwhelming, our police are being urged to do more, and the bulging prison population places a heavy strain on the economy of the country.

Clearly, crime is a complex problem that defies simple explanations or solutions. Although the more familiar crimes of murder, rape, assault, and drug law violations are still with us, international terrorism has become a pressing worry. The debate also continues over how to best handle juvenile offenders, sex offenders, and those who commit acts of domestic violence. The increasing prevalence of Internet crime also demands attention from the criminal justice system.

Article   Prepared by: Joanne Naughton

What Is the Sequence of Events in the Criminal Justice System?

Learning Outcomes

After reading this article, you will be able to:

- Name the agencies that make up the criminal justice system.

- State the various steps from the time someone is arrested for a crime.

The Private Sector Initiates the Response to Crime

This first response may come from individuals, families, neighborhood associations, business, industry, agriculture, educational institutions, the news media, or any other private service to the public.

It involves crime prevention as well as participation in the criminal justice process once a crime has been committed. Private crime prevention is more than providing private security or burglar alarms or participating in neighborhood watch. It also includes a commitment to stop criminal behavior by not engaging in it or condoning it when it is committed by others.

Citizens take part directly in the criminal justice process by reporting crime to the police, by being a reliable participant (for example, a witness or a juror) in a criminal proceeding and by accepting the disposition of the system as just or reasonable. As voters and taxpayers, citizens also participate in criminal justice through the policymaking process that affects how the criminal justice process operates, the resources available to it, and its goals and objectives. At every stage of the process from the original formulation of objectives to the decision about where to locate jails and prisons to the reintegration of inmates into society, the private sector has a role to play. Without such involvement, the criminal justice process cannot serve the citizens it is intended to protect.

The Response to Crime and Public Safety Involves Many Agencies and Services

Many of the services needed to prevent crime and make neighborhoods safe are supplied by noncriminal justice agencies, including agencies with primary concern for public health, education, welfare, public works, and housing. Individual citizens as well as public and private sector organizations have joined with criminal justice agencies to prevent crime and make neighborhoods safe.

Criminal Cases Are Brought by the Government Through the Criminal Justice System

We apprehend, try, and punish offenders by means of a loose confederation of agencies at all levels of government. Our American system of justice has evolved from the English common law into a complex series of procedures and decisions. Founded on the concept that crimes against an individual are crimes against the State, our justice system prosecutes individuals as though they victimized all of society. However, crime victims are involved throughout the process and many justice agencies have programs that focus on helping victims.

There is no single criminal justice system in this country. We have many similar systems that are individually unique. Criminal cases may be handled differently in different jurisdictions, but court decisions based on the due process guarantees of the U.S. Constitution require that specific steps be taken in the administration of criminal justice so that the individual will be protected from undue intervention from the State.

The description of the criminal and juvenile justice systems that follows portrays the most common sequence of events in response to serious criminal behavior.

Entry into the System

The justice system does not respond to most crime because so much crime is not discovered or reported to the police. Law enforcement agencies learn about crime from the reports of victims or other citizens, from discovery by a police officer in the field, from informants, or from investigative and intelligence work.

Once a law enforcement agency has established that a crime has been committed, a suspect must be identified and apprehended for the case to proceed through the system. Sometimes, a suspect is apprehended at the scene; however, identification of a suspect sometimes requires an extensive investigation. Often, no one is identified or apprehended. In some instances, a suspect is arrested and later the police determine that no crime was committed and the suspect is released.

Prosecution and Pretrial Services

After an arrest, law enforcement agencies present information about the case and about the accused to the prosecutor, who will decide if formal charges will be filed with the court. If no charges are filed, the accused must be released. The prosecutor can also drop charges after making efforts to prosecute (*nolle prosequi*).

A suspect charged with a crime must be taken before a judge or magistrate without unnecessary delay. At the initial appearance, the judge or magistrate informs the accused of the charges and decides whether there is probable cause to detain the accused person. If the offense is not very serious, the determination of guilt and assessment of a penalty may also occur at this stage.

Often, the defense counsel is also assigned at the initial appearance. All suspects prosecuted for serious crimes have a right to be represented by an attorney. If the court determines the suspect is indigent and cannot afford such representation, the court will assign counsel at the public's expense.

A pretrial-release decision may be made at the initial appearance, but may occur at other hearings or may be changed at another time during the process. Pretrial release and bail were traditionally intended to ensure appearance at trial. However, many jurisdictions permit pretrial detention of defendants accused of serious offenses and deemed to be dangerous to prevent them from committing crimes prior to trial.

The court often bases its pretrial decision on information about the defendant's drug use, as well as residence, employment, and family ties. The court may decide to release the accused on his/her own recognizance or into the custody of a third party after the posting of a financial bond or on the promise of satisfying certain conditions such as taking periodic drug tests to ensure drug abstinence.

In many jurisdictions, the initial appearance may be followed by a preliminary hearing. The main function of this hearing is to discover if there is probable cause to believe that the accused committed a known crime within the jurisdiction of the court. If the judge does not find probable cause, the case is dismissed; however, if the judge or magistrate finds probable cause for such a belief, or the accused waives his or her right to a preliminary hearing, the case may be bound over to a grand jury.

A grand jury hears evidence against the accused presented by the prosecutor and decides if there is sufficient evidence to cause the accused to be brought to trial. If the grand jury finds sufficient evidence, it submits to the court an indictment, a written statement of the essential facts of the offense charged against the accused.

Where the grand jury system is used, the grand jury may also investigate criminal activity generally and issue indictments called grand jury originals that initiate criminal cases. These investigations and indictments are often used in drug and conspiracy cases that involve complex organizations. After such an indictment, law enforcement tries to apprehend and arrest the suspects named in the indictment.

Misdemeanor cases and some felony cases proceed by the issuance of an information, a formal, written accusation submitted to the court by a prosecutor. In some jurisdictions, indictments may be required in felony cases. However, the accused may choose to waive a grand jury indictment and, instead, accept service of an information for the crime.

In some jurisdictions, defendants, often those without prior criminal records, may be eligible for diversion from prosecution subject to the completion of specific conditions such as drug treatment. Successful completion of the conditions may result in the dropping of charges or the expunging of the criminal record where the defendant is required to plead guilty prior to the diversion.

Adjudication

Once an indictment or information has been filed with the trial court, the accused is scheduled for arraignment. At the arraignment, the accused is informed of the charges, advised of the rights of criminal defendants, and asked to enter a plea to the charges. Sometimes, a plea of guilty is the result of negotiations between the prosecutor and the defendant.

If the accused pleads guilty or pleads *nolo contendere* (accepts penalty without admitting guilt), the judge may accept or reject the plea. If the plea is accepted, no trial is held and the offender is sentenced at this proceeding or at a later date. The plea may be rejected and proceed to trial if, for example, the judge believes that the accused may have been coerced.

If the accused pleads not guilty or not guilty by reason of insanity, a date is set for the trial. A person accused of a serious crime is guaranteed a trial by jury. However, the accused may ask for a bench trial where the judge, rather than a jury, serves as the finder of fact. In both instances the prosecution and defense present evidence by questioning witnesses while the judge decides on issues of law. The trial results in acquittal or conviction on the original charges or on lesser included offenses.

After the trial a defendant may request appellate review of the conviction or sentence. In some cases, appeals of convictions are a matter of right; all States with the death penalty provide for automatic appeal of cases involving a death sentence. Appeals may be subject to the discretion of the appellate court and may be granted only on acceptance of a defendant's petition for a *writ of certiorari*. Prisoners may also appeal their sentences through civil rights petitions and *writs of habeas corpus* where they claim unlawful detention.

Sentencing and Sanctions

After a conviction, sentence is imposed. In most cases the judge decides on the sentence, but in some jurisdictions the sentence is decided by the jury, particularly for capital offenses.

In arriving at an appropriate sentence, a sentencing hearing may be held at which evidence of aggravating or mitigating circumstances is considered. In assessing the circumstances surrounding a convicted person's criminal behavior, courts often rely on presentence investigations by probation agencies or other designated authorities. Courts may also consider victim impact statements.

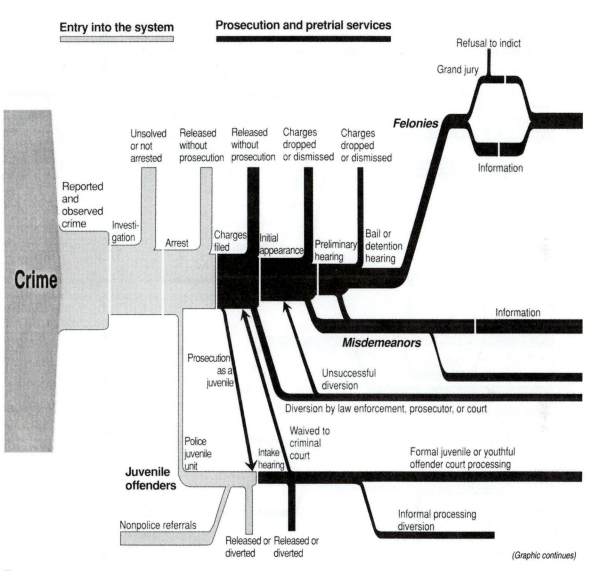

Figure 1

Note: This chart gives a simplified view of caseflow through the criminal justice system. Procedures vary among jurisdictions. The weights of the lines are not intended to show the actual size of caseloads.

The sentencing choices that may be available to judges and juries include one or more of the following:

- the death penalty
- incarceration in a prison, jail, or other confinement facility
- probation—allowing the convicted person to remain at liberty but subject to certain conditions and restrictions such as drug testing or drug restrictions such as drug testing or drug treatment
- fines—primarily applied as penalties in minor offenses
- restitution—requiring the offender to pay compensation to the victim. In some jurisdictions, offenders may be

sentenced to alternatives to incarceration that are considered more severe than straight probation but less severe than a prison term. Examples of such sanctions include boot camps, intense supervision often with drug treatment and testing, house arrest and electronic monitoring, denial of Federal benefits, and community service.

In many jurisdictions, the law mandates that persons convicted of certain types of offenses serve a prison term. Most jurisdictions permit the judge to set the sentence length within certain limits, but some have determinate sentencing laws that stipulate a specific sentence length that must be served and cannot be altered by a parole board.

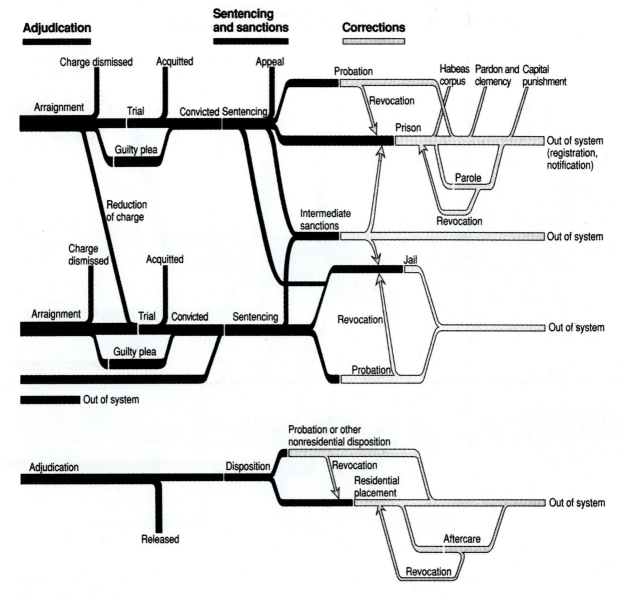

Figure 1 *(continued)*

Source: Adapted from *The challenge of crime in a free society*. President's Commission on Law Enforcement and Administration of Justice, 1967. This revision, a result of the Symposium on the 30th Anniversary of the President's Commission, was prepared by the Bureau of Justice Statistics in 1997.

Corrections

Offenders sentenced to incarceration usually serve time in a local jail or a State prison. Offenders sentenced to less than 1 year generally go to jail; those sentenced to more than 1 year go to prison. Persons admitted to the Federal system or a State prison system may be held in prison with varying levels of custody or in a community correctional facility.

A prisoner may become eligible for parole after serving a specific part of his or her sentence. Parole is the conditional release of a prisoner before the prisoner's full sentence has been served. The decision to grant parole is made by an authority such as a parole board, which has power to grant or revoke parole or to discharge a parolee altogether. The way parole decisions are made varies widely among jurisdictions.

Offenders may also be required to serve out their full sentences prior to release (expiration of term). Those sentenced under determinate sentencing laws can be released only after they have served their full sentence (mandatory release) less any "goodtime" received while in prison. Inmates get goodtime

Discretion Is Exercised throughout the Criminal Justice System

Discretion is "an authority conferred by law to act in certain conditions or situations in accordance with an official's or an official agency's own considered judgment and conscience."[1] Discretion is exercised throughout the government. It is a part of decision making in all government systems from mental health to education, as well as criminal justice. The limits of discretion vary from jurisdiction to jurisdiction.

Concerning crime and justice, legislative bodies have recognized that they cannot anticipate the range of circumstances surrounding each crime, anticipate local mores, and enact laws that clearly encompass all conduct that is criminal and all that is not.[2]

Therefore, persons charged with the day-to-day response to crime are expected to exercise their own judgment within limits set by law. Basically, they must decide—

- whether to take action
- where the situation fits in the scheme of law, rules, and precedent
- which official response is appropriate.[3]

To ensure that discretion is exercised responsibly, government authority is often delegated to professionals. Professionalism requires a minimum level of training and orientation, which guide officials in making decisions. The professionalism of policing is due largely to the desire to ensure the proper exercise of police discretion.

The limits of discretion vary from State to State and locality to locality. For example, some State judges have wide discretion in the type of sentence they may impose. In recent years, other states have sought to limit the judge's discretion in sentencing by passing mandatory sentencing laws that require prison sentences for certain offenses.

Notes

1. Roscoe Pound, "Discretion, dispensation and mitigation: The problem of the individual special case," *New York University Law Review* (1960) 35:925, 926.
2. Wayne R. LaFave, *Arrest: The decision to take a suspect into custody* (Boston: Little, Brown & Co., 1964), pp. 63–184.
3. Memorandum of June 21, 1977, from Mark Moore to James Vorenberg, "Some abstract notes on the issue of discretion."

Bureau of Justice Statistics (www.ojp.usdoj.gov/bjs/). January 1998. NCJ 167894. To order: 1-800-732-3277.

Who Exercises Discretion?

These criminal justice officials . . .	must often decide whether or not or how to—
Police	Enforce specific laws Investigate specific crimes; Search people
Prosecutors	File charges or petitions for adjudication Seek indictments Drop cases Reduce charges
Judges or magistrates	Set bail or conditions for release Accept pleas Determine delinquency Dismiss charges Impose sentence Revoke probation
Correctional officials	Assign to type of correctional facility Award privileges Punish for disciplinary infractions
Paroling authorities	Determine date and conditions of parole Revoke parole

credits against their sentences automatically or by earning them through participation in programs.

If released by a parole board decision or by mandatory release, the releasee will be under the supervision of a parole officer in the community for the balance of his or her unexpired sentence. This supervision is governed by specific conditions of release, and the releasee may be returned to prison for violations of such conditions.

Recidivism

Once the suspects, defendants, or offenders are released from the jurisdiction of a criminal justice agency, they may be processed through the criminal justice system again for a new crime. Long term studies show that many suspects who are arrested have prior criminal histories and those with a greater number of prior arrests were more likely to be arrested again. As the courts take prior criminal history into account at sentencing, most prison inmates have a prior criminal history and many have been incarcerated before. Nationally, about half the inmates released from State prison will return to prison.

The Juvenile Justice System

Juvenile courts usually have jurisdiction over matters concerning children, including delinquency, neglect, and adoption. They also handle "status offenses" such as truancy and running away, which are not applicable to adults. State statutes define which persons are under the original jurisdiction of the juvenile court. The upper age of juvenile court jurisdiction in delinquency matters is 17 in most States.

The processing of juvenile offenders is not entirely dissimilar to adult criminal processing, but there are crucial differences. Many juveniles are referred to juvenile courts by law enforcement officers, but many others are referred by school officials, social services agencies, neighbors, and even parents, for behavior or conditions that are determined to require intervention by the formal system for social control.

At arrest, a decision is made either to send the matter further into the justice system or to divert the case out of the system, often to alternative programs. Examples of alternative programs include drug treatment, individual or group counseling, or referral to educational and recreational programs.

When juveniles are referred to the juvenile courts, the court's intake department or the prosecuting attorney determines whether sufficient grounds exist to warrant filing a petition that requests an adjudicatory hearing or a request to transfer jurisdiction to criminal court. At this point, many juveniles are released or diverted to alternative programs.

All States allow juveniles to be tried as adults in criminal court under certain circumstances. In many States, the legislature *statutorily excludes* certain (usually serious) offenses from the jurisdiction of the juvenile court regardless of the age of the accused. In some States and at the Federal level under certain circumstances, prosecutors have the *discretion* to either file criminal charges against juveniles directly in criminal courts or proceed through the juvenile justice process. The juvenile court's intake department or the prosecutor may petition the juvenile court to *waive* jurisdiction to criminal court. The juvenile court also may order *referral* to criminal court for trial as adults. In some jurisdictions, juveniles processed as adults may upon conviction be sentenced to either an adult or a juvenile facility.

In those cases where the juvenile court retains jurisdiction, the case may be handled formally by filing a delinquency petition or informally by diverting the juvenile to other agencies or programs in lieu of further court processing.

If a petition for an adjudicatory hearing is accepted, the juvenile may be brought before a court quite unlike the court with jurisdiction over adult offenders. Despite the considerable discretion associated with juvenile court proceedings, juveniles are afforded many of the due-process safeguards associated with adult criminal trials. Several States permit the use of juries in juvenile courts; however, in light of the U.S. Supreme Court holding that juries are not essential to juvenile hearings, most States do not make provisions for juries in juvenile courts.

In disposing of cases, juvenile courts usually have far more discretion than adult courts. In addition to such options as probation, commitment to a residential facility, restitution, or fines, State laws grant juvenile courts the power to order removal of children from their homes to foster homes or treatment facilities. Juvenile courts also may order participation in special programs aimed at shoplifting prevention, drug counseling, or driver education.

Once a juvenile is under juvenile court disposition, the court may retain jurisdiction until the juvenile legally becomes an adult (at age 21 in most States). In some jurisdictions, juvenile offenders may be classified as youthful offenders, which can lead to extended sentences.

Following release from an institution, juveniles are often ordered to a period of aftercare that is similar to parole supervision for adult offenders. Juvenile offenders who violate the conditions of aftercare may have their aftercare revoked, resulting in being recommitted to a facility. Juveniles who are classified as youthful offenders and violate the conditions of aftercare may be subject to adult sanctions.

The Governmental Response to Crime Is Founded in the Intergovernmental Structure of the United States

Under our form of government, each State and the Federal Government has its own criminal justice system. All systems must respect the rights of individuals set forth in court interpretation of the U.S. Constitution and defined in case law.

State constitutions and laws define the criminal justice system within each State and delegate the authority and responsibility for criminal justice to various jurisdictions, officials, and institutions. State laws also define criminal behavior and groups of children or acts under jurisdiction of the juvenile courts.

Municipalities and counties further define their criminal justice systems through local ordinances that proscribe the local agencies responsible for criminal justice processing that were not established by the State.

Congress has also established a criminal justice system at the Federal level to respond to Federal crimes such as bank robbery, kidnaping, and transporting stolen goods across State lines.

The Response to Crime Is Mainly a State and Local Function

Very few crimes are under exclusive Federal jurisdiction. The responsibility to respond to most crime rests with State and local governments. Police protection is primarily a function of cities and towns. Corrections is primarily a function of State governments. Most justice personnel are employed at the local level.

Critical Thinking

1. Explain discretion and how it is exercised in the criminal justice system.
2. What are the steps that follow once a suspect is arrested by police and charged with a crime?
3. How are young people who violate the law treated?

Create Central

www.mhhe.com/createcentral

Internet References

Bureau of Justice Statistics
    www.bjs.gov/content/justsys.cfm

The National Center for Victims of Crime
    www.victimsofcrime.org/help-for-crime-victims/get-help-bulletins-for-crime-victims/the-criminal-justice-system

U.S. Department of Justice, 1998.

Article   Prepared by: Joanne Naughton

Can a Jury Believe What It Sees?

Videotaped Confessions Can Be Misleading

Jennifer L. Mnookin

Learning Outcomes

After reading this article, you will be able to:

- Discuss the advantages of videotaping confessions of criminal suspects.
- Explain what recent research shows about such recordings.

Los Angeles—Last week the FBI, the Drug Enforcement Administration and other federal law enforcement agencies instituted a policy of recording interrogations of criminal suspects held in custody. Only a minority of states and local governments have a similar requirement, but the new rule, which applies to nearly every federal interrogation, will most likely spur more jurisdictions to follow suit. It's not far-fetched to think that such recordings may soon become standard police practice nationwide.

Supporters of the practice present recordings as a solution for a host of problems, from police misconduct to false confessions. But while there are lots of good reasons to require them, they are hardly a panacea; in fact, the very same qualities that make them useful—their seeming vividness and objectivity—also risk making them misleading, and possibly even an inadvertent tool for injustice.

Support for electronic recording has been accelerating in recent years, and its backers now come from all sides of the criminal-justice process. Though some in law enforcement remain critical of the idea, firsthand experience with recording tends to turn law enforcers into supporters—it eliminates uncertainty about police conduct and lets investigators focus on the interrogation rather than taking detailed notes.

Likewise, criminal prosecutors find that when a defendant confesses or provides incriminating information, the video offers vivid and powerful evidence. At the same time, it aids defendants because the very presence of the camera is likely to reduce the use of coercive or unfair tactics in interrogation, and documents illegitimate behavior if and when it does occur. And a recording provides judges and juries with information about what took place in a more objective form.

Given this chorus of support, what's not to like?

The short answer is that, according to recent research, interrogation recording may in fact be too vivid and persuasive. Even seemingly neutral recordings still require interpretation. As advertisers and Hollywood directors know well, camera angles, close-ups, lenses, and dozens of other techniques shape our perception of what we see without our being aware of it.

In a series of experiments led by the psychologist G. Daniel Lassiter of Ohio University, mock juries were shown exactly the same interrogation, but some saw only the defendant, while others had a wider-angle view that included the interrogator. When the interrogator isn't shown on camera, jurors are significantly less likely to find an interrogation coercive, and more likely to believe in the truth and accuracy of the confession that they hear—even when the interrogator explicitly threatens the defendant.

Professor Lassiter and other psychologists have consistently shown this "camera perspective bias" across a substantial series of experiments, finding in one study that even professionals like judges and police interrogators are not immune.

Experiments like these feed a larger concern: whether the police, prosecutors, defense lawyers, judges, or jurors can actually tell the difference between true and false confessions, even with the more complete record of interactions that recorded interrogations provide.

We know that false confessions really do occur, even in very serious crimes, and probably more frequently than most people expect. But why? We know something about certain interrogation techniques, as well as defendant vulnerabilities like youth

Can a Jury Believe What It Sees? Videotaped Confessions Can Be Misleading by Jennifer L. Mnookin

13

or mental disability, that may create heightened risks for false confessions. But we don't yet know enough about the psychology of false confessions to be able to accurately "diagnose" the reliability of a given confession just by watching it.

The problem is that many of the red flags that frequently occur in false confessions—like unusually long interrogations, the inclusion of inaccurate details, or the police "feeding" some crime-related information to the suspect—can also occur in the confessions of the guilty. This means there's no surefire way to tell false confessions and true confessions apart by viewing a recording, except in extreme cases.

And yet by making confessions so vivid to juries, recording could paper over such complications, and sometimes even make the problem worse. The emotional impact of a suspect declaring his guilt out loud, on video, is powerful and hard to dislodge, even if the defense attorney points out reasons to doubt its accuracy.

This doesn't mean that mandating recording of interrogations is a bad idea. Routine recording will serve to make them fairer and less coercive—and this might well help reduce the number of false confessions.

But we need to recognize that by itself, video recording cannot stop all the problems with interrogations, prevent false confessions or guarantee that we will spot them when they do occur.

We are still a long way from fully understanding why the innocent confess during interrogations, and why we believe them when they do—regardless of what we see on camera.

Critical Thinking

1. What are some factors that may create heightened risks for false confessions?

2. Describe Lassiter's work regarding confessions.

3. How can false confessions be distinguished from valid ones?

Internet References

IZA
  ftp.iza.org
U.S. Department of Justice
  www.justice.gov

JENNIFER L. MNOOKIN is a professor of law at the University of California, Los Angeles.

Article   Prepared by: Joanne Naughton

Maze of Gun Laws in U.S. Hurts Gun Control Efforts

EILEEN SULLIVAN

Learning Outcomes

After reading this article, you will be able to:

- Appreciate the difficulty of regulating guns in the United States.
- Describe the roadblock created by Congressional opposition to new gun laws.

There is a legal avenue to try to get any gun you want somewhere in the U.S., thanks to the maze of gun statutes across the country and the lack of certain federal laws.

That undermines gun-control efforts in communities with tougher gun laws—and pushes advocates of tighter controls to seek a federal standard. Gun rights proponents say enforcing all existing laws makes more sense than passing new ones.

An Associated Press analysis found that there are thousands of laws, rules and regulations at the local, county, state and federal levels. The laws and rules vary by state, and even within states, according to a 2011 compilation of state gun laws by the Bureau of Alcohol, Tobacco, Firearms and Explosives.

These laws and regulations govern who can carry a firearm, what kind of firearm is legal, the size of ammunition magazines, and more. In some places, a person can buy as many guns as desired.

Not only can people acquire military-style assault weapons, they can also get gangster-style Tommy guns, World War II-era bazookas and even sawed-off shotguns.

"If you regulate something on the local or state level, you are still a victim to guns coming into other localities or states," said Laura Cutilletta, a senior staff attorney at the California-based Law Center to Prevent Gun Violence.

In California, most guns come from Nevada, where there is almost no regulation of firearms, Cutilletta said, and in Arizona, gun owners don't need a permit.

President Barack Obama earlier this month announced a $500 million plan to tighten federal gun laws. The December shooting massacre in Newtown, Conn., that killed 20 children and six adults at an elementary school launched the issue of gun control policy to a national focus not seen in decades.

Obama is urging Congress to pass new laws, some of which would set a minimum standard for the types of firearms and ammunition that are commercially available. Sen. Dianne Feinstein, D-Calif., on Thursday said she was introducing a new assault weapons ban.

The powerful gun lobby says the problem lies in enforcement of existing laws.

"Which begs the question: Why are we putting more laws on the books if we're not enforcing the laws we already have on the books?" said Andrew Arulanandam, spokesman for the National Rifle Association.

New gun laws will face tough opposition in Congress, particularly from members who rely on the NRA during election campaigns. The NRA contributed more than $700,000 to members of Congress during the 2012 election cycle, according to the Center for Responsive Politics.

Recognizing the opposition in Congress, states already are passing their own new gun laws while officials from some states are promising to ignore any new federal mandates. As the national debate on gun control and Second Amendment rights escalates, the terms being used won't mean the same thing everywhere, due to the thousands of laws, rules and regulations across the country.

"The patchwork of laws in many ways means that the laws are only as effective as the weakest law there is," said Gene Voegtlin of the International Association of Chiefs of Police. "Those that are trying to acquire firearms and may not be able to do that by walking into their local gun shop will try to find a way to do that. This patchwork of laws allows them to seek out the weak links and acquire weapons."

Obama wants to address this, in part, by passing federal gun-trafficking laws that carry heavy penalties. It's difficult to crack down on trafficking because the penalties are too low to serve as a deterrent, and federal prosecutors decline many cases because of a lack of evidence. For instance, in order to charge someone with willfully participating in a business of selling firearms without a license, the ATF needs to prove that the guns were not sold out of the suspect's private collection, the Justice Department inspector general has said.

Obama has also called for a new federal law banning magazines that carry more than 10 rounds of ammunition—a measure that was in effect during the previous assault weapons ban, between 1994 and 2004. High-capacity magazines have been used in recent deadly mass shootings, including those in Newtown, and in the suburban Denver movie theater attack last summer.

A high-capacity ammunition magazine means different things in different places.

In California, considered by many to have some of the strongest gun laws in the country, a large-capacity magazine is one that holds more than 10 rounds. In Illinois there is no state law regarding magazines. Yet, there are laws regarding magazines in Chicago where the threshold is more than 12 rounds. But about 40 miles away in Aurora, Ill., this type of magazine is called a large-capacity ammunition feeding device and means anything more than 15 rounds.

In 44 states, including Arizona, Colorado, Connecticut, Texas and Virginia where these magazines have been used in deadly mass shootings, there are no laws against using them, according to a 2012 analysis by the Law Center to Prevent Gun Violence. If a federal law banned magazines that hold more than 10 rounds, it would become the minimum standard.

The definition of "assault weapon" also varies. There is no federal definition of an assault weapon, and the meaning of the term is inconsistent even within the gun industry. California defines an assault weapon as a "firearm (that) has such a high rate of fire and capacity for fire-power that its function as a legitimate sports or recreational firearm is substantially outweighed by the danger that it can be used to kill and injure human beings." The law specifically lists 60 rifles, 14 pistols and five shotguns. Neighboring states Nevada and Arizona have no assault weapon restrictions.

Federal law does not prohibit the ownership of any weapon, said Ginger Colbrun, a Bureau of Alcohol, Tobacco, Firearms and Explosives spokeswoman in Washington. In order to buy or own certain firearms, including automatic weapons, machine guns and bazookas, people do have to apply for permission from the federal government. But as long as the application for a restricted firearm is approved, and there is no state law barring ownership of that type of gun, it's legal.

"There is such a variation in the number of laws that regulate the distribution of guns that there is no adequate minimum standard," said Richard Aborn, president of the New York-based Citizens Crime Commission. "The federal government has an obligation to establish at least minimum standards that have to be complied with before a gun can be sold anywhere in America."

Critical Thinking

1. What kind of gun laws would be most effective at controlling gun violence?
2. Would federal definitions be beneficial?

Create Central

www.mhhe.com/createcentral

Internet References

Bureau of Alcohol, Tobacco, Firearms and Explorsives
www.atf.gov
Law Center to Prevent Gun Violence
http://smartgunlaws.org

Article   Prepared by: Joanne Naughton

Teen Marijuana Use Remains Flat Nationwide As More States Legalize

Matt Ferner

Learning Outcomes

After reading this article, you will be able to:

- Show what change, if any, in marijuana use among U.S. high school students had occurred from 2011 to 2013.

- Show what change, if any, in cigarette and alcohol use among U.S. high school students has occurred since 1991.

As marijuana's national popularity continues to grow and more states have legalized either medical or recreational use of it, a new federal survey shows that those shifting attitudes have not produced a surge in teen use.

The biennial High School Youth Risk Behavior Surveillance System survey from the Centers for Disease Control and Prevention revealed that the rate of marijuana use among U.S. high school students remained virtually unchanged from 2011 to 2013. It's also about 3 percent less than the peak of teen marijuana use in 1999, when nearly 27 percent of teens said they had recently used marijuana, according to the CDC data.

In 2013, 23.4 percent of American high-school-aged teens used marijuana one or more times in the 30 days before the survey, the data show. That's nearly even with 23.1 percent in 2011.

From 2011 to 2013, five more states—Delaware, Connecticut, Massachusetts, Illinois, and New Hampshire—legalized marijuana for medical use. Currently, 22 states and the District of Columbia have legal medical cannabis programs. Also during that period, Colorado and Washington state became the first two states in the nation to legalize recreational marijuana.

The CDC's findings are similar to those in a recent report published in the *Journal of Adolescent Health,* which compared 20 years of CDC YRBS data about high school teens' marijuana habits in states that have legalized medical marijuana compared with neighboring states that continue to ban the plant. It found that legalization of marijuana for medical purposes did not result in greater illicit use of the substance by high school students.

The YRBS data also showed that the rate of alcohol and cigarette use by U.S. teens has been steadily declining since 1991 when about 50 percent of high school students had at least one drink of alcohol and 27 percent had smoked a cigarette on at least one day during the 30 days before the survey.

Both cigarettes and alcohol are of course legal and regulated for adults, and Marijuana Policy Project's Mason Tvert suggests this data may show that the legal regulation of marijuana could also help curb teen use.

"Rates of teen alcohol and cigarette use have dropped, and we didn't have to arrest any adults for using them," Tvert said. "We could see the same results by regulating marijuana. Regulation works."

Unfortunately, the CDC survey did not report specific Colorado or Washington data in 2013, so a localized look at how recreational marijuana laws are affecting those state populations is not available.

Data was available for Colorado from 2009 to 2011, during a period of rapid medical marijuana dispensary expansion in the state, which ballooned to around 500 shops statewide. That data showed Colorado high school students' marijuana use decreased by nearly 3 percent.

Critical Thinking

1. How were the changes in cigarette and alcohol consumption by U.S. teens accomplished?
2. Could marijuana use by U.S. teens be affected in the same way?

Internet References

Centers for Disease Control and Prevention
   nccd.cdc.gov/youthonline/app/results
IZA
   ftp.iza.org
Journal of Adolescent Health
   www.jahonline.org

Article   Prepared by: Joanne Naughton

An About-Face on Crime

CHARLIE SAVAGE AND ERICA GOODE

Learning Outcomes

After reading this article, you will be able to:

- Explain how fear of crime has caused some policing tactics to go too far.
- Show how mandatory minimum sentence laws came about.

Two decisions Monday, one by a federal judge in New York and the other by Attorney General Eric H. Holder Jr., were powerful signals that the pendulum has swung away from the tough-on-crime policies of a generation ago. Those policies have been denounced as discriminatory and responsible for explosive growth in the prison population.

Critics have long contended that draconian mandatory minimum sentence laws for low-level drug offenses, as well as stop-and-frisk police policies that target higher-crime and minority neighborhoods, have a disproportionate impact on members of minority groups. On Monday, Mr. Holder announced that federal prosecutors would no longer invoke the sentencing laws, and a judge found that stop-and-frisk practices in New York were unconstitutional racial profiling.

While the timing was a coincidence, Barbara Arnwine, the president of the Lawyers Committee for Civil Rights Under Law, said that the effect was "historic, groundbreaking, and potentially game-changing."

"I thought that the most important significance of both events was the sense of enough is enough," said Ms. Arnwine, who attended the speech in San Francisco where Mr. Holder unveiled the new Justice Department policy. "It's a feeling that this is the moment to make needed change. This just can't continue, this level of extreme heightened injustice in our policing, our law enforcement and our criminal justice system."

A generation ago, amid a crack epidemic, state and federal lawmakers enacted a wave of tough-on-crime measures that resulted in an 800 percent increase in the number of prisoners in the United States, even as the population grew by only a third. The spike in prisoners centered on an increase in the number of African-American and Hispanic men convicted of drug crimes; blacks are about six times as likely as whites to be incarcerated.

But the crack wave has long since passed and violent crime rates have plummeted to four-decade lows, in the process reducing crime as a salient political issue. Traditionally conservative states, driven by a need to save money on building and maintaining prisons, have taken the lead in scaling back policies of mass incarceration. Against that backdrop, the move away from mandatory sentences and Judge Shira A. Scheindlin's ruling on stop-and-frisk practices signaled that a course correction on two big criminal justice issues that disproportionately affect minorities has finally been made, according to the advocates who have pushed for those changes.

"I think that there is a sea change now of thinking around the impact of over-incarceration and selective enforcement in our criminal justice system on racial minorities," said Vanita Gupta of the American Civil Liberties Union. "These are hugely significant and symbolic events, because we would not have either of these even five years ago."

Michelle Alexander, an Ohio State University law professor who wrote "The New Jim Crow: Mass Incarceration in the Age of Colorblindness," an influential 2010 book about the racial impact of policies like stop-and-frisk and mandatory minimum drug sentences, said the two developments gave her a sense of "cautious optimism."

"For those of us who have become increasingly alarmed over the years at the millions of lives that have been wasted due to the drug war and the types of police tactics that have been deployed in the get-tough-on-crime movement, today's announcements give us fresh hope that there is, in fact, a growing public consensus that the path that we, the nation, have been on for the past 40 years has been deeply misguided and has caused far more harm and suffering than it has prevented," she said.

But not everyone was celebrating. William G. Otis, a former federal prosecutor and an adjunct professor at Georgetown Law School, described Mr. Holder's move as a victory for drug dealers that would incentivize greater sales of addictive contraband, and he suggested that the stop-and-frisk ruling could be overturned on appeal.

Mr. Otis also warned that society was becoming "complacent" and forgetting that the drug and sentencing policies enacted over the last three decades had contributed to the falling crime rates.

Yet Chuck Wexler, executive director of the Police Executive Research Forum, a Washington-based research group, said many police chiefs agreed that it was time to rethink mandatory sentencing for low-level drug offenses. And he said departments across the country would examine the stop-and-frisk ruling in New York "to see if their practices pass muster."

But he added: "You can't get away from the fact that in most large cities, crime is concentrated in poor areas which are predominantly minority. The question becomes, what tactics are acceptable in those communities to reduce crime? And there is a trade-off between the tactics that may be used and the issue of fairness."

David Rudovsky, a civil rights lawyer in Philadelphia who has been involved in a lawsuit over stop-and-frisk in that city, said both Holder's announcement and the ruling were "part of a national re-examination of criminal justice policy that has been spurred for the last 40 years by a fear of crime."

As that fear has lessened, he added, there has been more room to be heard for critics who say that some policies have gone too far and may be counterproductive. Those critics cite the low rate of finding guns with stop-and-frisk actions, and say that the experience of being searched—and the consequences if drugs are discovered—alienate people in targeted communities, making them less willing to give the police information about more serious violent crimes.

"There was the thought that if we stop, frisk, arrest and incarcerate huge numbers of people, that will reduce crime," Rudovsky said. "But while that may have had some effect on crime, the negative parts outweighed the positive parts."

Critics have argued that aggressive policing in minority neighborhoods can distort overall crime statistics. Federal data show, for example, that black Americans were nearly four times as likely as whites to be arrested on charges of marijuana possession in 2010, even though the two groups used the drug at similar rates.

"There is just as much drugs going on in the Upper East Side of New York or Cleveland Park in D.C.," said Jamie Fellner, a specialist on race and criminal drug law enforcement for Human Rights Watch, citing predominantly affluent and white neighborhoods. "But that is not where police are doing their searches for drugs."

Alfred Blumstein, a Carnegie Mellon professor who has studied race and incarceration issues, said Mr. Holder's speech and Judge Scheindlin's stop-and-frisk ruling both addressed policies that "were attempts to stop crime, but they weren't terribly effective."

Together, he said, the events indicated that society was "trying to become more effective and more targeted and, in the process, to reduce the heavy impact on particularly African-Americans."

Critical Thinking

1. What's wrong with the tough-on-crime policies of a generation ago?
2. Do you believe William Otis's warning is valid?

Create Central

www.mhhe.com/createcentral

Internet References

Drug War Facts
www.drugwarfacts.org/cms/Mandatory_Minimum_Sentencing#sthash.Jl4rCKxz.dpbs

The Sentencing Project
www.sentencingproject.org/detail/news.cfm?news_id=1659

Article   Prepared by: Joanne Naughton

The Injustice of Marijuana Arrests

Jesse Wegman

Learning Outcomes

After reading this article, you will be able to:

- Enumerate some of the costs of arresting people for violating marijuana laws.

- Describe what is meant by racial disparity in the enforcement of drug laws.

- State some of the lifelong consequences that can occur as a result of a marijuana conviction.

America's four-decade war on drugs is responsible for many casualties, but the criminalization of marijuana has been perhaps the most destructive part of that war. The toll can be measured in dollars—billions of which are thrown away each year in the aggressive enforcement of pointless laws. It can be measured in years—whether wasted behind bars or stolen from a child who grows up fatherless. And it can be measured in lives—those damaged if not destroyed by the shockingly harsh consequences that can follow even the most minor offenses.

In October 2010, Bernard Noble, a 45-year-old trucker and father of seven with two previous nonviolent offenses, was stopped on a New Orleans street with a small amount of marijuana in his pocket. His sentence: more than 13 years.

At least he will be released. Jeff Mizanskey, a Missouri man, was arrested in December 1993, for participating (unknowingly, he said) in the purchase of a five-pound brick of marijuana. Because he had two prior nonviolent marijuana convictions, he was sentenced to life without parole.

Outrageously long sentences are only part of the story. The hundreds of thousands of people who are arrested each year but do not go to jail also suffer; their arrests stay on their records for years, crippling their prospects for jobs, loans, housing and benefits. These are disproportionately people of color, with marijuana criminalization hitting black communities the hardest.

Meanwhile, police departments that presumably have far more important things to do waste an enormous amount of time and taxpayer money chasing a drug that two states have already legalized and that a majority of Americans believe should be legal everywhere.

A Costly, Futile Strategy The absurdity starts on the street, with a cop and a pair of handcuffs. As the war on drugs escalated through the 1980s and 1990s, so did the focus on common, low-level offenses—what became known as "broken windows" policing. In New York City, where the strategy was introduced and remains popular today, the police made fewer than 800 marijuana arrests in 1991. In 2010, they made more than 59,000.

Nationwide, the numbers are hardly better. From 2001 to 2010, the police made more than 8.2 million marijuana arrests; almost 9 in 10 were for possession alone. In 2011, there were more arrests for marijuana possession than for all violent crimes put together.

The costs of this national obsession, in both money and time, are astonishing. Each year, enforcing laws on possession costs more than $3.6 billion, according to the American Civil Liberties Union. It can take a police officer many hours to arrest and book a suspect. That person will often spend a night or more in the local jail, and be in court multiple times to resolve the case. The public-safety payoff for all this effort is meager at best: According to a 2012 Human Rights Watch report that tracked 30,000 New Yorkers with no prior convictions when they were arrested for marijuana possession, 90 percent had no subsequent felony convictions. Only 3.1 percent committed a violent offense.

The strategy is also largely futile. After three decades, criminalization has not affected general usage; about 30 million Americans use marijuana every year. Meanwhile, police forces across the country are strapped for cash, and the more resources they devote to enforcing marijuana laws, the less they have to go after serious, violent crime. According to FBI. data, more than half of all violent crimes nationwide, and four in five property crimes, went unsolved in 2012.

The Racial Disparity The sheer volume of law enforcement resources devoted to marijuana is bad enough. What makes the situation far worse is racial disparity. Whites and blacks use marijuana at roughly the same rates; on average, however, blacks are 3.7 times more likely than whites to be arrested for possession, according to a comprehensive 2013 report by the ACLU.

In Iowa, blacks are 8.3 times more likely to be arrested, and in the worst-offending counties in the country, they are up to 30 times more likely to be arrested. The war on drugs aims its firepower overwhelmingly at African-Americans on the street, while white users smoke safely behind closed doors.

Only about 6 percent of marijuana cases lead to a felony conviction; the rest are often treated as misdemeanors resulting in fines or probation, if the charges aren't dismissed completely. Even so, every arrest ends up on a person's record, whether or not it leads to prosecution and conviction. Particularly in poorer minority neighborhoods, where young men are more likely to be outside and repeatedly targeted by law enforcement, these arrests accumulate. Before long a person can have an extensive "criminal history" that consists only of marijuana misdemeanors and dismissed cases. That criminal history can then influence the severity of punishment for a future offense, however insignificant.

While the number of people behind bars solely for possessing or selling marijuana seems relatively small—20,000 to 30,000 by the most recent estimates, or roughly 1 percent of America's 2.4 million inmates—that means nothing to people, like Jeff Mizanskey, who are serving breathtakingly long terms because their records contained minor previous offenses. Nor does it mean anything to the vast majority of these inmates who have no history of violence (about nine in 10, according to a 2006 study). And as with arrests, the racial disparity is vast: Blacks are more than 10 times as likely as whites to go to prison for drug offenses. For those on probation or parole for any offense, a failed drug test on its own can lead to prison time—which means, again, that people can be put behind bars for smoking marijuana.

Even if a person never goes to prison, the conviction itself is the tip of the iceberg. In a majority of states, marijuana convictions—including those resulting from guilty pleas—can have lifelong consequences for employment, education, immigration status, and family life.

A misdemeanor conviction can lead to, among many other things, the revocation of a professional license; the suspension of a driver's license; the inability to get insurance, a mortgage or other bank loans; the denial of access to public housing; and the loss of student financial aid.

In some states, a felony conviction can result in a lifetime ban on voting, jury service, or eligibility for public benefits like food stamps. People can be fired from their jobs because of a marijuana arrest. Even if a judge eventually throws the case out, the arrest record is often available online for a year, free for any employer to look up.

Correcting an Old Inequity As recently as the mid-1970s, politicians and the public generally agreed that marijuana abuse was handled better by treatment than by prosecution and incarceration. Jimmy Carter ran for president and won while supporting decriminalization. But that view lost out as the war on drugs broadened and intensified, sweeping marijuana along with it.

In recent years, public acceptance of marijuana has grown significantly. Thirty-five states and the District of Columbia now permit some form of medical marijuana, and Colorado and Washington fully legalized it for recreational use in 2012. And yet even as "ganjapreneurs" scramble to take economic advantage, thousands of people remain behind bars, or burdened by countless collateral punishments that prevent them from full and active membership in society.

In a March interview, Michelle Alexander, a law professor whose book, *The New Jim Crow,* articulated the drug war's deeper costs to black men in particular, noted the cruel paradox at play in Colorado and Washington. She pointed to "40 years of impoverished black kids getting prison time for selling weed, and their families and futures destroyed," and said, "Now, white men are planning to get rich doing precisely the same thing?"

As pioneers in legalization, those two states should set a further example by providing relief to people convicted of crimes that are no longer crimes, including overturning convictions. A recent ruling by a Colorado appeals court overturned two 2011 convictions because of the changed law, and the state's Legislature has enacted laws in the last 2 years to give courts more power to seal records of drug convictions and to make it easier for defendants to get jobs and housing after a conviction. These are both important steps into an uncharted future.

Critical Thinking

1. Inasmuch as the number of people incarcerated solely for possessing or selling marijuana is relatively small, why should we be concerned?

2. How do some of the "collateral punishments" for drug law violations prevent people from full and active membership in society?

3. What effect has enforcing marijuana laws had, nationwide, on the ability of police departments to solve violent crime and property crimes in 2012?

Internet References

ACLU
www.aclu.org/files/assets/1114413-mj-report-rfs-rel1.pdf#77

Drug Policy Alliance
www.drugpolicy.org/news/2014/louisianan-given-13-year-sentence-possession-two-marijuana-cigarettes

River Front Times
rftblogs.riverfronttimes.com/dailyrft/2013missouri_man_serving_life_in_p.php

Article

Prepared by: Joanne Naughton

Eric Holder Warns About America's Disturbing Attempts at Precrime

PETER SUDERMAN

Learning Outcomes

After reading this article, you will be able to:

- Illustrate the concept of precrime.

- Explain Holder's position on programs that attempt to offer risk assessments of offenders.

- Show that, although race could not be an explicit factor, it could be built into a system implicitly.

The premise of the 2002 science fiction movie *Minority Report* was that police in a near-future Washington, DC had developed an innovative system to stop crime before it happens. The system, called precrime, was based on the visions of a trio of psychics who could sense criminal activity shortly before it happened. That allowed cops to arrive on the scene and preemptively arrest offenders. It was the end of crime in the District, with criminals apprehended just before they could offend.

America doesn't quite practice precrime yet, but in several states it's edging closer. One difference between the reality and the movie is that instead of psychics we use actuaries.

States such as Pennsylvania, Virginia, and Missouri have developed programs that attempt to offer risk assessments of offenders. Those risk assessments, which are based on a variety of factors including age, education level, and neighborhood of residence as well as past criminality, are meant to guide judges in sentencing. The explicit goal is to reduce future instances of criminality, which means that instead of sentencing people for crime already committed, sentences based on these risk assessments are instead sentencing people for crimes that they, or people like them, might commit.

In a speech last week to the National Association of Criminal Defense Lawyers (which *Reason*'s Jacob Sullum previously noted here), Attorney General Eric Holder warned against the use of such risk assessments:

> *When it comes to front-end applications—such as sentencing decisions, where a handful of states are now attempting to employ this methodology—we need to be sure the use of aggregate data analysis won't have unintended consequences.*

> *Here in Pennsylvania and elsewhere, legislators have introduced the concept of "risk assessments" that seek to assign a probability to an individual's likelihood of committing future crimes and, based on those risk assessments, make sentencing determinations. Although these measures were crafted with the best of intentions, I am concerned that they may inadvertently undermine our efforts to ensure individualized and equal justice. By basing sentencing decisions on static factors and immutable characteristics—like the defendant's education level, socioeconomic background, or neighborhood—they may exacerbate unwarranted and unjust disparities that are already far too common in our criminal justice system and in our society.*

> *Criminal sentences must be based on the facts, the law, the actual crimes committed, the circumstances surrounding each individual case, and the defendant's history of criminal conduct. They should not be based on unchangeable factors that a person cannot control, or on the possibility of a future crime that has not taken place. Equal justice can only mean individualized justice, with charges, convictions, and sentences befitting the conduct of each defendant and the particular crime he or she commits.*

It's not hard to understand the surface appeal of such tools to policymakers. It looks reasonable. It feels scientific. The goal is to identify likely reoffenders and prevent them from committing a second crime. As a 2011 article in the *Federal Sentencing Reporter* put it, it's a shift away from the traditional "backward-looking retributive approach" toward a "formalized, forward-looking, utilitarian" goal.

But Holder is right to be concerned about what is, in effect, a kind of actuarial profiling.

It's a troubling approach. Individuals should be sentenced based on what they have done, not what they might do, and especially not what other members of some group they belong to are likely, on average, to do.

The latter issue is particularly worrying. If a risk assessment recommends longer sentences for people from a particular neighborhood, and a judge follows that recommendation, then the result is effectively to sentence an individual for what his or her neighbors have done.

Even if this approach can be shown to prevent some types or instances of crime, that's not how a criminal justice system is supposed to work. By a roughly similar logic, we could lock up everyone—or even just everyone with the right risk profile, regardless of what crimes they have or have not already committed—from a high crime neighborhood, and call it a success when crime goes down.

Indeed, the same reasoning could lead to support for explicitly race-based sentencing. As a report on Virginia's risk assessment model notes, the state sentencing commission settled on 11 different identifiers to use in determining an offender's risk profile. In the end, race was explicitly excluded from the model, but in the initial analysis, it was "strongly significant" as a factor.

If you follow the "forward-looking utilitarian" logic of the idea to its ugly end, then it's all too easy to imagine a system that explicitly singles out certain races for harsher sentences, not because of the individual particulars of the crime in question, but because of the aggregate actions of other people who share that person's race.

Now, as Virginia's guidelines also suggest, it's unlikely that any state would ever decide to make race an explicit factor. And if that did happen, it's virtually certain that the courts wouldn't let it stand. But even if race is never made an explicit factor, it could be built into the system implicitly, with nonrace identifiers that have the practical effect of singling out certain races. (It's worth noting that there's already some evidence that, intentionally or not, prosecutors end up offering harsher plea deals to minorities.)

If anything, then, it's a system that could lead to something worse than the psychic-powered precrime of *Minority Report*. In the movie, cops targeted specific individuals who were just hours or minutes from committing a crime. Under a system that relied heavily on the sort of data-driven sentencing that Holder describes in his speech, we'd be targeting not individuals so much as large groups of people, and punishing them for what other people who they resemble have done, or might possibly do, months or years in the future.

Critical Thinking

1. What's wrong with programs that seek to determine who is likely to commit crimes, if they can be shown to prevent some types of crimes?

2. Do you believe it makes good sense for a judge to be able to sentence a guilty person from a high crime neighborhood to a longer sentence than someone from another neighborhood?

Internet References

Reason.com

reason.com/blog/2014/08/01/eric-holder-says-mandatory- minimums-are

The National Center for State Courts

www.vcsc.virginia.gov/risk_off_rept.pdf

U.S. Department of Justice

www.justice.gov/opa/speech/attorney-general-eric-holder-speaks-national-association-criminal-defense-lawyers-57th

Vera Institute of Justice

www.vera.org/pubs/special/race-and-prosecution-manhattan

Unit 2

UNIT

Victimology

Prepared by: Joanne Naughton

For many years, crime victims were not considered to be an important topic for criminological study. Now, however, criminologists consider that focusing on victims and victimization is essential to understanding the phenomenon of crime. The popularity of this area of study can be attributed to the early work of several criminologists such as Hans von Hentig and, later, Stephen Schafer, who examined victim-offender interactions and stressed reciprocal influences and role reversals.

Victimology focuses on the relationship of the victim to the criminal offender: whether they were strangers, mere acquaintances, friends, family members, or even intimates; and why a particular person or place was targeted.

The victim's role in the criminal justice process has received increasing attention from a growing number of criminologists in recent years, and as more criminologists focus their attention on the victim's role in the process, victimology will take on even greater importance.

Article _____   Prepared by: Joanne Naughton

Telling the Truth about Damned Lies and Statistics

JOEL BEST

Learning Outcomes

After reading this article, you will be able to:

- Evaluate statistics more critically.
- Understand how statistics can be misinterpreted.

The dissertation prospectus began by quoting a statistic—a "grabber" meant to capture the reader's attention. The graduate student who wrote this prospectus undoubtedly wanted to seem scholarly to the professors who would read it; they would be supervising the proposed research. And what could be more scholarly than a nice, authoritative statistic, quoted from a professional journal in the student's field?

So the prospectus began with this (carefully footnoted) quotation: "Every year since 1950, the number of American children gunned down has doubled." I had been invited to serve on the student's dissertation committee. When I read the quotation, I assumed the student had made an error in copying it. I went to the library and looked up the article the student had cited. There, in the journal's 1995 volume, was exactly the same sentence: "Every year since 1950, the number of American children gunned down has doubled."

This quotation is my nomination for a dubious distinction: I think it may be the worst—that is, the most inaccurate—social statistic ever.

What makes this statistic so bad? Just for the sake of argument, let's assume that "the number of American children gunned down" in 1950 was one. If the number doubled each year, there must have been two children gunned down in 1951, four in 1952, eight in 1953, and so on. By 1960, the number would have been 1,024. By 1965, it would have been 32,768 (in 1965, the F.B.I. identified only 9,960 criminal homicides in the entire country, including adult as well as child victims). By 1970, the number would have passed one million; by 1980, one billion (more than four times the total U.S. population in that year). Only three years later, in 1983, the number of American children gunned down would have been 8.6 billion (nearly twice the earth's population at the time). Another milestone would have been passed in 1987, when the number of gunned-down

American children (137 billion) would have surpassed the best estimates for the total human population throughout history (110 billion). By 1995, when the article was published, the annual number of victims would have been over 35 trillion—a really big number, of a magnitude you rarely encounter outside economics or astronomy.

Thus my nomination: estimating the number of American child gunshot victims in 1995 at 35 trillion must be as far off—as hilariously, wildly wrong—as a social statistic can be. (If anyone spots a more inaccurate social statistic, I'd love to hear about it.)

Where did the article's author get this statistic? I wrote the author, who responded that the statistic came from the Children's Defense Fund, a well-known advocacy group for children. The C.D.F.'s *The State of America's Children Yearbook 1994* does state: "The number of American children killed each year by guns has doubled since 1950." Note the difference in the wording—the C.D.F. claimed there were twice as many deaths in 1994 as in 1950; the article's author reworded that claim and created a very different meaning.

It is worth examining the history of this statistic. It began with the C.D.F. noting that child gunshot deaths had doubled from 1950 to 1994. This is not quite as dramatic an increase as it might seem. Remember that the U.S. population also rose throughout this period; in fact, it grew about 73 percent—or nearly double. Therefore, we might expect all sorts of things—including the number of child gunshot deaths—to increase, to nearly double, just because the population grew. Before we can decide whether twice as many deaths indicate that things are getting worse, we'd have to know more. The C.D.F. statistic raises other issues as well: Where did the statistic come from? Who counts child gunshot deaths, and how? What is meant by a "child" (some C.D.F. statistics about violence include everyone under age 25)? What is meant by "killed by guns" (gunshot-death statistics often include suicides and accidents, as well as homicides)? But people rarely ask questions of this sort when they encounter statistics. Most of the time, most people simply accept statistics without question.

Certainly, the article's author didn't ask many probing, critical questions about the C.D.F.'s claim. Impressed by the statistic, the author repeated it—well, meant to repeat it. Instead, by rewording the C.D.F.'s claim, the author created a mutant statistic, one garbled almost beyond recognition.

But people treat mutant statistics just as they do other statistics—that is, they usually accept even the most implausible claims without question. For example, the journal editor who accepted the author's article for publication did not bother to consider the implications of child victims doubling each year. And people repeat bad statistics: The graduate student copied the garbled statistic and inserted it into the dissertation prospectus. Who knows whether still other readers were impressed by the author's statistic and remembered it or repeated it? The article remains on the shelf in hundreds of libraries, available to anyone who needs a dramatic quote. The lesson should be clear: Bad statistics live on; they take on lives of their own.

Some statistics are born bad—they aren't much good from the start, because they are based on nothing more than guesses or dubious data. Other statistics mutate; they become bad after being mangled (as in the case of the author's creative rewording). Either way, bad statistics are potentially important: They can be used to stir up public outrage or fear; they can distort our understanding of our world; and they can lead us to make poor policy choices.

The notion that we need to watch out for bad statistics isn't new. We've all heard people say, "You can prove anything with statistics." The title of my book, *Damned Lies and Statistics*, comes from a famous aphorism (usually attributed to Mark Twain or Benjamin Disraeli): "There are three kinds of lies: lies, damned lies, and statistics." There is even a useful little book, still in print after more than 40 years, called *How to Lie With Statistics*.

We shouldn't ignore all statistics, or assume that every number is false. Some statistics are bad, but others are pretty good. And we need good statistics to talk sensibly about social problems.

Statistics, then, have a bad reputation. We suspect that statistics may be wrong, that people who use statistics may be "lying"—trying to manipulate us by using numbers to somehow distort the truth. Yet, at the same time, we need statistics; we depend upon them to summarize and clarify the nature of our complex society. This is particularly true when we talk about social problems. Debates about social problems routinely raise questions that demand statistical answers: Is the problem widespread? How many people—and which people—does it affect? Is it getting worse? What does it cost society? What will it cost to deal with it? Convincing answers to such questions demand evidence, and that usually means numbers, measurements, statistics.

But can't you prove anything with statistics? It depends on what "prove" means. If we want to know, say, how many children are "gunned down" each year, we can't simply guess—pluck a number from thin air: 100, 1,000, 10,000, 35 trillion,

whatever. Obviously, there's no reason to consider an arbitrary guess "proof" of anything. However, it might be possible for someone—using records kept by police departments or hospital emergency rooms or coroners—to keep track of children who have been shot; compiling careful, complete records might give us a fairly accurate idea of the number of gunned-down children. If that number seems accurate enough, we might consider it very strong evidence—or proof.

The solution to the problem of bad statistics is not to ignore all statistics, or to assume that every number is false. Some statistics are bad, but others are pretty good, and we need statistics—good statistics—to talk sensibly about social problems. The solution, then, is not to give up on statistics, but to become better judges of the numbers we encounter. We need to think critically about statistics—at least critically enough to suspect that the number of children gunned down hasn't been doubling each year since 1950.

A few years ago, the mathematician John Allen Paulos wrote *Innumeracy*, a short, readable book about "mathematical illiteracy." Too few people, he argued, are comfortable with basic mathematical principles, and this makes them poor judges of the numbers they encounter. No doubt this is one reason we have so many bad statistics. But there are other reasons, as well.

Social statistics describe society, but they are also products of our social arrangements. The people who bring social statistics to our attention have reasons for doing so; they inevitably want something, just as reporters and the other media figures who repeat and publicize statistics have their own goals. Statistics are tools, used for particular purposes. Thinking critically about statistics requires understanding their place in society.

While we may be more suspicious of statistics presented by people with whom we disagree—people who favor different political parties or have different beliefs—bad statistics are used to promote all sorts of causes. Bad statistics come from conservatives on the political right and liberals on the left, from wealthy corporations and powerful government agencies, and from advocates of the poor and the powerless.

In order to interpret statistics, we need more than a checklist of common errors. We need a general approach, an orientation, a mind-set that we can use to think about new statistics that we encounter. We ought to approach statistics thoughtfully. This can be hard to do, precisely because so many people in our society treat statistics as fetishes. We might call this the mind-set of the awestruck—the people who don't think critically, who act as though statistics have magical powers. The awestruck know they don't always understand the statistics they hear, but this doesn't bother them. After all, who can expect to understand magical numbers? The reverential fatalism of the awestruck is not thoughtful—it is a way of avoiding thought. We need a different approach.

One choice is to approach statistics critically. Being critical does not mean being negative or hostile—it is not cynicism. The critical approach statistics thoughtfully; they avoid the extremes of both naïve acceptance and cynical rejection of the numbers they encounter. Instead, the critical attempt to evaluate numbers, to distinguish between good statistics and bad statistics.

The critical understand that, while some social statistics may be pretty good, they are never perfect. Every statistic is a way of summarizing complex information into relatively simple numbers. Inevitably, some information, some of the complexity, is lost whenever we use statistics. The critical recognize that this is an inevitable limitation of statistics. Moreover, they realize that every statistic is the product of choices—the choice between defining a category broadly or narrowly, the choice of one measurement over another, the choice of a sample. People choose definitions, measurements, and samples for all sorts of reasons: Perhaps they want to emphasize some aspect of a problem; perhaps it is easier or cheaper to gather data in a particular way—many considerations can come into play. Every statistic is a compromise among choices. This means that every definition—and every measurement and every sample—probably has limitations and can be criticized.

Being critical means more than simply pointing to the flaws in a statistic. Again, every statistic has flaws. The issue is whether a particular statistic's flaws are severe enough to damage its usefulness. Is the definition so broad that it encompasses too many false positives (or so narrow that it excludes too many false negatives)? How would changing the definition alter the statistic? Similarly, how do the choices of measurements and samples affect the statistic? What would happen if different measures or samples were chosen? And how is the statistic used? Is it being interpreted appropriately, or has its meaning been mangled to create a mutant statistic? Are the comparisons that are being made appropriate, or are apples being confused with oranges? How do different choices produce the conflicting numbers found in stat wars? These are the sorts of questions the critical ask.

A s a practical matter, it is virtually impossible for citizens in contemporary society to avoid statistics about social problems. Statistics arise in all sorts of ways, and in almost every case the people promoting statistics want to persuade us. Activists use statistics to convince us that social problems are serious and deserve our attention and concern. Charities use statistics to encourage donations. Politicians use statistics to persuade us that they understand society's problems and that they deserve our support. The media use statistics to make their reporting more dramatic, more convincing, more compelling. Corporations use statistics to promote and improve their products. Researchers use statistics to document their findings and support their conclusions. Those with whom we agree use statistics to reassure us that we're on the right side, while our opponents use statistics to try and convince us that we are wrong. Statistics are one of the standard types of evidence used by people in our society.

It is not possible simply to ignore statistics, to pretend they don't exist. That sort of head-in-the-sand approach would be too costly. Without statistics, we limit our ability to think thoughtfully about our society; without statistics, we have no accurate ways of judging how big a problem may be, whether it is getting worse, or how well the policies designed to address that problem actually work. And awestruck or naïve attitudes toward statistics are no better than ignoring statistics; statistics have no magical properties, and it is foolish to assume that all statistics are equally valid. Nor is a cynical approach the answer; statistics are too widespread and too useful to be automatically discounted.

It would be nice to have a checklist, a set of items we could consider in evaluating any statistic. The list might detail potential problems with definitions, measurements, sampling, mutation, and so on. These are, in fact, common sorts of flaws found in many statistics, but they should not be considered a formal, complete checklist. It is probably impossible to produce a complete list of statistical flaws—no matter how long the list, there will be other possible problems that could affect statistics.

The goal is not to memorize a list, but to develop a thoughtful approach. Becoming critical about statistics requires being prepared to ask questions about numbers. When encountering a new statistic in, say, a news report, the critical try to assess it. What might be the sources for this number? How could one go about producing the figure? Who produced the number, and what interests might they have? What are the different ways key terms might have been defined, and which definitions have been chosen? How might the phenomena be measured, and which measurement choices have been made? What sort of sample was gathered, and how might that sample affect the result? Is the statistic being properly interpreted? Are comparisons being made, and if so, are the comparisons appropriate? Are there competing statistics? If so, what stakes do the opponents have in the issue, and how are those stakes likely to affect their use of statistics? And is it possible to figure out why the statistics seem to disagree, what the differences are in the ways the competing sides are using figures?

At first, this list of questions may seem overwhelming. How can an ordinary person—someone who reads a statistic in a magazine article or hears it on a news broadcast—determine the answers to such questions? Certainly news reports rarely give detailed information on the processes by which statistics are created. And few of us have time to drop everything and investigate the background of some new number we encounter. Being critical, it seems, involves an impossible amount of work.

In practice, however, the critical need not investigate the origin of every statistic. Rather, being critical means appreciating the inevitable limitations that affect all statistics, rather than being awestruck in the presence of numbers. It means not being too credulous, not accepting every statistic at face value. But it also means appreciating that statistics, while always imperfect, can be useful. Instead of automatically discounting every statistic, the critical reserve judgment. When confronted with an interesting number, they may try to learn more, to evaluate, to weigh the figure's strengths and weaknesses.

Of course, this critical approach need not—and should not—be limited to statistics. It ought to apply to all the evidence we encounter when we scan a news report, or listen to a speech—whenever we learn about social problems.

Claims about social problems often feature dramatic, compelling examples; the critical might ask whether an example is likely to be a typical case or an extreme, exceptional instance. Claims about social problems often include quotations from different sources, and the critical might wonder why those sources have spoken and why they have been quoted: Do they have particular expertise? Do they stand to benefit if they influence others? Claims about social problems usually involve arguments about the problem's causes and potential solutions. The critical might ask whether these arguments are convincing. Are they logical? Does the proposed solution seem feasible and appropriate? And so on. Being critical—adopting a skeptical, analytical stance when confronted with claims—is an approach that goes far beyond simply dealing with statistics.

Statistics are not magical. Nor are they always true—or always false. Nor need they be incomprehensible. Adopting a critical approach offers an effective way of responding to the numbers we are sure to encounter. Being critical requires more thought, but failing to adopt a critical mind-set makes us powerless to evaluate what others tell us. When we fail to think critically, the statistics we hear might just as well be magical.

Critical Thinking

1. Why are there bad statistics?
2. How can one approach statistics critically?
3. What was wrong with the following statement made in 1995: "Every year since 1950 the number of American children gunned down has doubled"?

Create Central

www.mhhe.com/createcentral

Internet References

Bureau of Justice Statistics
www.bjs.gov

Federal Bureau of Investigation (F.B.I.)
www.fbi.gov/about-us/cjis/ucr/ucr-statistics-their-proper-use

JOEL BEST is a professor of sociology and criminal justice at the University of Delaware. This essay is excerpted from *Damned Lies and Statistics: Untangling Numbers from the Media, Politicians, and Activists*, published by the University of California Press and reprinted by permission. Copyright © 2001 by the Regents of the University of California.

As seen in *Chronicle of Higher Education*, May 4, 2001, pp. B7–B9; originally appeared in *Damned Lies and Statistics: Untangling Numbers from the Media, Politicians, and Activists* by Joel Best (University of California Press, 2001). Copyright © 2001 by University of California Press. Reprinted by permission via Rightslink.

Article   Prepared by: Joanne Naughton

Stop Panicking About Bullies

Childhood is safer than ever before, but today's parents need to worry about something. Nick Gillespie on why busybodies and bureaucrats have zeroed in on bullying.

NICK GILLESPIE

Learning Outcomes

After reading this article, you will be able to:

- Argue that some reactions to bullying can be excessive.

- Show that it is important to check stated facts for accuracy.

"When I was younger," a remarkably self-assured, soft-spoken 15-year-old kid named Aaron tells the camera, "I suffered from bullying because of my lips—as you can see, they're kind of unusually large. So I would kind of get [called] 'Fish Lips'—things like that a lot—and my glasses too, I got those at an early age. That contributed. And the fact that my last name is Cheese didn't really help with the matter either. I would get [called] 'Cheeseburger,' 'Cheese Guy'—things like that, that weren't really very flattering. Just kind of making fun of my name—I'm a pretty sensitive kid, so I would have to fight back the tears when I was being called names."

It's hard not to be impressed with—and not to like—young Aaron Cheese. He is one of the kids featured in the new Cartoon Network special "Stop Bullying: Speak Up," which premiered last week and is available online. I myself am a former geekish, bespectacled child whose lips were a bit too full, and my first name (as other kids quickly discovered) rhymes with two of the most-popular slang terms for male genitalia, so I also identified with Mr. Cheese. My younger years were filled with precisely the sort of schoolyard taunts that he recounts; they led ultimately to at least one fistfight and a lot of sour moods on my part.

As the parent now of two school-age boys, I also worry that my own kids will have to deal with such ugly and destructive behavior. And I welcome the common-sense antibullying strategies relayed in "Stop Bullying": Talk to your friends, your parents and your teachers. Recognize that you're not the problem. Don't be a silent witness to bullying.

But is America really in the midst of a "bullying crisis," as so many now claim? I don't see it. I also suspect that our fears about the ubiquity of bullying are just the latest in a long line of well intentioned yet hyperbolic alarms about how awful it is to be a kid today.

I have no interest in defending the bullies who dominate sandboxes, extort lunch money and use Twitter to taunt their classmates. But there is no growing crisis. Childhood and adolescence in America have never been less brutal. Even as the country's overprotective parents whip themselves up into a moral panic about kid-on-kid cruelty, the numbers don't point to any explosion of abuse. As for the rising wave of laws and regulations designed to combat meanness among students, they are likely to lump together minor slights with major offenses. The antibullying movement is already conflating serious cases of gay-bashing and vicious harassment with things like . . . a kid named Cheese having a tough time in grade school.

How did we get here? We live in an age of helicopter parents so pushy and overbearing that Colorado Springs banned its annual Easter-egg hunt on account of adults jumping the starter's gun and scooping up treat-filled plastic eggs on behalf of their winsome kids. The Department of Education in New York City—once known as the town too tough for Al Capone—is seeking to ban such words as "dinosaurs," "Halloween," and "dancing" from citywide tests on the grounds that they could "evoke unpleasant emotions in the students," it was reported this week. (Leave aside for the moment that perhaps the whole point of tests is to "evoke unpleasant emotions.")

And it's not only shrinking-violet city boys and girls who are being treated as delicate flowers. Early versions of new labor restrictions still being hashed out in Congress would have barred children under 16 from operating power-driven farm equipment and kept anyone under 18 from working at agricultural co-ops and stockyards (the latest version would let kids keep running machines on their parents' spreads). What was once taken for granted—working the family farm, October tests with jack-o-lantern-themed questions, hunting your own Easter eggs—is being threatened by paternalism run amok.

Now that schools are peanut-free, latex-free, and soda-free, parents, administrators, and teachers have got to worry about something. Since most kids now have access to cable TV, the Internet, unlimited talk and texting, college and a world of opportunities that was unimaginable even 20 years ago, it seems that adults have responded by becoming ever more overprotective and thin-skinned.

Kids might be fatter than they used to be, but by most standards they are safer and better-behaved than they were when I was growing up in the 1970s and '80s. Infant and adolescent mortality, accidents, sex and drug use—all are down from their levels of a few decades ago. Acceptance of homosexuality is up, especially among younger Americans. But given today's rhetoric about bullying, you could be forgiven for thinking that kids today are not simply reading and watching grim, postapocalyptic fantasies like "The Hunger Games" but actually inhabiting such terrifying terrain, a world where "Lord of the Flies" meets "Mad Max 2: The Road Warrior," presided over by Voldemort.

Even President Barack Obama has placed his stamp of approval on this view of modern childhood. Introducing the Cartoon Network documentary, he solemnly intones: "I care about this issue deeply, not just as the president, but as a dad. . . . We've all got more to do. Everyone has to take action against bullying."

The state of New Jersey was well ahead of the president. Last year, in response to the suicide of the 18-year-old gay Rutgers student Tyler Clementi, the state legislature passed "The Anti-Bullying Bill of Rights." The law is widely regarded as the nation's toughest on these matters. It has been called both a "resounding success" by Steve Goldstein, head of the gay-rights group Garden State Equality, and a "bureaucratic nightmare" by James O'Neill, the interim school superintendent of the township of Roxbury. In Congress, New Jersey Sen. Frank Lautenberg and Rep. Rush Holt have introduced the federal Tyler Clementi Higher Education Anti-Harassment Act.

The Foundation for Individual Rights in Education has called the Lautenberg-Holt proposal a threat to free speech because

its "definition of harassment is vague, subjective and at odds with Supreme Court precedent." Should it become law, it might well empower colleges to stop some instances of bullying, but it would also cause many of them to be sued for repressing speech. In New Jersey, a school anti-bullying coordinator told the Star-Ledger that "The Anti-Bullying Bill of Rights" has "added a layer of paperwork that actually inhibits us" in dealing with problems. In surveying the effects of the law, the Star-Ledger reports that while it is "widely used and has helped some kids," it has imposed costs of up to $80,000 per school district for training alone and uses about 200 hours per month of staff time in each district, with some educators saying that the additional effort is taking staff "away from things such as substance-abuse prevention and college and career counseling."

One thing seems certain: The focus on bullying will lead to more lawsuits against schools and bullies, many of which will stretch the limits of empathy and patience. Consider, for instance, the current case of 19-year-old Eric Giray, who is suing New York's tony Calhoun School and a former classmate for $1.5 million over abuse that allegedly took place in 2004. Such cases can only become more common.

Which isn't to say that there aren't kids who face terrible cases of bullying. The immensely powerful and highly acclaimed documentary "Bully," whose makers hope to create a nationwide movement against the "bullying crisis," opens in selected theaters this weekend. The film follows the harrowing experiences of a handful of victims of harassment, including two who killed themselves in desperation. It is, above all, a damning indictment of ineffectual and indifferent school officials. No viewer can watch the abuse endured by kids such as Alex, a 13-year-old social misfit in Sioux City, Iowa, or Kelby, a 14-year-old lesbian in small-town Oklahoma, without feeling angry and motivated to change youth culture and the school officials who turn a blind eye.

But is bullying—which the stopbullying.gov website of the Department of Health and Human Services defines as "teasing," "name-calling," "taunting," "leaving someone out on purpose," "telling other children not to be friends with someone," "spreading rumors about someone," "hitting/kicking/pinching," "spitting," and "making mean or rude hand gestures"—really a growing problem in America?

Despite the rare and tragic cases that rightly command our attention and outrage, the data show that things are, in fact, getting better for kids. When it comes to school violence, the numbers are particularly encouraging. According to the National Center for Education Statistics, between 1995 and 2009, the percentage of students who reported "being afraid of attack or harm at school" declined to 4% from 12%. Over the same period, the victimization rate per 1,000 students declined fivefold.

When it comes to bullying numbers, long-term trends are less clear. The makers of "Bully" say that "over 13 million American kids will be bullied this year," and estimates of the percentage of students who are bullied in a given year range from 20% to 70%. NCES changed the way it tabulated bullying incidents in 2005 and cautions against using earlier data. Its biennial reports find that 28% of students ages 12-18 reported being bullied in 2005; that percentage rose to 32% in 2007, before dropping back to 28% in 2009 (the most recent year for which data are available). Such numbers strongly suggest that there is no epidemic afoot (though one wonders if the new anti-bullying laws and media campaigns might lead to more reports going forward).

The most common bullying behaviors reported include being "made fun of, called names, or insulted" (reported by about 19% of victims in 2009) and being made the "subject of rumors" (16%). Nine percent of victims reported being "pushed, shoved, tripped, or spit on," and 6% reported being "threatened with harm." Though it may not be surprising that bullying mostly happens during the school day, it is stunning to learn that the most common locations for bullying are inside classrooms, in hallways and stairwells, and on playgrounds—areas ostensibly patrolled by teachers and administrators.

None of this is to be celebrated, of course, but it hardly paints a picture of contemporary American childhood as an unrestrained Hobbesian nightmare. Before more of our schools' money, time and personnel are diverted away from education in the name of this supposed crisis, we should make an effort to distinguish between the serious abuse suffered by the kids in "Bully" and the sort of lower-level harassment with which the Aaron Cheeses of the world have to deal.

In fact, Mr. Cheese, now a sophomore in high school with hopes of becoming a lawyer, provides a model in dealing with the sort of jerks who will always, unfortunately, be a presence in our schools. At the end of "Stop Bullying," he tells younger kids, "Just talk to somebody and I promise to you, it's going to get better." For Aaron, it plainly has: "It has been turned around actually. I am a generally liked guy. My last name has become something that's a little more liked. I have a friend named Mac and so together we are Mac and Cheese. That's cool."

Indeed, it is cool. And if we take a deep breath, we will realize that there are many more Aaron Cheeses walking the halls of today's schools than there are bullies. Our problem isn't a world where bullies are allowed to run rampant; it's a world where kids like Aaron are convinced that they are powerless victims.

Critical Thinking

1. Why do people file lawsuits when they believe they have been wronged?
2. Where would you draw the line between bullying and "lower-level harassment"?
3. Is working on a family farm a dangerous occupation, according to the Bureau of Labor Statistics?

Internet References

New Jersey Department of Education
www.nj.gov/education/students/safety/behavior/hib/guidance.pdf
New York City Department of Education
http://schools.nyc.gov/RulesPolicies/default.htm

MR. GILLESPIE is editor in chief of Reason.com and Reason.tv and the coauthor of *The Declaration of Independents: How Libertarian Politics Can Fix What's Wrong With America.*

Article   Prepared by: Joanne Naughton

Cyberbullying and Sexting: Law Enforcement Perceptions

JUSTIN W. PATCHIN, JOSEPH A. SCHAFER, AND SAMEER HINDUJA

Learning Outcomes

After reading this article, you will be able to:

- Define and give examples of cyberbullying.

- Explain sexting and how it generally occurs.

- Understand how the gender of a law enforcement officer, and whether he or she had young children, affected the officer's perceptions.

L aw enforcement officers often struggle to determine their proper role in addressing bullying behavior. Emerging social networking and other communication tools and their accompanying roles in the shift in youth behavior complicate the situation. Historically, bullying occurred within or in close proximity to a school or neighborhood; however, technology allows present-day bullies to extend their reach.

Problem

Defined as "willful and repeated harm inflicted through the use of computers, cell phones, and other electronic devices," cyberbullying has become a growing concern.[1] It includes sending threatening texts, posting or distributing libelous or harassing messages, and uploading or distributing hateful or humiliating images or videos to harm someone else.[2] Estimates of the number of youth who experience cyberbullying range from 5 to 72 percent, depending on the age of the group and the definition of cyberbullying.[3]

Sexting is another issue involving teens and technology that poses a public concern. Sexting involves "sending or receiving sexually explicit or sexually suggestive nude or seminude images or video, generally via cell phone."[4] Often individuals initially send these images to romantic partners or interests, but the pictures can find their way to others.[5] Estimates of the number of youth who have participated in sexting range from 4 to 31 percent.[6] In 2010 surveys from 4,400 middle and high school students indicated that 8 percent had sent naked or seminude images of themselves to others, and 13 percent reported receiving such pictures from classmates.[7]

Cyberbullying and sexting are significant problems facing teens and schools because of the psychological, emotional, behavioral, and physical repercussions that can stem from victimization.[8] School administrators recognize the severity of these issues, and promising practices provide these educators what they need to know about cyberbullying and sexting, their prevention, and the proper responses when incidents arise. Questions of law enforcement's role linger and deserve an answer.

Survey

Law enforcement officers, especially those assigned to school settings, likely will encounter cyberbullying, sexting, and other forms of online impropriety. The authors collected two separate samples for their investigation of these problems. The first, taken in May 2010, involved 336 school resource officers (SROs) who completed an online survey about cyberbullying and sexting. The second sample included law enforcement leaders attending the FBI National Academy (FBINA), a 10-week residential career development experience at the FBI Academy in Quantico, Virginia. The authors collected data from surveys administered to 643 officers from three FBINA classes in 2010 and 2011.

The SRO and FBINA samples were predominantly male (77 and 92 percent, respectively) and Caucasian (82 and 83 percent) with 73 percent being between the ages of 36 and 50 years old. The FBINA participants averaged 20 years experience in law enforcement, compared with 15 years for the SROs. Twenty-three percent of FBINA participants and 95 percent of SROs had school assignment experience. Both groups responded to comparable surveys on experiences with cyberbullying and sexting cases, as well as perceptions of their primary professional role in preventing and responding to such incidents.

School Resource Officers

Ninety-four percent of SROs agreed that cyberbullying was a serious problem warranting a law enforcement response. Seventy-eight percent stated that they conducted cyberbullying investigations (an average of 16 separate incidents) during the previous school year. Of the 336 respondents, 93 percent indicated that sexting was an important concern for law enforcement officers. Sixty-seven percent reported investigating an average of five sexting incidents in the previous year. Approximately 50 percent of the SROs commented that the school in which they worked had a policy on cyberbullying; however, only 25 percent said there was a sexting policy. Eighteen percent of the respondents were unsure whether there were policies in place.

Officers reported that most cyberbullying occurred through social networking or text messaging. One officer described an incident that involved female students spreading defamatory information about one classmate's sexual activities, choice of boyfriends, and other associations. Officers, school administrators, and parents worked together to alleviate the problem by advising the involved students that their behavior possibly could be criminal and that subsequent harassment would involve the court system.

Generally, sexting incidents involve romantic partners. One SRO stated that boyfriends and girlfriends send pictures to each other, sometimes with the boy sharing the girl's photos with his friends. Images sent and received as part of a consensual relationship received informal handling with officers talking to students and parents about the seriousness of the situation. When coercion or unauthorized distribution occurred, formal prosecution was likely. An officer conveyed a situation where a girl made an obscene video for her boyfriend, who distributed it to multiple other people, resulting in a child pornography investigation.

FBI National Academy Participants

Eighty-two percent of the FBINA respondents recognized that cyberbullying was a significant issue necessitating police involvement. Ten percent of the officers indicated that they had experience investigating cyberbullying cases, averaging two cases during the previous school year. While 78 percent of the FBINA respondents determined that sexting was a considerable concern for law enforcement, only 7 percent (averaging three

cases each in the previous year) reported that they investigated sexting incidents.

Research Findings

Using hypothetical cyberbullying scenarios (Table 1), all respondents rated the extent to which law enforcement should play a significant role. They perceived the greatest law enforcement role in situations involving a threat of physical harm. For example, they used a scale with 0 being no role and 10 being a significant role to rate the appropriate responsibility of officers in the following situation: A male student received an e-mail from an unknown person threatening to kill him at school the next day. The average rating was 9.1 for the SROs and 8.6 for the FBINA respondents.

Participants indicated that a formal law enforcement response was not essential in situations involving potential violations of student codes of conduct. They rated the following scenario: A teacher confiscates a cell phone from a student in class and wants to determine if it contains any information that is in violation of school policy. SROs rated the law enforcement role on average as 2.4, and FBINA respondents reported 1.4. Law enforcement officers understand their role more clearly when the behavior is an obvious violation of state or local law and less if there is no immediate safety concern.

Experience with cyberbullying and sexting cases, gender of the officer, and whether the officer had young children living at home all were predictors of perceptions about the role of law enforcement. Officers who recently investigated a cyberbullying or sexting case were more likely to view these issues as a significant law enforcement concern. This finding explains why SROs reported a greater law enforcement role than the FBINA respondents in all of the scenarios. SROs had direct experience with cyberbullying and sexting. Female officers and police with children aged 18 or younger living at home agreed that law enforcement played a significant role in dealing with these problems.

The research indicated that more young people will encounter a cyberbully than be groomed, abducted, and assaulted by a stranger on the Internet.[9] However, over 80 percent of study participants indicated that they needed additional training on preventing and responding to cyberbullying. Twenty-five percent of the SROs and over 40 percent of the FBINA officers surveyed did not know if their state had a law specific to cyberbullying. As of this writing, 49 states had laws regarding bullying, and 45 of those mentioned electronic forms of harassment.[10]

Best Practices

Law enforcement officers, especially SROs, need an awareness and understanding of their state statutes to grasp the legal implications of cyberbullying. The growth of cell phones and

Table 1 Law Enforcement Perceptions Regarding Responsibility in Dealing with Cyberbullying

With 0 being no law enforcement role or responsibility and 10 being a very important or significant role or responsibility, to what degree should law enforcement be involved?	School Resource Officers N = 336 Mean	FBI National Academy N = 643 Mean
A male student receives an e-mail from an unknown person threatening to kill him at school tomorrow	9.1	8.6
A female student, Jenny, covertly takes a picture of another female student, Margaret, in her underwear in the girl's locker room and posts it on a website without permission that allows the rest of the student body to rate or judge Margaret's physical appearance	8.9	7.8
A parent calls to report that her son has a naked image of a female student from his school on his cell phone	8.3	6.3
A parent calls the police department to report that her son is being cyberbullied by another youth in their neighborhood	7.8	6.5
A student creates a Facebook Fan Page called "Give Mary a Wedgie Day." Mary is a student at a school in your jurisdiction	5.8	3.8
A male student reveals another classmate's sexual orientation (without permission) via Twitter to the rest of the student body	5.7	4.0
A female student receives a text message from another classmate calling her a slut	4.2	3.4
A student creates a webpage making fun of the school principal	4.1	2.6
A teacher confiscates a cell phone from a student in class and wants to determine if it contains any information that violates school policy	2.4	1.4

N = Number of respondents.

Internet usage among teens has altered youth social and conduct norms. Cyberbullying is one of the most significant new issues law enforcement has to address. Anecdotal and research-based accounts from police across the nation depicted a lack of clear guidance, training, and support. This is unfortunate because bullying is an age-old problem with recent forms often relying on technological devices and mediums. Research has indicated a strong link between online and offline bullying.[11]

Even if no criminal statute on cyberbullying exists, law enforcement should not ignore these behaviors or dismiss the issue. Officers must help other professionals, such as school administrators, understand legal obligations and authority regarding cyberbullying. School officials can discipline students for their behavior when there is a policy prohibiting such conduct—even when the student is away from campus—if the official can demonstrate that the behavior substantially disrupted the learning environment at school.[12] When educating the community about cyberbullying, law enforcement officers should stress that different levels of responsibility exist; the matter is serious; an investigation will occur; and parents, schools, and the criminal justice system could punish the offender if warranted.

Online harassment not covered by specific cyberbullying laws may fall under traditional statutes. Officers have charged students for disorderly conduct in incidents that interrupt the main educational purpose of schools (e.g., making embarrassing videos at school and distributing them online) or infringe upon the rights of others. It is important for authorities to take cyberbullying situations more seriously that appear motivated by race, class, gender, or sexual orientation. While directed solely at one person, these events reflect malice and bias toward an entire group of people. Police should consult their district attorney liaisons to determine what existing criminal statutes apply.

Criminal law often pertains when stalking, coercion, sexually explicit images, or the sexual exploitation of youth are involved. High-profile cases of criminal prosecution against teens who engage in sexting illustrate the complexity of addressing this behavior. Legal and political authorities often factor in the age of participants and the relational context in which the sexting incident occurred.[13] Many states have introduced or enacted legislation that addresses sexting, with penalties ranging from educational programming for first-time offenders to fines, felony charges, or short-term incarceration.[14]

Sexting occurs along a continuum, ranging from typical teenage behavior to significant and intentional victimization of others.[15] Due to the sensitive nature of the images and the potential for these photos to remain publicly available, law enforcement involvement at all levels is important.

Conclusion

Law enforcement officers, especially those assigned to schools, are called upon to act after incidents and will need to address cyberbullying at some point during their tenure. Even if the cyberbullying behavior is not at a criminal level, officers should handle the situation in a way that is appropriate for the circumstances. A discussion of the legal issues may be enough to deter some first-time bullies from future misbehavior. Officers should talk to parents about their child's conduct and the seriousness of online harassment. Law enforcement's response will vary based on how the case was discovered, what harm has occurred, how evidence was collected, who was involved, and what level of training officers have received.

Cyberbullying and sexting still are relatively new social problems, and officers involved in this study agreed that they need more training to help them understand and respond to these behaviors. Some participants perceived that when these issues occurred away from school, the school could not take any action. One school resource officer stated, "The incident began on Facebook and was done outside of school hours, so the school was unable to do anything about the cyberbullying." Another noted, "Most of the time the school district does not get involved because cyberbullying does not happen on school time." A third officer pointed out that "Most of these occurred outside of school, so there was no school punishment."

It is important that law enforcement officers understand that schools can discipline students for their off-campus behavior when it infringes on the rights of other students or results in or has a foreseeable likelihood of causing substantial and material disruption of the learning environment of the school.[16] Even when the behavior does not violate the law, schools can and should apply appropriate discipline. Law enforcement officers play an important role in ensuring that proper responses are provided to minimize the future risk and harm that cyberbullying and sexting may create.

Notes

1. Sameer Hinduja and J.W. Patchin, *Bullying Beyond the Schoolyard: Preventing and Responding to Cyberbullying* (Thousand Oaks, CA: Sage Publications, Corwin Press, 2009), p. 5.

2. Sameer Hinduja and J.W. Patchin, *Bullying Beyond the Schoolyard*, p. 5.

3. J.W. Patchin and Sameer Hinduja, *Preventing and Responding to Cyberbullying: Expert Perspectives* (Thousand Oaks, CA: Routledge, 2012).

4. Sameer Hinduja and J.W. Patchin, *School Climate 2.0: Reducing Teen Technology Misuse by Reshaping the Environment* (Thousand Oaks, CA: Sage Publications, Corwin Press, 2012).

5. L.E. Soronen, N. Vitale, and K.A. Haase, "Sexting at School: Lessons Learned the Hard Way, Inquiry and Analysis," *http://www.nsba.org/* (accessed January 30, 2013); J. Leshnoff, "Sexting, Not Just for Kids," *http://www.aarp.org/relationships/love-sex/info-11-2009/sexting_not_just_for_kids.html* (accessed January 30, 2013); and J. Wolak and D. Finkelhor, "Sexting: A Typology," *http://www.unh.edu/ccrc/pdf/CV231_Sexting%20Typology%20Bulletin_4-6-11_revised.pdf* (accessed January 30, 2013).

6. S. Hinduja and J.W. Patchin, *Reducing Teen Technology;* V. Stuart-Cassel, A. Bell, and J.F. Springer, "Analysis of State Bullying Laws and Policies," *http://www2.ed.gov/rschstat/eval/bullying/state-bullying-laws/state-bullying-laws.pdf* (accessed January 30, 2013).

7. S. Hinduja and J.W. Patchin, *Reducing Teen Technology.*

8. M.L. Ybarra, M. Diener-West, and P.J. Leaf, "Examining the Overlap in Internet Harassment and School Bullying: Implications for School Intervention," *Journal of Adolescent Health* 41 (2007): S42-S50; and S. Hinduja and J.W. Patchin, "Bullying, Cyberbullying, and Suicide," *Archives of Suicide Research* 14, no. 3 (2010): 206–221.

9. J.G. Palfrey, D. Boyd, and D. Sacco, "Enhancing Child Safety and Online Technologies: Final Report of the Internet Safety Technical Task Force," (Durham, NC: Carolina Academic Press, 2009).

10. S. Hinduja and J.W. Patchin, "Bullying and Cyberbullying Laws," *http://www.clyberbullying.us/Bullying_and_Cyberbullying_Laws.pdf* (accessed February 28, 2013).

11. S. Hinduja and J.W. Patchin, *Bullying Beyond the Schoolyard,* p. 5; and J.W. Patchin and S. Hinduja, "Traditional and Nontraditional Bullying Among Youth: A Test of General Strain Theory," *Youth and Society* 43, no. 2 (2011): 727–751.

12. S. Hinduja and J.W. Patchin, "Cyberbullying: A Review of the Legal Issues Facing Educators," *Preventing School Failure* 55, no. 2 (2010): 1–8.

13. T.J. Dishion, D.M. Capaldi, and K. Yoerger, "Middle Childhood Antecedents to Progressions in Male Adolescent Substance Use: An Ecological Analysis of Risk and Protection," *Journal of Adolescent Research* 14 (1999): 175–205.

14. D.L. Haynie, "Delinquent Peers Revisited: Does Network Structure Matter?" *American Journal of Sociology* 106, (2001): 1013–1057.

15. N.E. Willard, 2010, "School Response to Cyberbullying and Sexting: The Legal Challenges," *Center for Safe and Responsible Internet Use,* *http://www.embracecivility.org* (accessed January 31, 2013).

16. S. Hinduja and J.W. Patchin, *Cyberbullying,* pp. 1–8.

Critical Thinking

1. If no criminal statute on cyberbullying exists, what should be the role of law enforcement when such conduct occurs?

2. When students engage in cyberbullying behavior that violates criminal law, should they always be arrested?

3. Is the use of law enforcement practices a good way to deal with this problem?

Internet References

University of New Hampshire, Crimes Against Children Research Center

www.unh.edu/ccrc/pdf/CV231_Sexting%20Typology%20Bulletin_4-6-11_revised.pdf

U.S. Department of Education

www2.ed.gov/rschstat/eval/bullying/state-bullying-laws/state-bullying-laws.pdf

Federal Bureau of Investigation, 2013.

Article   Prepared by: Joanne Naughton

This Is How a Domestic Violence Victim Falls Through the Cracks

MELISSA JELTSEN

Learning Outcomes

After reading this article, you will be able to:

- Explain the ways a victim can be controlled by an abuser.

- Understand why a victim will stay with an abuser instead of just leaving.

- Show the effect of guns on domestic violence in Arkansas.

Berryville, Arkansas—Two days before she died, Laura Aceves stood on the side of the road and frantically dialed the police for the last time.

It was early afternoon and the 21-year-old had finished her shift at the Berryville Tyson Foods plant, where she worked on an assembly line deboning chicken. Moments after pulling out of the parking lot, her car broke down. At the nearest service station, a mechanic identified the problem: Someone had poured bleach in her gas tank.

Laura knew who was responsible. Her abusive ex-boyfriend, Victor Acuna-Sanchez, was out on bail and had a history of destroying her stuff. "No one else would have done this," she told police.

According to family members and court records, Laura spent the last year of her life being terrorized by Acuna-Sanchez. He allegedly beat her with a baseball bat, dragged her behind a car, strangled her until she blacked out on the floor and told her over and over how he would kill her if she ever left him.

At the time, Acuna-Sanchez, 18, was awaiting trial for charges stemming from two prior attacks on Laura, including a felony for aggravated assault. He was out on bail, under court order to have no contact with Laura and to check in with probation by phone each week.

At the gas station, Laura told police where she thought Acuna-Sanchez might be staying and pleaded for their help. An officer said he'd search for him, but came up empty-handed. That evening, Laura, who had three young children, posted a vague message on Facebook hinting at her troubles: *It is gonna be a long night.*

Less than 48 hours later, she was found in her apartment with a gunshot wound to the head. Her four-month-old son was crying by her side, coated in so much blood that EMTs thought he'd been shot too. Laura had an open casket funeral. No amount of makeup could conceal her black eyes.

A year and a half has passed since her murder. On a clear day in April, her mother, Laura Ponce, drives to her last apartment and stands in the driveway, holding back tears.

The apartment complex is on the outskirts of town, on a steep, twisting ridge in the Ozarks. In the spring, the shrubs lining the road flush with tiny purple flowers. It's the road that leaves town, the path out of Carroll County.

"She was trying to get as far away as she could," Ponce says. "It wasn't enough."

As with many women who are killed in domestic violence homicides, Laura's death was foreshadowed by a documented trail of warning signs. But in this small town in rural Arkansas, those red flags went unheeded. Despite Acuna-Sanchez's history of brutal attacks and repeated violations of his bail conditions, the justice system failed to keep him away from the woman he vowed to kill.

"Everybody knew she was in danger," Ponce says. "A police officer came to my house and I told him everything in detail: How Victor beat her up, how he told us we were all going to be murdered, and that he had guns. Why couldn't anyone stop him?"

Robert Hancock, a neighbor, spots Ponce through his window and comes outside to talk. He was home the night Laura died. His mother owns the 12-unit apartment complex, which is now for sale. They haven't been able to rent Laura's unit since her death. Everyone knows what happened there.

"You have to trust that God will take care of it, one way or another," he says. "Are you a Christian—do you believe in God?"

"I do," Ponce says, her voice strained. "But I don't believe in the justice of Berryville."

Sheriff Bob Grudek, 71, sits in his office at the jail where Acuna-Sanchez is being held on capital murder charges and rattles off a list of small-town problems facing Carroll County.

Theft, mostly of farm equipment. People stripping copper wire off the chicken houses and selling it. Kids stealing their parents' prescription drugs. DUIs. Some methamphetamine. And a lot of domestic violence.

In the last decade, Arkansas has frequently been ranked as one of the 10 worst states in the nation when it comes to men killing women, according to annual reports by the Violence Policy Center. The ranking is based on FBI data on incidents in which a sole male offender kills a single female victim, a typical indicator of domestic homicide.

In Arkansas, the combination of lots and lots of guns and lax firearm laws contributes to the problem. Research has shown if a batterer has access to a gun, the victim is eight times more likely to be killed. According to an analysis by the Center for American Progress, in 2010 Arkansas had the third-worst gun murder rate for women in the nation.

In the aftermath of Laura's gruesome murder, a blame game between the sheriff and prosecutor's office played out in the local press.

Acuna-Sanchez was out on bail at the time of Laura's death, awaiting trial for earlier assaults against her. In the month leading up to her death, he repeatedly broke the conditions of his pretrial release, but faced few consequences.

Just three weeks before she was killed, police arrested him for violating a no-contact order. Despite a record of escalating violence against Laura, he was released without bail the following day.

In a local newspaper, Grudek blamed Acuna-Sanchez's release on gaps in communication between the prosecutor and the judge. Since he had violated the no-contact order, prosecutors could have asked the judge to hold him pending trial, but they didn't.

Deputy prosecuting attorney Devon Closser said that was because they didn't know about his most recent arrest. She told The Lovely County Citizen that there was no procedure

in place to inform prosecutors when protective orders had been violated—and that the system could use "fine-tuning."

In an interview with *The Huffington Post,* Closser declined to discuss the case, but said it was "not unusual" for offenders to be released quickly if they were arrested simply for violating a no-contact order.

Records also show that Acuna-Sanchez wasn't checking in with a probation officer, as he was ordered to do as a condition of bail, but no one noticed.

Grudek said he couldn't comment on Acuna-Sanchez's case specifically. But he shared his perspective on the problem of domestic violence, which he said he formulated by watching Dr. Phil.

"This is a very serious social problem," he said, speculating that the crime was related to the breakdown of the traditional family structure. "Maybe if our culture goes back to when we had different values . . . I don't remember when I was a kid hearing about any domestic violence."

In fact, the opposite is true. Domestic violence has been on a steady decline in the U.S. for the past 20 years. Since the landmark Violence Against Women Act was passed in 1994, annual rates of domestic violence have plummeted by 64 percent. But the U.S. still has the highest rate of domestic violence homicide of any industrialized country.

Each day on average, three women are murdered by intimate partners—husbands and ex-husbands, boyfriends, and estranged lovers. Compared to men, women are far more often murdered by someone they know. In 2010, 39 percent of U.S. female homicide victims were killed by an intimate partner. Just 3 percent of men suffered the same fate.

When asked how Carroll County could improve its handling of domestic violence cases, Grudek said he was unconvinced that a more proactive response—like setting high bail for serial abusers, or requiring GPS tracking for offenders who violate restraining orders—would make a substantial difference.

"The question you're asking me is what's wrong with the courts," he said. "I'm asking you, what's wrong with the women?"

Grudek said domestic violence prevention should focus on why women return to their abusers, and that it wasn't "logical or responsible" to think the criminal justice system could solve the problem.

But across the country, many people are hopeful that it can play a pivotal role to help reduce domestic violence deaths.

While one in four women will be victims of domestic violence at some point in their lives, only a small fraction of cases turn lethal. The trick, many experts now believe, is identifying which women are at highest risk of death so they can be targeted for intervention.

Twenty-five years ago, Jacquelyn Campbell, now viewed as the country's leading expert on domestic homicide, created a screening tool that helps police, court personnel and victim advocates identify the women who are at the greatest risk of being killed.

Victims of domestic abuse are asked 20 questions, including: Do you believe he is capable of killing you? Does he own a gun? Is he violently and constantly jealous of you?

"We now know enough about the risk factors that we need to assess perpetrators for risk of homicide," Campbell said in an interview.

At the time of her death, Laura would have scored an 18—in "extreme danger"—on Campbell's lethality screening test, according to calculations by *The Huffington Post*. "The system might have worked best together to identify that perpetrator as high-risk and manage that case in a more proactive way," Campbell said.

Jurisdictions in at least 33 states are now screening domestic violence victims, in a process dubbed "lethality assessment." A number of different screening tools are in use, all stemming from Campbell's seminal research in the 80s.

States that have adopted some form of lethality assessment are showing impressive progress. Over the past 6 years, an ambitious lethality assessment program in Maryland reduced its domestic violence homicide rate by 25 percent. A team in Newburyport, Massachusetts, has intervened in 129 high-risk cases since 2005 and has had zero homicides.

Last year, encouraged by these success stories, the U.S. Justice Department began funding 12 pilot programs across the country to train police in lethality assessment. In a speech announcing the initiative, Vice President Joe Biden hailed the approach.

"Lives are being saved—we know how to do it," Biden said. "We know what risk factors put someone in greater danger of being killed by the person they love—and that also means we have the opportunity to step in and try to prevent these murders."

Legislators in Oklahoma recently passed a bill requiring police to screen victims with an 11-question checklist to determine if they are at high risk of being killed or severely assaulted. Once a woman is determined to be at high risk, police inform her about the danger she is in, encourage her to seek help and connect her with key resources.

In neighboring Arkansas, police are not currently being trained to screen women using lethality assessment. When asked about the value of identifying high-risk victims, Grudek said he would use a screening tool if the state introduced it, but expressed skepticism.

"It doesn't make any difference what kind of training officers get. You can tell that person they are at risk. But they will

keep going back," he said. "Women continue to live in that environment. Why don't you do a study on why victims go back to these abusers? Why do they do that?"

There are many complex reasons why women stay with abusive partners. Leaving can be economically impossible, as well as dangerous. Research has shown that women are at greatest risk of homicide at the point of separation or after leaving a violent partner.

Fixating on that question—why doesn't the woman just leave—reveals a fundamental misunderstanding about the realities of domestic abuse, said Kim Gandy, president of the National Network to End Domestic Violence.

"So often, when people say, 'Why didn't she just leave?' the reality is that she did leave, or tried to," Gandy said. "Often she has reached out for help repeatedly, to the police, to the courts, sometimes to friends or family. Often she has a protective order and he assaults her anyway."

Blaming the victim for not leaving indicates ignorance about the power and control that is an integral part of domestic abuse, she said.

"If these kinds of police attitudes are common—the idea that it's really the victim's fault for being in that situation—then it would certainly deter a victim from seeking police help or protection," she said. "These kinds of attitudes are one of the reasons that abusers feel they can do whatever they want, and not have to answer for their violence."

Linda Tyler, a former state representative who fought to strengthen domestic violence laws in Arkansas, said that police, prosecutors and judges across the state aren't adequately educated about domestic violence and don't do a good enough job protecting victims from abusers.

"We consistently have no-contact orders violated, and victims subsequently assaulted or killed," she said in an interview.

In 2009, she spearheaded a bill that gives judges the power to put GPS tracking on offenders who violate restraining orders. Keeping tabs on domestic abusers during the pretrial period has shown to be effective—a 2012 study found that when offenders out on bail are made to wear GPS trackers, they rarely try to contact their victims.

As Tyler traveled the state seeking support for the bill, she was dismayed by what she found.

"There were so many cases, over and over, where law enforcement just didn't believe the victim," she said. "I had prosecutors tell me that women made this stuff up. It's unfortunately still an environment of—I'm a husband and I think I have the right to beat my wife, if that's what I feel like I need to do. That goes with marital privileges."

Her bill passed but has not been embraced by Arkansas' judges. She said she knew of only three counties out of 75 that have used GPS tracking in response to the bill.

"I'm frustrated that it's not used more often," she said. "It may not be the only tool to use to curb domestic violence, but it is at least a tool and we seem to have so few of them, so we should really consider using it more than we do."

Tyler said more training is urgently needed for police, prosecutors and judges, as is increased data gathering on domestic violence.

"We don't effectively collect data on a statewide basis that allows us to compare performance from one jurisdiction to the other," she said. "We should identify the areas where we have significant issues of violations of protective orders and hold those jurisdictions accountable, or at the very least make the information public so that the voters are informed. As you know, we do elect our county prosecutors, judges and sheriff."

Laura was 2 years older than Acuna-Sanchez, and the two didn't move in the same circles. But Berryville is a small place. In 2011, at a friend's birthday party, they connected and started dating.

She was 19 and had two kids from a previous relationship. He was just 17. Within days, they were a couple.

From the very beginning, Ponce said, Acuna-Sanchez was violent. As is often the case with batterers, his methods of abuse went far beyond physical beatings. Ponce described a harrowing cycle of harassment, where he would brutally assault Laura, steal or destroy her belongings—a form of economic abuse— and threaten to kill her and her kids if she left him.

"He beat her on a weekly basis," Ponce said. "She suffered like you wouldn't imagine. Daytime, nighttime. It was a living hell."

Acuna-Sanchez had a reputation around town for violent behavior.

According to a woman who went to high school with him, he "wasn't ever afraid to fight." In a court-ordered mental health evaluation, he told a psychiatrist that he fought in school constantly, starting in elementary school, where he was eventually expelled. At 11, he said he was ordered to receive mental health treatment due to "anger problems." He said his father hit him a lot, "hard enough to where you're bleeding," and his mother married a string of violent men who beat her in front of him.

A woman who witnessed the relationship and who asked to remain anonymous said Acuna-Sanchez was deeply controlling. "Laura acted like she always had to do what he wanted and if she didn't, there'd be hell to pay," she said. "Sometimes they were happy but most of the time she was scared of him."

In one case, Laura fled to her mother after an assault and asked her for a copy of her passport. Acuna-Sanchez had destroyed the original by burning it in the kitchen sink, along with her social security card and birth certificate.

"She had her hair over her eyes. I grabbed her, tipped her face up—all purple," Ponce said. "I screamed and said I was going to call the cops. She said, 'Please, no mama, he will kill us all.'"

In March 2012, less than a year after they started dating, Laura became pregnant with Acuna-Sanchez's child. She filed a restraining order soon after.

"I have tried to leave him before, but he always finds me and makes my life miserable by taking my things or my mom's things until I get back with him," she wrote in the restraining order. "He told me he wouldn't leave me alone."

Researchers are split on how effective restraining orders are at protecting victims. At the most basic level, they serve as documentation of misbehavior that can be used to arrest offenders. But they are often ignored—abusers violate restraining orders an estimated 40 percent of the time—and there's no way to track how many domestic abuse homicide victims had restraining orders against their killers at their time of death.

Even after filing a restraining order, Laura struggled to separate from Acuna-Sanchez. The two briefly rekindled their relationship, though Ponce describes Laura's participation as involuntary.

"I don't like to call it 'dating,'" she said. "Laura did not want to continue the relationship. He was forcing her to be with him. If she didn't do what he said, she had to pay."

Each time she tried to leave him, he would intimidate her with threats, beat her and destroy her belongings. "She was so exhausted," Ponce said. "Every time he would ruin her things, and she had to start over. She didn't have much money."

At the court hearing to make the restraining order permanent, Laura declined to pursue it and the petition was dismissed.

But after Laura gave birth to their baby boy, Jordan, the abuse accelerated.

A week after Jordan was born, on Sept. 1, police responded to a 911 call at Laura's house. She told police that Acuna-Sanchez had hit her in the face, then smashed her car with a hammer and destroyed the baby's car seat by tearing all the stuffing out.

He was arrested for domestic battery that day. On Sept. 4, he was released on bail with a protective order to have no contact with Laura. But two days later, Acuna-Sanchez returned to her apartment.

In the police report, Laura said she heard a noise outside and opened the door to peek out. Acuna-Sanchez pushed his way in and tried to kiss her. When she refused, she told police, he tackled her to the ground and strangled her. She blacked out. When she regained consciousness, she said, her newborn baby was lying by her side and Acuna-Sanchez had fled, stealing her cell phone and car keys. When police arrived, "she was crying and holding her two-week-old child," the officer wrote.

It took over a month for Acuna-Sanchez to be arrested. It is not clear why police did not apprehend him earlier.

On Oct. 3, he was arrested and charged with aggravated assault on a family member, a felony, and with violating the no-contact order. This time he was held in jail for a month. On November 15, he was granted bail, and told he wasn't allowed to contact Laura. He was also ordered to call the probation office two times a week.

But due to an apparent error at the courthouse, the probation office was never notified that Acuna-Sanchez was on probation and therefore required to stay in close contact with an officer. He never once called in.

In a letter sent to prosecutors, Kent Villines, assistant area manager of the Arkansas Department of Community Correction, confirmed the Berryville office had been unaware of the order. "I checked with all the personnel . . . and no one knew anything about this situation," he wrote, "therefore Victor Acuna has not been checking in with this office at any time."

Villines told *The Huffington Post* that it was the prosecutor's responsibility to send over the order, and that it was "rare" for an order to fall through the cracks. "Usually, with this system we have set up, things don't disappear, but sometimes they do," he said.

In early December, Acuna-Sanchez was arrested for violating the no-contact order once more, after police spotted him in a car with Laura. The next day, Berryville District Judge Scott Jackson released him on his personal recognizance; no bail. That was the last time he was in police custody while Laura was still alive.

At Christmas, Ponce said, Laura told Acuna-Sanchez that she was leaving town. She had been saving money and was planning to rent an apartment in Missouri with her best friend.

"That was her biggest mistake, telling him," Ponce said. "He wasn't going to just let her go."

Laura didn't make it to the New Year.

On New Year's Eve, 2011, police found her dying on the floor of her apartment. Hours later, they arrested Acuna-Sanchez at his mother's house. He was found hiding in the shower, armed with a 22-caliber handgun. In the pocket of his overalls were 39 bullets and the key to Laura's apartment.

He is now awaiting trial on capital murder charges. If convicted, he will face death or life imprisonment without parole.

On a Saturday night in early April, locals gather outside the courthouse for a memorial for Laura. Little has changed in Carroll County since her death. As far as Ponce can tell, there's been no real effort to reform how domestic violence cases are handled. And there's been no acknowledgement that anything went wrong.

"The only thing I've been told is the system needs 'fine-tuning,'" Ponce says. "Nothing is different."

She's dejected by the lack of progress and alarmed that no steps have been taken to prevent this kind of tragedy from happening again. That's her biggest fear. Ponce organized the memorial—plastering the town with posters and posting an ad in the local newspaper—hoping to raise awareness about domestic violence in the community. She doesn't want Laura's death to be for nothing. It has to mean something.

At dusk, she pulls up in a minivan with Laura's three kids in tow. After Laura's death, she abruptly became the caretaker of a newborn, as well as Laura's two school-aged children.

"I had no baby clothes," Ponce recalls. Now, her life revolves around the kiddos, as she calls them.

Jordan, who will be 2 in August, still wakes up screaming most nights. Christopher, Laura's other son, is 6. And then there's Josie, her only daughter, who is 8.

All three are in therapy over their mother's brutal death. Research has shown that kids who grow up witnessing domestic violence suffer lasting emotional effects and are more likely to have behavioral problems.

The kids sit on the ground and wait quietly for the memorial to start. The crowd is mostly Latino, but there are at least a dozen Caucasians in the crowd of around 40. Kids outnumber adults two to one.

Someone hands out purple ribbons. An oversized sketch of Laura, donated by a local artist, is displayed on an easel. Pamphlets about domestic violence support are scattered across a table.

There is no shelter for battered women in all of Carroll County. The director of the closest shelter, The Sanctuary, located 30 miles away in Harrison, speaks to the crowd about their services: temporary accommodation, a 24-hour crisis line, support groups and assistance with protective orders and court advocacy. The director of community outreach translates afterwards in Spanish.

Ponce chokes up when it's her turn to take the microphone.

"I want to turn Laura's tragedy into a way to help other people," she says. "If anyone is in that situation, do not wait. A restraining order is just a piece of paper. Leave, get into a shelter, move out, don't wait."

Her point is clear—Women won't get help here. The only recourse is to flee. She offers to drive them.

Ponce directs her harshest words toward the local justice system, which she says failed her family.

"They have to do their jobs more seriously and they need to communicate," she says. "I'm just going to keep fighting and fighting until I see justice served."

Josie, Laura's firstborn, tries not to cry. She prefers to remember the good times with her mom. They used to bake cookies together and play in the park. And whenever her mom got sad, she'd play "Don't Worry, Be Happy," and the two would dance around and everything would be better.

She stays very still while her grandmother talks. She listens.

When the 21 balloons are released—one for each year of Laura's life—Josie cranes her head upward and watches the purple spheres become smaller and smaller in the distance, until they are just little dots and then nothing at all.

Need help? In the U.S., call 1-800-799-SAFE (7233) for the National Domestic Violence Hotline.

Critical Thinking

1. Could any one in the criminal justice system have done anything that might have prevented Laura's death?

2. What do you think of Jacquelyn Campbell's screening tool?

3. Based on what Linda Tyler learned, should GPS tracking devices be used on violators of restraining orders?

Internet References

Center for American Progress
cdn.americanprogress.org/wp-content/uploads/2013/04/americaUnder TheGun-2.pdf

Violence Policy Center
www.vpc.org/domesticviolence.htm

Article

Prepared by: Joanne Naughton

Human Sex Trafficking

AMANDA WALKER-RODRIGUEZ AND RODNEY HILL

Learning Outcomes

After reading this article, you will be able to:

- Outline the scope of human sex trafficking.

- Describe how victims are recruited into the business of human sex trafficking.

Human sex trafficking is the most common form of modern-day slavery. Estimates place the number of its domestic and international victims in the millions, mostly females and children enslaved in the commercial sex industry for little or no money.[1] The terms *human trafficking* and *sex slavery* usually conjure up images of young girls beaten and abused in faraway places, like Eastern Europe, Asia, or Africa. Actually, human sex trafficking and sex slavery happen locally in cities and towns, both large and small, throughout the United States, right in citizens' backyards.

Appreciating the magnitude of the problem requires first understanding what the issue is and what it is not. Additionally, people must be able to identify the victim in common trafficking situations.

Human Sex Trafficking

Many people probably remember popular movies and television shows depicting pimps as dressing flashy and driving large fancy cars. More important, the women—adults—consensually and voluntarily engaged in the business of prostitution without complaint. This characterization is extremely inaccurate, nothing more than fiction. In reality, the pimp *traffics* young women (and sometimes men) completely against their will by force or threat of force; this is human sex trafficking.

The Scope

Not only is human sex trafficking slavery but it is big business. It is the fastest-growing business of organized crime and the third-largest criminal enterprise in the world.[2] The majority of sex trafficking is international, with victims taken from such places as South and Southeast Asia, the former Soviet Union, Central and South America, and other less developed areas and moved to more developed ones, including Asia, the Middle East, Western Europe, and North America.[3]

Unfortunately, however, sex trafficking also occurs domestically.[4] The United States not only faces an influx of international victims but also has its own homegrown problem of interstate sex trafficking of minors.[5]

> **The United States not only faces an influx of international victims but also has its own homegrown problem of interstate sex trafficking of minors.**

Although comprehensive research to document the number of children engaged in prostitution in the United States is lacking, an estimated 293,000 American youths currently are at risk of becoming victims of commercial sexual exploitation.[6] The majority of these victims are runaway or thrown-away youths who live on the streets and become victims of prostitution.[7] These children generally come from homes where they have been abused or from families who have abandoned them. Often, they become involved in prostitution to support themselves financially or to get the things they feel they need or want (like drugs).

Other young people are recruited into prostitution through forced abduction, pressure from parents, or through deceptive agreements between parents and traffickers. Once these children become involved in prostitution, they often are forced to travel far from their homes and, as a result, are isolated from their friends and family. Few children in this situation can develop new relationships with peers or adults other than the person victimizing them. The lifestyle of such youths revolves around violence, forced drug use, and constant threats.[8]

Among children and teens living on the streets in the United States, involvement in commercial sex activity is a problem of epidemic proportion. Many girls living on the street engage in formal prostitution, and some become entangled in nationwide organized crime networks where they are trafficked nationally. Criminal networks transport these children around the United States by a variety of means—cars, buses, vans, trucks, or planes—and often provide them counterfeit identification to use in the event of arrest. The average age at which girls first become victims of prostitution is 12 to 14. It is not only the girls on the streets who are affected; boys and transgender youth enter into prostitution between the ages of 11 and 13 on average.[9]

The Operation

Today, the business of human sex trafficking is much more organized and violent. These women and young girls are sold to traffickers, locked up in rooms or brothels for weeks or months, drugged, terrorized, and raped repeatedly.[10] These continual abuses make it easier for the traffickers to control their victims. The captives are so afraid and intimidated that they rarely speak out against their traffickers, even when faced with an opportunity to escape.

> **Today, the business of human sex trafficking is much more organized and violent.**

Generally, the traffickers are very organized. Many have a hierarchy system similar to that of other criminal organizations. Traffickers who have more than one victim often have a "bottom," who sits atop the hierarchy of prostitutes. The bottom, a victim herself, has been with the trafficker the longest and has earned his trust. Bottoms collect the money from the other girls, discipline them, seduce unwitting youths into trafficking, and handle the day-to-day business for the trafficker.

Traffickers represent every social, ethnic, and racial group. Various organizational types exist in trafficking. Some perpetrators are involved with local street and motorcycle gangs, others are members of larger nationwide gangs and criminal organizations, and some have no affiliation with any one group or organization. Traffickers are not only men—women run many established rings.

> **Traffickers represent every social, ethnic, and racial group.**

Traffickers use force, drugs, emotional tactics, and financial methods to control their victims. They have an especially easy time establishing a strong bond with young girls. These perpetrators may promise marriage and a lifestyle the youths often did not have in their previous familial relationships. They claim they "love" and "need" the victim and that any sex acts are for their future together. In cases where the children have few or no positive male role models in their lives, the traffickers take advantage of this fact and, in many cases, demand that the victims refer to them as "daddy," making it tougher for the youths to break the hold the perpetrator has on them.

Sometimes, the traffickers use violence, such as gang rape and other forms of abuse, to force the youths to work for them and remain under their control. One victim, a runaway from Baltimore County, Maryland, was gang raped by a group of men associated with the trafficker, who subsequently staged a "rescue." He then demanded that she repay him by working for him as one of his prostitutes. In many cases, however, the victims simply are beaten until they submit to the trafficker's demands.

In some situations, the youths have become addicted to drugs. The traffickers simply can use their ability to supply them with drugs as a means of control.

Traffickers often take their victims' identity forms, including birth certificates, passports, and drivers' licenses. In these cases, even if youths do leave they would have no ability to support themselves and often will return to the trafficker.

These abusive methods of control impact the victims both physically and mentally. Similar to cases involving Stockholm Syndrome, these victims, who have been abused over an extended period of time, begin to feel an attachment to the perpetrator.[11] This paradoxical psychological phenomenon makes it difficult for law enforcement to breach the bond of control, albeit abusive, the trafficker holds over the victim.

National Problem with Local Ties

The Federal Level

In 2000, Congress passed the Trafficking Victims Protection Act (TVPA), which created the first comprehensive federal law to address trafficking, with a significant focus on the international dimension of the problem. The law provides a three-pronged approach: *prevention* through public awareness programs overseas and a State Department-led monitoring and sanctions program; *protection* through a new T Visa and services for foreign national victims; and *prosecution* through new federal crimes and severe penalties.[12]

As a result of the passing of the TVPA, the Office to Monitor and Combat Trafficking in Persons was established in October 2001. This enabling legislation led to the creation of a bureau within the State Department to specifically address human trafficking and exploitation on all levels and to take legal action against perpetrators.[13] Additionally, this act was designed to enforce all laws within the 13th Amendment to the U.S. Constitution that apply.[14]

U.S. Immigration and Customs Enforcement (ICE) is one of the lead federal agencies charged with enforcing the TVPA. Human trafficking represents significant risks to homeland security. Would-be terrorists and criminals often can access the same routes and use the same methods as human traffickers. ICE's Human Smuggling and Trafficking Unit works to identify criminals and organizations involved in these illicit activities.

The FBI also enforces the TVPA. In June 2003, the FBI, in conjunction with the Department of Justice Child Exploitation and Obscenity Section and the National Center for Missing and Exploited Children, launched the Innocence Lost National Initiative. The agencies' combined efforts address the growing problem of domestic sex trafficking of children in the United States. To date, these groups have worked successfully to rescue nearly 900 children. Investigations successfully have led to the conviction of more than 500 pimps, madams, and their associates who exploit children through prostitution. These convictions have resulted in lengthy sentences, including multiple 25-year-to-life sentences and the seizure of real property, vehicles, and monetary assets.[15]

Both ICE and the FBI, along with other local, state, and federal law enforcement agencies and national victim-based advocacy groups in joint task forces, have combined resources and expertise on the issue. Today, the FBI participates in approximately 30 law enforcement task forces and about 42 Bureau of Justice Assistance (BJA)-sponsored task forces around the nation.[16]

In July 2004, the Human Smuggling Trafficking Center (HSTC) was created. The HSTC serves as a fusion center for information on human smuggling and trafficking, bringing together analysts, officers, and investigators from such agencies as the CIA, FBI, ICE, Department of State, and Department of Homeland Security.

The Local Level

With DOJ funding assistance, many jurisdictions have created human trafficking task forces to combat the problem. BJA's 42 such task forces can be demonstrated by several examples.[17]

- In 2004, the FBI's Washington field office and the D.C. Metropolitan Police Department joined with a variety of nongovernment organizations and service providers to combat the growing problem of human trafficking within Washington, D.C.
- In January 2005, the Massachusetts Human Trafficking Task Force was formed, with the Boston Police Department serving as the lead law enforcement entity. It uses a two-pronged approach, addressing investigations focusing on international victims and those focusing on the commercial sexual exploitation of children.
- The New Jersey Human Trafficking Task Force attacks the problem by training law enforcement in the methods of identifying victims and signs of trafficking, coordinating statewide efforts in the identification and provision of services to victims of human trafficking, and increasing the successful interdiction and prosecution of trafficking of human persons.
- Since 2006, the Louisiana Human Trafficking Task Force, which has law enforcement, training, and victim services components, has focused its law enforcement and victim rescue efforts on the Interstate 10 corridor from the Texas border on the west to the Mississippi border on the east. This corridor, the basic northern border of the hurricane-ravaged areas of Louisiana, long has served as a major avenue of illegal immigration efforts. The I-10 corridor also is the main avenue for individuals participating in human trafficking to supply the labor needs in the hurricane-damaged areas of the state.
- In 2007, the Maryland Human Trafficking Task Force was formed. It aims to create a heightened law enforcement and victim service presence in the community. Its law enforcement efforts include establishing roving operations to identify victims and traffickers, deputizing local law enforcement to assist in federal human trafficking investigations, and providing training for law enforcement officers.

Anytown, USA

In December 2008, Corey Davis, the ringleader of a sex-trafficking ring that spanned at least three states, was sentenced in federal court in Bridgeport, Connecticut, on federal civil rights charges for organizing and leading the sex-trafficking operation that exploited as many as 20 females, including minors. Davis received a sentence of 293 months in prison followed by a lifetime term of supervised release. He pleaded guilty to multiple sex-trafficking charges, including recruiting a girl under the age of 18 to engage in prostitution. Davis admitted that he recruited a minor to engage in prostitution; that he was the organizer of a sex-trafficking venture; and that he used force, fraud, and coercion to compel the victim to commit commercial sex acts from which he obtained the proceeds.

According to the indictment, Davis lured victims to his operation with promises of modeling contracts and a glamorous lifestyle. He then forced them into a grueling schedule of dancing and performing at strip clubs in Connecticut, New York, and New Jersey. When the clubs closed, Davis forced the victims to walk the streets until 4 or 5 A.M. propositioning customers. The indictment also alleged that he beat many of the victims to force them to work for him and that he also used physical abuse as punishment for disobeying the stringent rules he imposed to isolate and control them.[18]

As this and other examples show, human trafficking cases happen all over the United States. A few instances would represent just the "tip of the iceberg" in a growing criminal enterprise. Local and state criminal justice officials must understand that these cases are not isolated incidents that occur infrequently. They must remain alert for signs of trafficking in their jurisdictions and aggressively follow through on the smallest clue. Numerous websites openly (though they try to mask their actions) advertise for prostitution. Many of these sites involve young girls victimized by sex trafficking. Many of the pictures are altered to give the impression of older girls engaged in this activity freely and voluntarily. However, as prosecutors, the authors both have encountered numerous cases of suspected human trafficking involving underage girls.

> **Local and state criminal justice officials must understand that these cases are not isolated incidents that occur infrequently.**

The article "The Girls Next Door" describes a conventional midcentury home in Plainfield, New Jersey, that sat in a nice middle-class neighborhood. Unbeknownst to the neighbors, the house was part of a network of stash houses in the New York area where underage girls and young women from dozens of countries were trafficked and held captive. Acting on a tip, police raided the house in February 2002, expecting to find an underground brothel. Instead, they found four girls between the ages of 14 and 17, all Mexican nationals without documentation.

However, they were not prostitutes; they were sex slaves. These girls did not work for profit or a paycheck. They were captives to the traffickers and keepers who controlled their every move. The police found a squalid, land-based equivalent of a 19th-century slave ship. They encountered rancid, doorless bathrooms; bare, putrid mattresses; and a stash of penicillin, "morning after" pills, and an antiulcer medication that can induce abortion. The girls were pale, exhausted, and malnourished.[19]

Human sex trafficking warning signs include, among other indicators, streetwalkers and strip clubs. However, a jurisdiction's lack of streetwalkers or strip clubs does not mean that it is immune to the problem of trafficking. Because human trafficking involves big money, if money can be made, sex slaves can be sold. Sex trafficking can happen anywhere, however unlikely a place. Investigators should be attuned to reading the signs of trafficking and looking closely for them.

Investigation of Human Sex Trafficking

ICE aggressively targets the global criminal infrastructure, including the people, money, and materials that support human trafficking networks. The agency strives to prevent human trafficking in the United States by prosecuting the traffickers and rescuing and protecting the victims. However, most human trafficking cases start at the local level.

Strategies

Local and state law enforcement officers may unknowingly encounter sex trafficking when they deal with homeless and runaway juveniles; criminal gang activity; crimes involving immigrant children who have no guardians; domestic violence calls; and investigations at truck stops, motels, massage parlors, spas, and strip clubs. To this end, the authors offer various suggestions and indicators to help patrol officers identify victims of sex trafficking, as well as tips for detectives who investigate these crimes.

Patrol Officers

- Document suspicious calls and complaints on a police information report, even if the details seem trivial.
- Be aware of trafficking when responding to certain call types, such as reports of foot traffic in and out of a house. Consider situations that seem similar to drug complaints.
- Look closely at calls for assaults, domestic situations, verbal disputes, or thefts. These could involve a trafficking victim being abused and disciplined by a trafficker, a customer having a dispute with a victim, or a client who had money taken during a sex act.
- Locations, such as truck stops, strip clubs, massage parlors, and cheap motels, are havens for prostitutes forced into sex trafficking. Many massage parlors and strip clubs that engage in sex trafficking will have cramped living quarters where the victims are forced to stay.
- When encountering prostitutes and other victims of trafficking, do not display judgment or talk down to them. Understand the violent nature in how they are forced into trafficking, which explains their lack of cooperation. Speak with them in a location completely safe and away from other people, including potential victims.

- Check for identification. Traffickers take the victims' identification and, in cases of foreign nationals, their travel information. The lack of either item should raise concern.

Detectives/Investigators

- Monitor websites that advertise for dating and hooking up. Most vice units are familiar with the common sites used by sex traffickers as a means of advertisement.
- Conduct surveillance at motels, truck stops, strip clubs, and massage parlors. Look to see if the girls arrive alone or with someone else. Girls being transported to these locations should raise concerns of trafficking.
- Upon an arrest, check cell phone records, motel receipts, computer printouts of advertisements, and tollbooth receipts. Look for phone calls from the jailed prostitute to the pimp. Check surveillance cameras at motels and toll facilities as evidence to indicate the trafficking of the victim.
- Obtain written statements from the customers; get them to work for you.
- Seek assistance from nongovernmental organizations involved in fighting sex trafficking. Many of these entities have workers who will interview these victims on behalf of the police.
- After executing a search warrant, photograph everything. Remember that in court, a picture may be worth a thousand words: nothing else can more effectively describe a cramped living quarter a victim is forced to reside in.
- Look for advertisements in local newspapers, specifically the sports sections, that advertise massage parlors. These businesses should be checked out to ensure they are legitimate and not fronts for trafficking.
- Contact your local U.S. Attorney's Office, FBI field office, or ICE for assistance. Explore what federal resources exist to help address this problem.

Other Considerations

Patrol officers and investigators can look for many other human trafficking indicators as well.[20] These certainly warrant closer attention.

General Indicators

- People who live on or near work premises
- Individuals with restricted or controlled communication and transportation
- Persons frequently moved by traffickers
- A living space with a large number of occupants
- People lacking private space, personal possessions, or financial records
- Someone with limited knowledge about how to get around in a community

Physical Indicators

- Injuries from beatings or weapons
- Signs of torture (e.g., cigarette burns)
- Brands or scarring, indicating ownership
- Signs of malnourishment

Financial/Legal Indicators

- Someone else has possession of an individual's legal/travel documents
- Existing debt issues
- One attorney claiming to represent multiple illegal aliens detained at different locations
- Third party who insists on interpreting. Did the victim sign a contract?

Brothel Indicators

- Large amounts of cash and condoms
- Customer logbook or receipt book ("trick book")
- Sparse rooms
- Men come and go frequently

Conclusion

This form of cruel modern-day slavery occurs more often than many people might think. And, it is not just an international or a national problem—it also is a local one. It is big business, and it involves a lot of perpetrators and victims.

Agencies at all levels must remain alert to this issue and address it vigilantly. Even local officers must understand the problem and know how to recognize it in their jurisdictions. Coordinated and aggressive efforts from all law enforcement organizations can put an end to these perpetrators' operations and free the victims.

Notes

1. www.routledgesociology.com/books/Human-Sex-Trafficking-isbn9780415576789 (accessed July 19, 2010).
2. www.unodc.org/unodc/en/human-trafficking/what-is-human-trafficking.html (accessed July 19, 2010).
3. www.justice.gov/criminal/ceos/trafficking.html (accessed July 19, 2010).
4. Ibid.
5. www.justice.gov/criminal/ceos/prostitution.html (accessed July 19, 2010).
6. Richard J. Estes and Neil Alan Weiner, *Commercial Sexual Exploitation of Children in the U.S., Canada, and Mexico* (University of Pennsylvania, Executive Summary, 2001).
7. Ibid.
8. http://fpc.state.gov/documents/organization/9107.pdf (accessed July 19, 2010).
9. Estes and Weiner.
10. www.womenshealth.gov/violence/types/human-trafficking.cfm (accessed July 19, 2010).
11. For additional information, see Nathalie De Fabrique, Stephen J. Romano, Gregory M. Vecchi, and Vincent B. Van Hasselt, "Understanding Stockholm Syndrome," *FBI Law Enforcement Bulletin,* July 2007, 10–15.
12. Trafficking Victims Protection Act, Pub. L. No. 106–386 (2000), codified at 22 U.S.C. § 7101, et seq.
13. Ibid.
14. U.S. CONST. amend. XIII, § 1: "Neither slavery nor involuntary servitude, except as a punishment for crime whereof the party shall have been duly convicted, shall exist within the United States, or any place subject to their jurisdiction."
15. U.S. Department of Justice, "U.S. Army Soldier Sentenced to Over 17 Years in Prison for Operating a Brothel from Millersville Apartment and to Drug Trafficking," www.justice.gov/usao/md/Public-Affairs/press_releases/press10a.htm (accessed September 30, 2010).
16. www.fbi.gov/hq/cid/civilrights/trafficking_initiatives.htm (accessed September 30, 2010).
17. www.ojp.usdoj.gov/BJA/grant/42HTTF.pdf (accessed September 30, 2010).
18. http://actioncenter.polarisproject.org/the-frontlines/recent-federal-cases/435-leader-of-expansive-multi-state-sex-trafficking-ring-sentenced (accessed July 19, 2010).
19. www.nytimes.com/2004/01/25/magazine/25SEXTRAFFIC.html (accessed July 19, 2010).
20. http://httf.wordpress.com/indicators/ (accessed July 19, 2010).

Critical Thinking

1. Do you believe prostitutes are victims of human sex traffickers?
2. How can sex traffickers compel anyone to become a sex worker against his or her will?
3. What laws have been enacted to deal with sex trafficking?

Create Central

www.mhhe.com/createcentral

Internet References

Polaris Project
www.polarisproject.org/human-trafficking/sex-trafficking-in-the-us
Science Daily
www.sciencedaily.com/releases/2013/09/130925132333.htm

From *FBI Law Enforcement Bulletin* by Amanda Walker-Rodriguez and Rodney Hill, March 2011. Published by Federal Bureau of Investigation. www.fbi.gov.

Article   Prepared by: Joanne Naughton

Reporting Rape and Wishing She Hadn't

How One College Handled a Sexual Assault Complaint

WALT BOGDANICH

Learning Outcomes

After reading this article, you will be able to:

- Understand some of the frustrations faced by some students when they report having been raped by a fellow student.

- See the effect a sexual assault can have on a victim.

Geneva, NY—She was 18 years old, a freshman, and had been on campus for just two weeks when one Saturday night last September her friends grew worried because she had been drinking and suddenly disappeared.

Around midnight, the missing girl texted a friend, saying she was frightened by a student she had met that evening. "Idk what to do," she wrote. "I'm scared." When she did not answer a call, the friend began searching for her.

In the early-morning hours on the campus of Hobart and William Smith Colleges in central New York, the friend said, he found her—bent over a pool table as a football player appeared to be sexually assaulting her from behind in a darkened dance hall with six or seven people watching and laughing. Some had their cellphones out, apparently taking pictures, he said.

Later, records show, a sexual-assault nurse offered this preliminary assessment: blunt force trauma within the last 24 hours indicating "intercourse with either multiple partners, multiple times or that the intercourse was very forceful." The student said she could not recall the pool table encounter, but did remember being raped earlier in a fraternity-house bedroom.

The football player at the pool table had also been at the fraternity house—in both places with his pants down—but denied raping her, saying he was too tired after a football game to get an erection. Two other players, also accused of sexually assaulting the woman, denied the charge as well. Even so, tests later found sperm or semen in her vagina, in her rectum and on her underwear.

It took the college just 12 days to investigate the rape report, hold a hearing and clear the football players. The football team went on to finish undefeated in its conference, while the woman was left, she said, to face the consequences—threats and harassment for accusing members of the most popular sports team on campus.

A *New York Times* examination of the case, based in part on hundreds of pages of disciplinary proceedings—usually confidential under federal privacy laws—offers a rare look inside one school's adjudication of a rape complaint amid a roiling national debate over how best to stop sexual assaults on campuses.

Whatever precisely happened that September night, the internal records, along with interviews with students, sexual-assault experts and college officials, depict a school ill prepared to evaluate an allegation so serious that, if proved in a court of law, would be a felony, with a likely prison sentence. As the case illustrates, school disciplinary panels are a world unto themselves, operating in secret with scant accountability and limited protections for the accuser or the accused.

At a time of great emotional turmoil, students who say they were assaulted must make a choice: Seek help from their school, turn to the criminal justice system or simply remain silent. The great majority—including the student in this case—choose their school, because of the expectation of anonymity and the belief that administrators will offer the sort of support that the police will not.

Yet many students come to regret that decision, wishing they had never reported the assault in the first place.

The woman at Hobart and William Smith is no exception. With no advocate to speak up for her at the disciplinary hearing, panelists interrupted her answers, at times misrepresented evidence and asked about a campus-police report she had not seen. The hearing proceeded before her rape-kit results were known, and the medical records indicating trauma were not shown to two of the three panel members.

One panelist did not appear to know what a rape exam entails or why it might be unpleasant. Another asked whether the football player's penis had been "inside of you" or had he been "having sex with you." And when the football player violated an order not to contact the accuser, administrators took five months to find him responsible, then declined to tell her if he had been punished.

Hobart and William Smith officials said they have "no tolerance for sexual assault" and treat all complaints seriously, offering emotional support, counseling and, when necessary, extra security and no-contact orders. They said the school's procedures offer students a fair hearing and were followed in this case. But they cited privacy laws in declining to answer specific questions.

"Campuses are really frustrated by knowing so much about a given case and how reasonable they were and they can't tell this story," said Brett A. Sokolow, a legal adviser to the school. "It's easy to paint them as the bad guy because they are in a position where they can't defend themselves."

Yet privacy laws did not stop Hobart and William Smith from disclosing the name of the woman—a possible rape victim—in letters to dozens of students. "I'm surprised they didn't attach my picture," she said.

After that disclosure, the woman spoke with her parents and agreed to have The Times use her first name, Anna, as well as her photograph.

The school said it was legally obligated to identify Anna to students who might have been called to testify in a possible criminal proceeding. The district attorney who was assessing the case disagreed, calling the identification "unnecessarily specific and, in my mind, a poor exercise of judgment."

A second female student at Hobart and William Smith, who was sexually assaulted at a fraternity party in October 2012, told The Times that one of her two assailants had had his punishment reduced on appeal because of poor questioning by the school's disciplinary panel. Like Anna, the student said friends of the accused had retaliated against her for reporting the assault.

Colleges nationwide are navigating the treacherous legal and emotional terrain of sexual assault. In May, the federal

Department of Education disclosed for the first time the names of colleges—55 in all, including Hobart and William Smith—under investigation for possibly violating federal rules aimed at stopping sexual harassment.

Afterward, Hobart and William Smith's president, Mark D. Gearan, sent letters to the college community, saying the school was confident it had not violated federal law. The school's policies and procedures "reflect our commitment to creating and maintaining an academic environment that is free from sexual harassment and misconduct," wrote Mr. Gearan, a former Peace Corps director and White House aide to Bill Clinton. This summer, a committee of faculty, staff and students is studying whether the school can deal more effectively with sexual misconduct.

Turning to the police may not offer a more equitable alternative. For example, as The Times reported in April, the Tallahassee police conducted virtually no investigation of a Florida State University student's rape complaint against the star quarterback Jameis Winston.

College administrators have their own incentive to deal with such cases on campus, since a public prosecution could frighten parents, prospective students and donors. Until last year, Hobart and William Smith's chief fund-raiser also helped oversee the school's handling of sexual assaults. The two functions are now separate.

While the school explained to Anna that talking to the police was an important option, she said, she decided against it after a school administrator said it would be a longer, drawn-out process. When she changed her mind six months later, the district attorney, R. Michael Tantillo, said he had "virtually nothing to work with" and quickly closed the case.

Although federal officials estimate that up to 20 percent of college students will be sexually assaulted in school, Mr. Tantillo said he rarely heard of such reports at Hobart and William Smith. "I guess that's your job to find out why," he told a reporter.

The Red Zone

Hobart and William Smith, on a hill overlooking Seneca Lake, deep in Finger Lakes wine country, is technically two small liberal-arts colleges—Hobart for men, William Smith for women. Its 2,300 students share the same campus, classes, dorms and overall administration, but receive degrees from their respective schools.

It took one visit for Anna to know this was where she wanted to be. "You could see out on the lake—literally, felt like this is what heaven looks like," she said.

Saying goodbye at the beginning of school, Anna's mother was comforted by a professor who had been in touch with her daughter. "'She really sounds like something,'" she recalled him saying. "He said: 'This is a very preppy place. I'm going to look out for her.'"

Anna, who considers herself anything but preppy, quickly grasped the challenge. "It was really a culture shock for me," she said. "A lot of the girls, they look alike, and I'm not small and have blonde hair and $500 sunglasses." So she searched for students "who didn't fit into that stereotypical William Smith girl."

There was something else: She had entered what is commonly known as the Red Zone, a period of vulnerability for sexual assaults, beginning when freshmen first walk onto campus until Thanksgiving break.

"Students arrive and you have a new environment, new social circle and the fear that goes with new expectations," said Robert S. Flowers, vice president for student affairs. That can lead to experimentation, including excessive drinking and attendant problems.

For that reason, the school held what students call rape seminars, the first in a program that, Mr. Flowers said, has made Hobart and William Smith a leader in preventing sexual violence.

Anna and her girlfriends often joked about how the national rape estimates might affect them. "They kept repeating the statistics," she said, and "every night we would go out we would be like, 'Oh, who's going to be the one?'"

It took just 14 days to find out, Anna said.

Whether one believes the accuser or the accused, it would be hard to dispute that what happened was a life-altering experience that ruptured Anna's nascent friendships, damaged her health, traumatized her family and derailed her college plans.

Emotionally battered, Anna later took a leave and returned home. "I do not recognize myself—I have become someone that I hate," she said. "It was such a toxic environment that I needed to be home and try and find myself again."

The fraternity houses, where so many parties occur, sit high above the lake. And it was at one fraternity, Kappa Sigma, where sometime between 9:30 and 10 P.M. on Sept. 7, Anna attended one of the year's first big social events—a "highlighter party," where students write on one another's clothes with a marker that glows under black light.

Later there was dancing. Anna and a senior football player she had just met were grinding to the music, rubbing their bodies together.

With so many students packed together in the basement, it became hot, and the football player escorted Anna upstairs, where smaller groups congregated in students' bedrooms. A friend tried to stop her, but she went anyway.

Anna said she had begun the evening drinking shots of rum mixed into Gatorade. She drank one beer at the dance, she said, and then the rest of an opened beer her dance partner had given her.

Around midnight, a fraternity member tried to enter his room, but found it locked. He opened the door with his key and caught a glimpse of what would become a pivotal episode in Anna's case: The senior football player was naked, and Anna was sitting on a bed with her top off, covering her breasts. The visitor quickly left.

About the same time, Anna texted the friend who had tried to intervene earlier; she had asked him to hold her keys because she had a hole in her pocket, and wanted them back. A subsequent message was darker, talking of hookups. "He got ten guys to try and hu with me," Anna wrote and added, "I'm scared." She would later tell the hearing panel that she had exaggerated the number to get her friend's attention.

She texted again for her keys, and then wrote, "He won't leave me."

Her friend tried calling, but got no response. Around 1 A.M., he asked another student to check Anna's room. She wasn't there. "We need to find her ASAP," he texted, adding, "She is so drunk."

Eventually he tracked her to a building called the Barn, a dance hall favored by students who do not belong to fraternities. Inside the dimly lit room, a D.J. played music near a couple of pool tables.

Around 1:25 A.M., after 10 minutes of searching, the friend said, he found Anna "bent over the pool table face down with her back towards the wall." She and the senior football player had their pants down, he said, "and it was clear they were having sex."

Anna "had a scared look on her face," he said, as six or seven people, perhaps five feet away, were "looking and laughing."

Anna's friend, a freshman who was also a football player, approached his teammate and told him that he was being disrespectful and had "crossed the line."

"It wasn't me, it was her," the teammate replied.

The friend walked Anna back to her dorm. On the way, another student saw her crying.

To this day, Anna says she remembers nothing about the Barn, the pool table or what happened there.

The Aftermath

It wasn't long before students in Anna's dorm realized something wasn't right. She was pale and disoriented. After she tried to vomit, classmates changed her clothes and put her to bed. Yet they continued to worry, fearing she had been drugged and raped.

One friend remembered that she had asked a football player earlier if he knew where Anna was. He smirked and made a crude allusion to a sexual act with Anna. "I felt very uncomfortable and got up and left," she said. Anna later identified him as one of her assailants.

Soon word spread that something untoward had happened at the Barn.

"The girls and I decided we should call campus security," one friend said. "We knew something was really wrong."

At 2:10 A.M., Sgt. Anthony Pluretti arrived to find 10 to 15 students outside Anna's room. After talking to her and realizing that she "could not remember how many drinks she had consumed and that she had no idea that she was at the Barn," Sergeant Pluretti called campus paramedics, he wrote in a report.

They recommended that a hospital evaluate her. The closest one with a trained sexual-assault nurse was 20 to 30 minutes away in Canandaigua.

The friend who had walked Anna home from the Barn accompanied her to the hospital. As the hours passed, he later told school officials, she began to talk about what had happened at Kappa Sigma: She was in a room with several boys and girls who left her alone with the football player; three times she refused his request for sex; two other football players entered the room, and she was sexually assaulted.

She did not go into great detail, the friend said, because she was "just beginning to remember what happened."

Around 7:30 in the morning, the nurse told Sergeant Pluretti that she had found "internal abrasions and heavy inflammation" and believed that Anna had suffered a forceful sexual assault. No date-rape drugs were found, but based on tests at the hospital, her blood-alcohol level at the time of the first sexual encounter would have been about twice what is considered legally drunk. While driving Anna back to her dorm, Sergeant Pluretti reported, he pulled over four times so she could vomit.

He tried to comfort her, explaining that the school "would respond in whatever manner that would support her," and that she should not feel rushed or pressured into deciding what to do, including whether to file a police report. She did express a desire to see a counselor after she had slept.

Back at Anna's home, around 2:30 on Sunday afternoon, her mother was entertaining guests when the phone rang. "The caller ID said Geneva, and I knew that was bad," she recalled. The caller identified herself as Maria Finger, a psychologist at the school.

"Are you sitting down?" she asked.

Behind Closed Doors

After a few hours of sleep, Anna gave a statement to the Office of Campus Safety. Other students provided their own statements, including the three accused football players. (They are not being identified in this article because the school cleared them.)

The first football player—who had pleaded guilty to a lesser charge in 2012 after being arrested for fighting and resisting arrest—was given a no-contact order, with a warning: "You

should not involve your friends in any manner to breach this order." Yet he twice asked one of the other two players to talk to Anna and check on her. He also texted one of Anna's friends, who then texted her: "He wants me to explain something to you. I don't necessarily believe him, but I wanna tell you his side to see if anything clicks considering that you don't remember some of it."

Now it was the school's responsibility under federal law to evaluate the allegations and, if necessary, hold a hearing.

At 3:14 P.M. on Tuesday, Sept. 17, a three-member panel convened behind closed doors to begin adjudicating Anna's complaint.

Such hearings are usually confidential. But The Times obtained a transcript of the proceedings.

The hearing, not dissimilar to what happens at many colleges, bore little resemblance to a court proceeding. Neither the accuser nor the accused were allowed to have lawyers or family members present. They could bring "advisers," but they would be voiceless advisers, prohibited from speaking.

The panelists could act pretty much as they wished, including questioning Anna about internal college reports and witness statements that she was not shown. Also absent were the usual courtroom checks and balances. The panel acted as prosecutor, judge and jury, questioning students and rendering judgment. All members were supposed to be trained for this delicate assignment.

The chairwoman, Sandra E. Bissell, vice president of human resources, was joined by Brien Ashdown, an assistant professor of psychology, and Lucille Smart, director of the campus bookstore, who the school said had expressed an interest in serving.

Boiled down, the complaint alleged that the senior football player had sexually assaulted Anna at the fraternity house while a second player inserted his penis into her mouth. At some point, a third player was alleged to have held her down. The senior was also accused of raping her later in the Barn.

The panel's initial questioning was based mostly on the investigative work of campus officers who aggressively sought out witnesses, followed leads and conducted interviews. According to the federal Education Department, a sexual-assault investigation typically takes around 60 calendar days. Hobart and William Smith did it in a little more than a week.

The hearing followed almost immediately. While a speedy adjudication can help all parties move on with their lives, in this case it left little time for the panel to study witness statements and prepare a cogent line of questioning. It also left Anna with little time to process events of that night, much less familiarize herself with the statements of others, some of which she had received the day before the hearing.

Anna was questioned first. "It was one of the hardest things I have ever gone through," she said later, adding, "I felt like I was talking to someone who knew nothing of any sort of social interaction; what happens at parties; what happens in sex."

She had to relive that evening through questions that jumped around in time, interrupted her answers and misrepresented witness statements. One question incorrectly quoted one of her friends asserting that at the dance Anna had told her that she wanted to go upstairs and have sex; in fact, the friend had said, Anna told her that the football player wanted to have sex.

At a critical point, Anna was about to describe what happened when she was alone upstairs with the first two football players—only to have the panel abruptly change the subject.

Q. OK, just the three of you?

A. Yeah.

Q. And then what happened?

Q: Can I just ask a question? OK, in your statement you do say that you were trying to text.

This is followed by a lengthy exchange about texting.

Later she was asked how the senior football player had tried to undress her, but the panelists cut her off.

Q. It helps us to understand what took place. You know, I'm going to apologize now because we have to ask difficult questions and I really apologize for that.

Q. And for all of us, as hard as it is, if you could be specific, if you are going to talk about a hand holding you, was his left or his right? And if there's a penis involved, is it flaccid, is it erect?

Q. Because the most detail you give us when you tell us the story, the less questions we have to ask for details. And if you want to break just let us know, we can give a couple of minutes.

Q. And as you start your story about this line of events, I just want to—you know what, can we just back up a little bit before that, because before this line of events starts to happen, there has or has not been any coke brought into the room?

This was followed by a discussion of Anna's allegation that some students in the room were using cocaine.

Two of the three panel members did not examine the medical records showing blunt force trauma—it was the chairwoman's prerogative not to share them. Instead, the panel asked what Anna had drunk, who she may have kissed and how she had danced. It was, Anna said, as if admitting you were grinding—a common way of dancing—"means you therefore consent to sex or should be raped."

The panel asked about the Barn—even though Anna stated that she did not remember being there—and whether the friend who found her there might have misconstrued her dancing as

sex. Anna responded that the pool-table witness had said she and the football player had their pants down. "I don't know who dances like that in public," she added.

It was during this discussion that one panelist asked if the witness had seen the player's penis in Anna's vagina or if he had just seen them having sex. "The questioning is absolutely stunning in its absurdity," Anna's lawyer, Inga L. Parsons, said later.

Anna's panelists were supposed to have "adequate training or knowledge" of sexual violence, according to federal guidelines. Even so, they pressed Anna on why she initially had not wanted a rape exam at the hospital.

"Does anyone really believe that it is pleasant to have rectal, vaginal, vulva and cervical swabs taken?" Ms. Parsons said. "Not to mention photographs of your private parts and dye injected into your vagina?"

A Locker-Room Meeting

The three football players then took their turns before the panel. Their accounts were quite different from their accuser's.

The senior player said Anna had given him a lap dance behind the fraternity bar. Upstairs, he said, she kissed him and then performed oral sex on him for two to three minutes. However, he said, he could not get an erection because he was tired from playing football and "a super long bus ride."

At the Barn, he said, she again pulled his pants down. "My flaccid penis was rubbing up against her vagina," he had told the campus police, adding that he had then realized their conduct "was inappropriate" and pulled up his pants.

The second football player said that while his teammate was in the room, Anna pulled down his pants and gave him oral sex. "I didn't consent," he said. "She's doing it all by herself. My hands are not touching her." After a brief period, he said, he told her to stop. "I zippered my pants up, put my belt on, and I walked out the door."

The third player, who faced the weakest case, acknowledged being in the fraternity room but said he left before the sexual encounter.

Anna's friend who recounted the pool-table scene chose not to testify, but, according to Anna, stands by his account.

Records show that the first two players had lied to campus officers when initially asked about Anna's allegations. The panel, though, chose not to ask about it.

The day after the episode, the senior football player told two campus officers that he could not recall Anna's name, even though he had spent much of the evening with her. The player denied having sexual contact with her during or after the fraternity party.

How the Suspects' Stories Changed

Two football players accused of sexual assault lied to the police and then changed basic parts of their accounts after witnesses contradicted them. The college panel that cleared both players failed to ask them any questions about why they had lied.

Player 1

First contacted by police

Did Not Have Sex

He told the police that he spent a few hours with the accuser but did not have sexual contact with her and didn't know her name.

Official police interview

Had Sexual Contact

He now said he received consensual oral sex from the accuser but was too tired from football to get an erection. Player 2 was not involved, he said.

A few days later

Both Players Were Involved

He said that he was "ready to come clean with the truth" and that Player 2 was in the room and received oral

sex. He said he had lied to protect himself against "false allegations."

Player 2

First contacted by police

Was Not There

He told a college official that he was "not involved in what-ever happened" with Player 1.

Official police interview

Was Not There

He told the police in two separate interviews that he was never in the room where the alleged assault took place.

A few days later

Had Sex For "A Few Seconds"

He now told police that he was in the room where the accuser said she was assaulted. He said she gave him oral sex for "a couple of seconds" before he got uncomfortable and left.

Source: The New York Times.

Only after the officers confronted him with reports to the contrary did he acknowledge having "sexual contact"—but not sex—at the Barn, and engaging in oral sex with Anna at the fraternity house.

The second player, during three separate interviews with campus officers, denied even being in the fraternity room. It wasn't until his fourth interview two days after the sexual encounter that he confessed to being in the room with his team-mate and having oral sex with Anna.

That same day, the football coach, Mike Cragg, summoned the three accused players, two team captains and the pool table witness for a private locker-room meeting where he heard their recollections, then passed on details of Anna's account, hearing transcripts show.

Two days after that meeting, the senior player changed his account a second time, telling the campus police that he "wanted us to know that he was ready to come clean about the truth," records show. A second player had in fact been with him at the fraternity house, the player said, and Anna had given both oral sex. He said he had lied to protect himself and his team-mate from Anna's false allegations.

Mr. Cragg declined to answer questions from The Times. But in a written statement he said, "If I were to learn that a

member of my team had behaved in a manner that violated our code of ethics or community standards, I would want him removed from the team immediately." He added: "I have never and would never encourage any player or players to coordinate stories to avoid disciplinary actions."

While the panel did not ask the players about their changed accounts, it did let the senior give an opening statement.

"I come from a wonderful family with strong Christian val-ues," he said. "I have been blessed with a beautiful mother, grandmothers, nieces and amazing aunts." And he added: "I treat women with the respect and honor they deserve."

The Panel Decides

The panel had to answer several basic questions: Did Anna give consent, was she capable of giving consent, and did the senior player violate the no-contact order either directly or through his friends? The standard of proof, mandated under federal guidelines, was preponderance of evidence—was it more likely than not that the students had sexually assaulted Anna?

Several hours after the last witness, the panel announced its decision clearing all three athletes on all counts.

The next day, the panel chairwoman sent Anna written confirmation of the decision, informing her that if she wished to appeal, she could find directions on Page 13 of the sexual-misconduct policy.

But Page 13 said nothing about appeals. Instead, it contained a section titled "False Allegations." The college admitted its mistake, Anna's mother said.

Anna's lawyer appealed the decision to clear the senior player. Mr. Flowers, the student-affairs administrator, granted the family additional time to file its appeal and reviewed the rape-kit results and hospital records. He upheld the panel's ruling, though he did find a violation of the no-contact order.

In an email response to The Times, the panel's chairwoman, Ms. Bissell, said the members were proud of their service. "A great deal of care and focus goes into this work, including extensive training in advance of our service, as well as refresher training prior to serving on a particular panel," she said.

As students returned after winter break, amid swirling rumors of a gang rape, they were greeted by a new mandate: Everyone had to watch an interactive video designed to educate them about sexual assault. The video contained hypotheticals and a series of questions. Answer them, students were told, or be denied campus housing.

The video generated instant controversy, beginning with its title—"ThinkLuv."

"So right from the start, it's the kind of program that's fun and playful and not something that needs to be taken seriously," said Kelsey Carroll, a recent graduate who founded a student group to combat sexism. "Rape is not about love. It is about violence and power."

The campus paper said the video attempted to educate students "while slut-shaming, generalizing, and even being sexist in the process."

Mr. Flowers defended the video, saying 94 percent of students had called it a positive experience.

On May 2, the day after the federal government announced that Hobart and William Smith was among the schools under investigation, the school sponsored an event used on other campuses called "Walk a Mile in Her Shoes," in which men walk around campus in high-heeled shoes to raise awareness of sexual assault. Campus meetings were also held to discuss the issue.

"I think the school has been receiving a lot of pressure from the press, alums and certainly from students to act," Ms. Carroll said. "As a campus we know it's not the case that rapes and sexual assaults are not happening on campus—it's that they aren't reported or the reporting system is failing."

Mr. Tantillo, the district attorney, said that after prosecuting a campus rape case 7 years ago, he had worked with the school to improve its handling of sexual-assault reports. He praised what he said was the thoroughness of its investigation of Anna's case.

But he also understands the questions that might lead a woman to stay silent. "Is this going to be publicized? Is everybody going to know about this? Am I going to be ostracized? Is this going to affect me for the rest of my life? Am I going to lose friends? Are people going to believe me?"

If a woman does decide to come forward, he said, she should do so immediately. "If you wait hours, days or weeks, that gives people plenty of time to get their stories together, to engage other witnesses to support them, and it makes it much, much more challenging."

Looking Back

Disappointment is a recurring theme among many students who ask their schools to adjudicate their sexual-assault complaints.

"Most of the students I work with say, 'Had I known how bad the school process was, I would not have reported at all,'" said Annie E. Clark, who counsels assault victims on their rights.

One reason for this disappointment is that many college hearing panelists lack even the most basic training, said Senator Claire McCaskill, a Missouri Democrat who has investigated the quality of campus rape investigations. The senator recently surveyed 440 colleges and universities and found that one-third had failed to properly train officials adjudicating claims.

A lack of transparency in student hearings makes it difficult, if not impossible, for students to evaluate the way their schools adjudicate complaints. "They are a little like snowflakes—they are all different," said Ms. McCaskill, a former sex-crimes prosecutor.

The police have their own shortcomings, she said, citing the flawed inquiry in the Jameis Winston case in Florida.

The Geneva police hardly distinguished themselves in Anna's case. Detective Brian E. Choffin, relying primarily on his reading of school records, sent the prosecutor an error-filled report.

Detective Choffin mischaracterized witness statements, put the words of one student in the mouth of another, and stated that he "never saw any discrepancies or alterations" in what the two football players told the authorities, even though they had initially lied about having sexual contact with their accuser. And while Anna's blood-alcohol tests had been done many hours after she last had a drink, he also stated unequivocally that her level "would not make a person impaired to the point of blacking out."

The detective defended his report, which disputed much of Anna's account, calling it "thorough and based on facts."

Looking back, Anna said she knows only too well the price of pursuing her complaint—physical threats and obscenities on her dormitory door, being pushed in the dining hall and asked to leave a fraternity party. Her roommate moved out with no explanation.

Mr. Flowers said the school continued to strengthen programs to stop sexual violence. Over the last 2 years, he said, seven students have undergone disciplinary hearings for sexual assaults; four were expelled.

Against her parents' wishes, Anna plans to return to Hobart and William Smith in the fall.

"Someone needs to help survivors there," she said.

Critical Thinking

1. Is it better to report the crime directly to the police rather than to the school?

2. If a woman gets drunk, shouldn't she be responsible for what happens to her?

3. What should the school have done differently, if anything?

Internet References

Create Central
www.mhhe.com/createcentral

The Herald
hwstheherald.com/wordpress/2014/02/20/federal-sexual-assault-investigation-questions-answerdsort/

U.S. Department of Education
www.ed.gov/news/press-releases/us-department-education-releases-list-higher-education-institutions-open-title-1

Unit 3

UNIT

Prepared by: Joanne Naughton

The Police

Police officers are the guardians of our rights under the Constitution and the law, and as such they have an awesome task which, in turn, requires furnishing police with immense powers. They are asked to maintain order, prevent crime, protect citizens, arrest wrongdoers, aid the sick, control juveniles, control traffic, and provide emergency services on a moment's notice. Sometimes in the service of these duties, police officers may sustain injuries or lose their lives.

In recent years, the job of the police officer has become even more complex and dangerous. Illegal drug use and trafficking are still major problems; racial tensions are explosive; and terrorism is now an alarming reality. As our population grows more numerous and diverse, the role of the police in America becomes ever more challenging, requiring skills that can only be obtained by greater training and professionalism. It is also vital that the public be aware of how their various police departments are carrying out their duties, providing citizen oversight.

Article   Prepared by: Joanne Naughton

The Changing Environment for Policing, 1985–2008

DAVID H. BAYLEY AND CHRISTINE NIXON

Learning Outcomes

After reading this article, you will be able to:

- State the differences between the policing environments in 1985 and 2008.
- Relate some of the challenges facing police executives today.
- Show how the growth of private security affects policing.

Introduction

In 1967, the President's Commission on Law Enforcement and the Administration of Justice published *The Challenge of Crime in a Free Society*. This publication is generally regarded as inaugurating the scientific study of the police in America in particular but also in other countries. Almost 20 years later, the John F. Kennedy School of Government, Harvard University, convened an Executive Session on the police (1985–1991) to examine the state of policing and to make recommendations for its improvement. Its approximately 30 participants were police executives and academic experts. Now, 20 years further on, the Kennedy School has again organized an Executive Session. Its purpose, like the first, is to combine professional with scholarly appraisals of the police and their contribution to public safety.

So the question naturally arises, what are the differences in the environment for policing between these two time periods? Are the problems as well as the institution of the police similar or different from one period to the next? Our thesis is that policing in the mid-1980s was perceived to be in crisis and there was a strong sense that fundamental changes were needed in the way it was delivered. In contrast, police are considered to be performing well 20 years later by both practitioners and outside observers. Crime has been falling for almost 18 years and any new challenges, including terrorism, appear to be manageable without the invention of new strategies for the delivery of police services. Past experience contains the lessons needed for the future. In our view, this assessment may be mistaken, not because existing policies are defective in controlling crime but because the institutions that

provide public safety are changing in profound ways that are not being recognized.

The Policing Environment in 1985

Policing in the United States was under siege in the 1980s for two reasons: (1) crime had been rising from the early 1960s, and (2) research had shown that the traditional strategies of the police were ineffective at coping with it. In 1960, the serious crime rate was 1,887 per 100,000 people. In 1985 it was 5,224, almost a threefold increase. This trend peaked in 1990 at 5,803. Violent crime (i.e., murder, rape, robbery and aggravated assault) rose from 161 per 100,000 people in 1960 to 558 in 1985, on the way to quadrupling by 1991 (Maguire and Pastore, 2007). Crime was, understandably, a big issue, feeding what could properly be called a moral panic.

Prompted by the President's Commission on Law Enforcement and the Administration of Justice in 1967, researchers in universities and private think-tanks began to study the effectiveness of standard police strategies. In the ensuing two decades, studies were published showing that crime rates were not affected by:

- Hiring more police (Loftin and McDowell, 1982; Krahn and Kennedy, 1985; Koenig, 1991; Laurie, 1970; Gurr, 1979; Emsley, 1983; Silberman, 1978; Reiner, 1985; Lane, 1980).
- Random motorized patrolling (Kelling et al., 1974; Kelling, 1985; Morris and Heal, 1981).
- Foot patrols (Police Foundation, 1981).
- Rapid response to calls for service (Tien, Simon and Larson, 1978; Bieck and Kessler, 1977; Spelman and Brown, 1981).
- Routine criminal investigation (Laurie, 1970; Burrows, 1986; Greenwood, Petersilia and Chaiken, 1977; Eck, 1982; Royal Commission on Criminal Procedure, 1981).

These conclusions, despite challenges to some of them on methodological grounds, were considered authoritative. They were so well accepted, in fact, that Bayley could say in 1994 that "one of the best kept secrets of modern life" was that the police do not prevent crime. "Experts know it, the police know it, and the public does not know it" (Bayley, 1994:3).

No wonder, then, that the first Executive Session concluded that fundamental changes were needed in police strategies. The Session took the lead in developing and legitimating a new model for the delivery of police services—community policing. The key recommendation was that police needed to be reconnected to the public in order both to enhance their crime-control effectiveness and to increase public respect. The strategy for doing this was community policing, including problem-oriented policing (Trojanowicz and Bucqueroux, 1990; Goldstein, 1990). Of the 17 studies published by the first Executive Session as *Perspectives on Policing,* eight featured "community" or "community policing" in the title, and several others discussed the importance of community. George Kelling and Mark Moore, members of the session, argued that the evolution of American policing could be described as movement from a politicized system to professionalism, then to constitutionalism, and ultimately to community policing (Kelling and Moore, 1988).

The first Executive Session also encouraged a new management style for policing, namely, one based on the analysis of crime and disorder problems and the evaluation of remediation programs. This process of description and analysis was to be carried out jointly by police and outside experts, such as academic scholars and management consultants.

The Policing Environment in 2008

When the second Executive Session met in January 2008, crime in the United States had declined dramatically since 1990. The serious crime rate (Part I crimes) had fallen to 3,808 per 100,000 people by 2006, a decline of 34 percent (Maguire and Pastore, 2007).[1] Even though the violent crime rate was still three times higher in 2006 than in 1960 (474 versus 161 per 100,000 people), it had declined by 37.5 percent since its peak in 1991, a huge change for the better. The police, in particular, feel that the decline vindicates their crime-control efforts, notably the strategy attributed to Bill Bratton of New York City, of the strict enforcement of laws against disorder and the management technique known as *zero tolerance,* managed through COMPSTAT (Bratton and Knobler, 1998; Eck and Maguire, 2000).

The decline has been so dramatic that it offset the continued questioning by analysts of the importance of police action in controlling crime (Eck and Maguire, 2000). Furthermore, there are now positive findings about the efficacy of certain police strategies. The most authoritative summary of this research comes from a panel of the National Research Council (Skogan and Frydl, 2004).

Reviewing all research conducted since the President's Commission (1967) and available in English, the panel reaffirmed the findings of the 1970s and 1980s that the standard practices of policing—employing more sworn officers, random motorized patrolling, rapid response and criminal investigation—failed to reduce crime when applied generally throughout a jurisdiction. It should be noted that most of the research on these topics, except for analysis of the effect of the number of

police employees on crime, dated from the earlier period. At the same time, the panel found that police could reduce crime when they focused operations on particular problems or places and when they supplemented law enforcement with other regulatory and abatement activities.

The strongest evidence for effectiveness was some form of problem solving, especially when focused on "hot spots," that is, locations accounting for a high volume of repeat calls for police service. Nonenforcement options included changing the physical design of buildings and public spaces, enforcing fire and safety codes, providing social services to dysfunctional families, reducing truancy and providing after-school programs for latch-key children.

By 2008, police executives could feel much happier about their efforts to control crime than they had 20 years before. Scholars, too, agreed that strategies used since the 1980s were efficacious, by and large.

This is not to say that police leaders currently feel that they can rest on their laurels nor that the environment for policing is entirely benign. Police executives understand that they are confronting several challenges, some new and some old:

- **Declining budgets and the rising cost of sworn police officers.** The cost of policing has quadrupled between 1985 and 2005, according to the Bureau of Justice Statistics (Gascón and Foglesong, 2009). The causes are rising labor costs for both sworn officers and civilian personnel, increased demand for police services and the growing complexity of police work. As a result, police budgets are increasingly at risk, with some cities reducing the number of police officers per capita.

- **Terrorism.** The primary impact of the Sept. 11 terrorist attack on state and local policing in the United States has been to improve their capacity for risk assessment of local vulnerabilities and first-responding in the event of terrorist incidents (Bayley and Weisburd, 2009). Although threat assessment and first-responding are understood to be core responsibilities of local police, their role with respect to counterterrorism intelligence gathering and analysis is more problematic. At the moment, most intelligence about terrorism comes from federal sources. Some observers take the view that local law enforcement, especially in the United States with its radically decentralized police system, does not have the personnel or skills to collect operational intelligence in a cost-effective way. Others argue, however, that local general-duties police who work among the population are essential for detecting precursor terrorist activities and building cooperative relations with the communities in which terrorists live (Bayley and Weisburd, 2009). Many police executives are critical of the federal government, therefore, for downgrading its law enforcement attention from nonterrorist crime and for reducing its support for local community-responsive and crime-prevention activities.

- **New immigrants, both legal and illegal.** Until recently, most American police departments took the view that enforcing immigration was a federal rather than a local responsibility. They took this view, in part, because they wanted illegal immigrants to feel free to approach police when they were victims of crime, particularly when they were exploited by employers. Police executives felt that even people who were in the country illegally deserved protection under the law. Recently, however, driven by growing anti-illegal immigration feelings in their jurisdictions, some police departments have begun to enforce immigration regulations. As anticipated, this has alienated these communities at the very moment when the importance of connecting with immigrants—legal as well as illegal—has become imperative as a response to terrorism. Not only may foreign terrorists take cover in immigrant communities but these communities, especially if they are disadvantaged and marginalized, may produce their own home-grown perpetrators. Great Britain and France have both experienced this phenomenon. Thus, the threat of terrorism raises difficult questions about the scope, intensity and methods of law enforcement in immigrant communities.

- **Racial discrimination.** Charges of unequal treatment on the basis of race have been a continual problem for police since the rise of civil rights consciousness in the 1960s. Concerns raised about the substantial amount of discretion possessed by frontline police was one of the first issues taken up by police researchers more than 40 years ago. Various aspects of policing have been implicated—arrests, use of force, shootings, street stops, search and seizure, offense charging and equality of coverage (Fridell et al., 2001; Skolnick and Fyfe, 1993; Walker, 2003). Not only is racial discrimination an enduring issue for police executives to manage but its potential for destroying the reputation of police agencies and the careers of officers is hard to exaggerate. It is the allegation that every police chief dreads.

- **Intensified accountability.** Oversight of police performance, with regard to effectiveness in controlling both crime and personal behavior, has grown steadily in the past few years. The monitoring of institutional performance has been part of a governmentwide movement to specify measurable performance indicators. External oversight of individual behavior has involved complaints commissions, citizen review panels and ombudsmen. Many would argue that the quality of policing with respect to crime control and personal behavior has improved over the last half of the 20th century as a result of these developments. The public, however, seems more skeptical, especially with respect to the behavior of individual officers. At least that would be a fair reading of the fact that in the United States as well as other English-speaking countries, the demand for greater oversight of police behavior continues to grow, fed by the media's insatiable appetite for stories about police misdeeds.

There are two aspects to what is being asked for: (1) holding the police to account for performing the services for which they were created—crime prevention and criminal investigation and (2) disciplining officers who behave improperly in the course of their duties.

Today, more than 100 of America's largest cities have some sort of civilian oversight of police behavior compared with only a handful in the early 1990s (Walker, 2003). Independent civilian review of complaints against the police has been established in the last three decades in Great Britain, New Zealand, Australia and Canada. But this is only the most visible tip of a larger iceberg. Oversight has also intensified in the form of tighter financial auditing, performance indicators mandated by governmental and quasi-governmental bodies, enactment of more stringent legal standards and federal consent decrees. This is in addition to what seems to police to be an unappeasable media appetite for revelations about police, and even ex-police, misbehavior.

- **Police unions.** While acknowledging the reasons that led to the growth of police unions, police executives complain about its impact on management. In particular, they criticize the reflexive defense of work rules that inhibit strategic innovation and organizational change, the elaborate procedures required to discipline poorly performing officers, and the inculcation of an occupational culture preoccupied with tangible rewards.

Although all of these current challenges certainly complicate their work, police executives do not view them as a crisis for policing as was the case in the mid-1980s. These challenges are complex and difficult but manageable within the competence of experienced executives. With the arguable exception of terrorism, they do not require a shift in the strategies of policing.

Embedded in this sense of achievement among police professionals is frustration with the gap between objective measures of public safety and public perceptions. Although crime may have declined, the public's fear has not. Police commonly attribute this discrepancy to the exaggeration of crime by the media and the failure to give credit where credit is due.

The Looming Watershed

We believe that policing may be approaching, if not well into, a period of change that will significantly affect what police do and how they do it. It may be as significant as the period after 1829 when Sir Robert Peel created the London Metropolitan Police. The choice of 1829 as the reference point is not rhetorical. This year marked the beginning of the gradual monopolization of the police function by government. Starting in 1829, governments in Anglo-Saxon countries, much earlier in Europe, assumed responsibility for policing—for hiring, paying, training and supervising. What is happening now is the reverse of that: nation-states are losing their monopoly on policing.

The pressures eroding the monopoly of governments within national boundaries to create and manage policing come from three directions:

- The internationalization of policing.
- The devolution of policing to communities.
- The growth of private policing.

In short, policing is being pushed up, down and sideways from its traditional mooring in government.

The Internationalization of Policing

Policing has shifted away from national governments because of the development of a genuinely international police capacity and increased international collaboration in law enforcement. The United Nations now has more than 11,000 police recruited from about 118 countries and deployed in 13 missions. The United States currently contributes 268 police to UNPOL (formerly CIVPOL). Although UNPOL's primary mission is "to build institutional police capacity in post-conflict environments" (Kroeker, 2007), its officers have been armed in Kosovo, Timor-Leste and Haiti and enforce laws alongside the local police. It is worth mentioning that this is part of a broader development of international institutions of justice, including the development of a portable international criminal code, courts and tribunals authorized to try individuals, and prisons for persons both convicted and under trial.

The United States now collaborates widely with law enforcement agencies abroad. As of February 2010, the FBI has offices in 70 cities overseas and the DEA has offices in almost 90 (see FBI and DEA home pages). The United States trains more than 10,000 police a year at its four International Law Enforcement Training Academies (located in Budapest, Bangkok, Gaborone and San Salvador) and brings many more trainees to the United States. The United States also participates in a host of international task forces and ad hoc law enforcement operations that focus on drugs, terrorism, trafficking in people and, more recently, cyber-crime, including pornography. The United States has also encouraged—some would say "pressured"—countries to bring their laws into conformity with American practice, for example, with respect to wiretapping, the use of informants, asset forfeiture, and the Racketeer Influenced and Corrupt Organizations Act (Nadelman, 1997; Snow, 1997). American influence, direct and indirect, has been so powerful that Chris Stone says there has been an "Americanization of global law enforcement" (Stone, 2003). The United States, furthermore, has begun to create a reserve force of police and other criminal justice experts that can be deployed at short notice to countries emerging from conflict.

If policing is a fundamental attribute of government, along with external defense, then the world has begun to create a world government of sorts. Although seeds of this movement preceded the first Executive Session, a major impetus was the fall of the Berlin Wall in 1989 and the subsequent implosion of the Soviet Union (Bayley, 2006).

The Devolution of Policing to Communities

The attitude of police generally in the Western world, but especially in its English-speaking democracies, toward collaborating with members of the public who act voluntarily to improve public security has undergone a major change since the 1980s. No longer viewed as nuisances or dangerous vigilantes, these people are now seen as "co-producers" of public safety. This transformation of view is attributable in large part to the acceptance of community policing, which the first Executive Session was instrumental in promoting. Police in democratic countries now actively encourage citizen participation by sharing information, training volunteers, consulting the public about priorities, mobilizing collaborative crime-prevention programs, enlisting the public as informants in problem solving, and soliciting help from city planners, architects and the designers of products to minimize criminal opportunities. Neighborhood Watch is probably the best known police-citizen partnership. Others include Business Improvement Districts, mobile CB-radio patrols, and private-sector programs for providing equipment and professional skills to police departments.

It has become axiomatic in policing that the public should be encouraged to take responsibility for enhancing public safety. As police themselves now recognize, they cannot do the job alone. Public participation is seen by police and academics alike as a critical contributor to police effectiveness and thus to public safety.

The Growth of Private Policing

Policing is being pushed sideways by the growth in the private security industry. Estimates of its strength are not exact because "private security" covers a wide range of activities—e.g., guarding, transporting valuables, investigating, installing protective technology and responding to alarms—and is supplied by companies commercially to others as well as by businesses to themselves. The U.S. Department of Labor estimated that there were slightly more than 1 million private security guards in 2005 (U.S. Bureau of Labor Statistics, 2005). That would be 49 percent more than the number of full-time sworn police officers in the same year (673,146). A report issued by the International Association of Chiefs of Police (IACP) and the Community Oriented Police Services (COPS) Office estimated, however, that in 2004, the number was about 2 million (IACP, 2005). If that were true, there would be almost three times as many private security personnel as full-time police officers. The discrepancy between figures of the Department of Labor and those of IACP-COPS may have arisen because the larger estimate includes in-house security provided by private organizations, whereas the Department of Labor figures only include the personnel of companies providing security services commercially. The larger figure is the one most often cited in commentaries on private policing (Cunningham and Taylor, 1985; Singer, 2003).

The growth of private security appears to be a phenomenon of the last quarter of the 20th century (Nalla and Newman, 1991). It was first documented in *The Hallcrest Report: Private Security and Police in America* (Cunningham and Taylor, 1985), which estimated the number at 1.5 million. This was more than twice the number of public police at that time. Although the use of private security was certainly visible to police officials in the 1980s, the number of *commercial* private security personnel has grown by as much as two-thirds. Their number rose sharply immediately after the Sept. 11 attack, fell in 2003 (although not to pre-Sept. 11 levels) and has continued to increase (U.S. Bureau of Labor Statistics, 2007). It is reasonable to assume that the number of *in-house* private security personnel has also increased, though perhaps not as much.

Worldwide, there are now more private police than government-run police: 348 versus 318 per 100,000, according to a survey by Jan Van Dijk (2008). The highest rates are in the United States, Canada and central Europe. Britain and Australia also have slightly more private security personnel than public police (Australian Bureau of Statistics, 2006; European Union, 2004). In the European Union, only Britain and Ireland have more private than public police (European Union, 2004). Statistics are not available for Latin America, Africa, and South and Southeast Asia, but private security is certainly very visible there.

The point to underscore is that worldwide, and dramatically in the United States, there has been a steady growth in the number of private "police." If visible guardians are a deterrent to crime, as the routine-activities theory of crime asserts and as police themselves strongly believe, then one reason for the decline in crime in the United States since the early 1990s might be the growth in private security. As far as we are aware, analyses of the crime drop in the United States have not tested for this possibility.

The effect of these three changes in the environment for policing is to diversify the providers of public safety. Governments, especially country-based governments, no longer direct or provide public safety exclusively. The domestic security function has spread to new levels of government but, more important, to nonstate actors, volunteers and commercial providers. The police role is now shared. This is not simply saying that there are now both public and private police. Public and private policing have blended and are often hard to distinguish. Governments hire private police to supplement their own police; private entrepreneurs hire public police. We are in an era of what Les Johnston refers to as hybrid policing (Johnston, 1992).

Until now, assessments of the police have focused on two questions: How can they be made more effective, and how can the behavior of individual officers be improved? Now, we suggest, a third question has arisen: Who is responsible for policing?

Changes within Public Policing

Not only are changes occurring in the environment that may affect the structure of policing but police themselves are in the process of changing the way they work. The factors driving this are (1) the threat of terrorism, (2) intelligence-led policing and (3) DNA analysis. Each of these developments transfers initiative in directing operations to specialists who collect and analyze information and away from both general-duties police and the public. Ironically, these changes could undo the signature contribution of the 1980s—community policing.

The Threat of Terrorism

Although many anti-terrorism experts understand the importance of working with communities, especially immigrant ones, counterterrorism centralizes decision making, shifting it upward in police organizations and making it less transparent. In the aftermath of Sept. 11, a new emphasis has been placed on the development of covert intelligence gathering, penetration and disruption. In the United States, the development of covert counterterrorism capacity has been unequally distributed, being more pronounced in larger police forces. Where it occurs, important questions arise about legal accountability as well as operational payoff. These issues are familiar to police, having arisen before in efforts to control illegal narcotics and organized crime.

Intelligence-Led Policing

Intelligence-led policing[2] utilizes crime mapping, data mining and the widespread use of closed-circuit television monitoring, which all rely on analysis based on information collected from impersonal sources. It thereby empowers senior commanders to develop their own agendas for law enforcement rather than consulting with affected communities.

DNA Analysis

DNA analysis allows crimes to be solved without witnesses or confessions. Research in the 1970s showed that the identification of suspects by victims and witnesses was essential to the solving of most crimes (Greenwood, Petersilia and Chaiken, 1977). Detectives, contrary to their fictional portrayals, work from the identification of suspects by the public back to the collection of evidence to prove guilt. DNA changes that, emphasizing forensic evidence over human testimony, promising a technological solution to criminal identification.

The effect of these developments—the threat of terrorism, intelligence-led policing and DNA analysis—impels the police to rely more on their own intellectual and physical resources and on centralized decision making for agendas and strategies. It lessens the importance of consulting with and mobilizing the disaggregate resources of communities. It also favors enforcement as the tool of choice over preventive strategies of regulation and abatement. These changes in orientation may be necessary and may raise police effectiveness, but they also represent a return to the sort of insular professionalism that characterized policing before the 1980s.

The Challenges of Change

The changes described both inside and outside the established police structures and functions create issues that will have to be confronted. With the expansion of private policing, public safety may become more inequitably distributed on the basis of economic class. The affluent sectors of society, especially its commercial interests, may be more protected, and the poor sectors less protected (Bayley and Shearing, 2001). This trend could be exacerbated if the tax-paying public at the same time withdraws its support from the public police in favor of private security. There are indications that this has already occurred in public education, where people with the means to pay for private schools are increasingly reluctant to support public education. If this should occur in policing, a dualistic system could evolve—responsive private policing for the affluent, and increasingly underfunded public policing for the poor (Bayley and Shearing, 2001). The political consequences of this could be calamitous.

Furthermore, who is to hold private policing to legal and moral account? Public police in the United States and other democracies have been made accountable in many ways.

Public police executives themselves often argue that they are too accountable, meaning they are scrutinized too closely, too mechanically and at a substantial cost in reporting. Private policing, however, is imperfectly regulated and it is unclear whether existing law provides sufficient leverage (Joh, 2004; Prenzler and Sarre, 2006).

So, an ironic question arises: Is there a continuing role for government in ensuring an equitable and lawful distribution of security at the very time that government is losing its monopoly control? Should it accomplish by regulation what it no longer can by ownership? If so, how should this be done? In particular, what agency of government would be responsible for it?

The internationalization of policing also raises issues of control and legitimacy. Simply put, whose interests will be served by policing under international auspices? Will it be collective interests articulated by constituent states and powerful organized interests, or by the needs of disaggregate populations represented through participative institutions? Democratic nation-states emphasize the needs of individuals in directing police. It is not at all clear that international institutions will do the same, although they have taken impressive steps on paper to articulate comprehensive standards of police conduct (U.N. High Commissioner for Human Rights, 1996).

Finally, we submit that policing may be facing a clash of cultures as the public increasingly demands participation in the direction and operation of policing while at the same time police agencies become more self-directing and self-sufficient in their use of intelligence resources. This issue is not new. It is the same issue that policing faced in the 1980s and that was tackled in the first Executive Session. How important is public legitimacy for police effectiveness and public safety? How can the support of the public be maintained while police take advantage of powerful new technologies that may decrease interaction with them?

Conclusion

In the United States and other developed democracies, changes are occurring that may undermine the monopoly of state-based policing as well as its community-based paradigm. In pointing out these changes between 1985 and 2008, we are not making value judgments about them. These changes may have made the police more effective at providing public safety without infringing human rights in unacceptable ways. We call attention to these changes because their potential effects are enormous and largely unappreciated. They constitute an invisible agenda as consequential as the problems discussed in the 1980s.

Twenty years ago, policing was in the throes of what is now regarded as a revolution in its operating approach. It shifted from a philosophy of "give us the resources and we can do the job" to realizing the importance of enlisting the public in the coproduction of public safety. Policing today faces much less obvious challenges. Current strategies and technologies seem to be sufficient to deal with foreseeable threats to public safety, with the possible exception of terrorism. If this is so, then policing will develop in an evolutionary way, fine-tuning operational techniques according to experience, particularly the findings of

evidence-based evaluations. If, however, changes in the environment are reshaping the structure and hence the governance of policing, and adaptations within the police are weakening the connection between police and public, then we may be entering a period of evolutionary discontinuity that could be greater than that of the 1980s, perhaps even of 1829. Both the role of police in relation to other security providers and the soul of the police in terms of how it goes about its work may be in play today in more profound ways than are being recognized.

References

Australian Bureau of Statistics. "2006 Census of Population and Housing, Australia, Occupation by Sex (Based on Place of Employment)." Accessed February 11, 2010, at www.censusdata.abs.gov.au.

Bayley, David H. *Police for the Future*. New York: Oxford University Press, 1994.

Bayley, David H. *Changing the Guard: Developing Democratic Police Abroad*. New York: Oxford University Press, 2006.

Bayley, David H. and Clifford Shearing. *The New Structure of Policing: Description, Conceptualization, and Research Agenda*. Final report. Washington, D.C.: U.S. Department of Justice, National Institute of Justice, July 2001. NCJ 187083.

Bayley, David H. and David Weisburd. "Cops and Spooks: The Role of the Police in Counterterrorism." In *To Protect and Serve: Policing in an Age of Terrorism*, ed. David Weisburd, Thomas E. Feucht, Idit Hakimi, Lois Felson Mock and Simon Perry. New York: Springer, 2009:81–100.

Bieck, William and David A. Kessler. *Response Time Analysis*. Kansas City, Mo.: Board of Police Commissioners, 1977.

Bratton, William and Peter Knobler. *Turnaround: How America's Top Cop Reversed the Crime Epidemic*. New York: Random House, 1998.

Burrows, John. *Investigating Burglary: The Measurement of Police Performance*. Research Study 88. London: Home Office, 1986.

Cunningham, William C. and Todd H. Taylor. *The Hallcrest Report: Private Security and Police in America*. Portland, Ore.: Chancellor Press, 1985.

Eck, John E. *Solving Crimes: The Investigation of Burglary and Robbery*. Washington, D.C.: Police Executive Research Forum, 1982.

Eck, John E. and Edward Maguire. "Have Changes in Policing Reduced Violent Crime? An Assessment of the Evidence." In *The Crime Drop in America*, ed. Alfred Blumstein and Joel Wallman. New York: Cambridge University Press, 2000:207–265.

Emsley, Clive. *Policing and Its Context, 1750–1870*. London: Macmillan, 1983.

European Union. "Panoramic Overview of Private Security Industry in the 25 Member States of the European Union." Presentation at Fourth European Conference on Private Security Services, Brussels, Belgium. Confederation of European Security Services and UNI-Europa, 2004. Accessed February 11, 2010, at www.coess.org/pdf/ panormal.pdf.

Fridell, Lori, Robert Lunney, Drew Diamond and Bruce Kubu. *Racially Biased Policing: A Principled Response*. Washington, D.C.: Police Executive Research Forum, 2001.

Gascón, George and Todd Foglesong. "How to Make Policing More Affordable: A Case Study of the Rising Costs of Policing in the United States." Draft paper submitted to the Second Harvard

Executive Session on Policing and Public Safety, Cambridge, Mass., 2009.

Goldstein, Herman. *Problem Oriented Policing.* Philadelphia, Penn.: Temple University Press, 1990.

Greenwood, Peter W., Joan Petersilia and Jan Chaiken. *The Criminal Investigation Process.* Lexington, Mass.: D.C. Heath, 1977.

Gurr, Ted R. "On the History of Violent Crime in Europe and America." In *Violence in America: Historical and Comparative Perspectives,* ed. H.D. Graham and Ted R. Gurr. Beverly Hills, Calif.: Sage Publications, 1979:353–374.

International Association of Chiefs of Police. *Post 9-11 Policing: The Crime Control–Homeland Security Paradigm—Taking Command of New Realities.* Alexandria, Va.: IACP, 2005.

Joh, Elizabeth E. "The Paradox of Private Policing." *Journal of Criminal Law and Criminology* 95(1):(2004)49–131.

Johnston, Les. *The Rebirth of Private Policing.* London: Routledge, 1992.

Kelling, George L. "Order Maintenance, the Quality of Urban Life, and Police: A Different Line of Argument." *In Police Leadership in America,* ed. William A. Geller. New York: Praeger Publishers, 1985:309–321.

Kelling, George L. and Mark H. Moore. *The Evolving Strategy of Policing.* Harvard University, Kennedy School of Government, Perspectives on Policing Series, No. 4. Washington, D.C.: National Institute of Justice, November 1988. NCJ 114213.

Kelling, George L., Antony M. Pate, Duane Dieckman and Charles Brown. *The Kansas City Preventive Patrol Experiment: Summary Report.* Washington, D.C.: Police Foundation, 1974.

Koenig, Daniel J. *Do Police Cause Crime? Police Activity, Police Strength and Crime Rates.* Ottawa, Ontario: Canadian Police College, 1991.

Krahn, Harvey and Leslie Kennedy. "Producing Personal Safety: The Effects of Crime Rates, Police Force Size, and Fear of Crime." *Criminology* 23 (1985): 697–710.

Kroeker, Mark. Informal presentation to biannual meeting of the International Police Advisory Commission, Abuja, Nigeria, January 2007.

Lane, Roger. "Urban Police and Crime in Nineteenth-Century America." In *Crime and justice,* ed. N. Morris and Michael Tonry. Chicago: University of Chicago Press, 1980.

Laurie, Peter. *Scotland Yard.* New York: Holt, Rinehart & Winston, 1970.

Loftin, Colin and David McDowell. "The Police, Crime, and Economic Theory: An Assessment." *American Sociological Review* 47 (1982): 393–401.

Maguire, Kathleen and Ann L. Pastore, eds. *Sourcebook of Criminal Justice Statistics.* Years 2000–2007. Washington, D.C.: U.S. Department of Justice, Bureau of Justice Statistics. Accessed February 11, 2010, at www.albany.edu/sourcebook /about.html.

Morris, Pauline and Kevin Heal. *Crime Control and the Police: A Review of Research.* Research Study 67. London: Home Office, 1981.

Nadelman, Ethan A. "The Americanization of Global Law Enforcement: The Diffusion of American Tactics and Personnel." In *Crime and Law Enforcement in the Global Village,* ed. William F. McDonald. Cincinnati, Ohio: Anderson Publishing, 1997:123–138.

Nalla, Mahesh and Graeme Newman. "Public versus Private Control: A Reassessment." *Journal of Criminal Justice* 19 (1991): 537–549.

Police Foundation. *The Newark Foot Patrol Experiment.* Washington, D.C.: Police Foundation, 1981.

Prenzler, Tim and Rick Sarre. "Private and Public Security Agencies: Australia." In *Plural Policing: A Comparative Perspective,* ed. T. Jones and T. Newburn. London: Routledge, 2006:169–189.

President's Commission on Law Enforcement and the Administration of Justice. *The Challenge of Crime in a Free Society.* Washington, D.C.: U.S. Government Printing Office, 1967.

Reiner, Robert. *The Politics of the Police.* New York: St. Martin's Press, 1985.

Royal Commission on Criminal Procedure. Research Study 17. London: HMSO, 1981.

Shearing, Clifford D. "The Relation Between Public and Private Policing." In *Modern Policing,* ed. N. Morris and Michael Tonry. Chicago: University of Chicago Press, 1992.

Silberman, Charles. *Criminal Violence, Criminal Justice.* New York: Random House, 1978.

Singer, Peter W. *Corporate Warriors: The Rise of the Privatized Military Industry.* Cornell Studies in Security Affairs. Ithaca, N.Y.: Cornell University Press, 2003.

Skogan, Wesley and Kathleen Frydl. *Fairness and Effectiveness in Policing: The Evidence.* Washington, D.C.: National Academies Press, 2004.

Skolnick, Jerome H. and James Fyfe. *Beyond the Law.* New York: Free Press, 1993.

Snow, Thomas. "Competing National and Ethical Interests in the Fight Against Transnational Crime: A U.S. Practitioners Perspective." In *Crime and Law Enforcement in the Global Village,* ed. William F. McDonald. Cincinnati: Anderson Publishing, 1997:169–186.

Spelman, William and Dale K. Brown. *"Calling the Police": Citizen Reporting of Serious Crime.* Washington, D.C.: Police Executive Research Forum, 1981.

Stone, Christopher. "Strengthening Accountability in the New Global Police Culture." Presentation at conference on Crime and the Threat to Democratic Governance, Woodrow Wilson International Center for Scholars, Washington, D.C., 2003.

Tien, James M., James W. Simon and Richard C. Larson. *An Alternative Approach to Police Patrol: The Wilmington Split-Force Experiment.* Washington, D.C.: U.S. Government Printing Office, 1978.

Trojanowicz, Robert C. and Bonnie Bucqueroux. *Community Policing: A Contemporary Perspective.* Cincinnati: Anderson Publishing, 1990.

United Nations High Commissioner for Human Rights. *International Human Rights Standards for Law Enforcement: A Pocket Book on Human Rights for Police.* Geneva, Switzerland: UNHCHR, 1996.

U.S. Bureau of Labor Statistics, U.S. Department of Labor. "May 2005 Occupational Employment and Wage Estimates." Accessed February 11, 2010, at www.bls.gOv/oes/oes_dl/htm#2005_m.

U.S. Bureau of Labor Statistics, U.S. Department of Labor. "Security Guard Employment Before and After 2001." Summary 07–08 (August 2007). Accessed March 22, 2010, at www.bls.gov/opub /ils/pdf/opbils61.pdf.

Van Dijk, Jan. *The World of Crime.* Los Angeles: Sage Publications, 2008.

Walker, Samuel. "The New Paradigm of Police Accountability: The U.S. Justice Department 'Pattern or Practice' Suits in Context." *St. Louis University Public Law Review* 22(1) (2003):3–52.

Notes

1. The FBI, which provides the statistics on crimes known to the police, stopped calculating a rate for the entire Part I index after 2001. It did, however, continue to publish rates for both violent and property crime, from which a total rate for all Part I crime can be calculated.

2. Intelligence-led policing may be confused with evidence-based policing. Intelligence-led policing refers to the targeting of operations on the basis of specific information, whereas evidence-based policing refers to shaping of operational strategies on the basis of evaluations of their efficacy.

Critical Thinking

1. Why was community policing developed?
2. What factors are affecting the way policing is done today?
3. Does the increase of private policing present the possibility of problems?
4. What has been the public's reaction to the fact that crime has declined?

Create Central

www.mhhe.com/createcentral

Internet References

Law Enforcement Guide to the World Wide Web
http://leolinks.com

National Institute of Justice/National Criminal Justice Reference Service
www.ncjrs.gov/policing/man199.htm

DAVID H. BAYLEY is Distinguished Professor in the School of Criminal Justice at the State University of New York, Albany. **CHRISTINE NIXON** is APM Chair, Victorian Bushfire Reconstruction and Recovery Authority, and State Commissioner of Police, Victoria, Australia (Retired). The authors acknowledge valuable research assistance provided by Baillie Aaron, Research Assistant, in the Program in Criminal Justice and Police Management, John F. Kennedy School of Government, Harvard University.

From *New Perspectives in Policing*, http://goo.gl/dvnJ3 (September 2010). Copyright © by John F. Kennedy School of Government at Harvard University with funding by the National Institute of Justice. This article is available free of charge online at: http://cms.hks.harvard.edu/var/ezp_site/storage/fckeditor/file/pdfs/centers-programs/programs/criminal-justice/NPIP-The-Changing-Environment-for-Policing-1985–2008.pdf.

Article   Prepared by: Joanne Naughton

Judge Rejects New York's Stop-and-Frisk Policy

JOSEPH GOLDSTEIN

Learning Outcomes

After reading this article, you will be able to:

- Understand the objections to "stop-and-frisk"

- Describe the remedies ordered by the judge in *Floyd v. City of New York.*

In a repudiation of a major element in the Bloomberg administration's crime-fighting legacy, a federal judge has found that the stop-and-frisk tactics of the New York Police Department violated the constitutional rights of minorities in New York, and called for a federal monitor to oversee broad reforms.

In a decision issued on Monday, the judge, Shira A. Scheindlin, ruled that police officers have for years been systematically stopping innocent people in the street without any objective reason to suspect them of wrongdoing. Officers often frisked these people, usually young minority men, for weapons or searched their pockets for contraband, like drugs, before letting them go, according to the 195-page decision.

These stop-and-frisk episodes, which soared in number over the last decade as crime continued to decline, demonstrated a widespread disregard for the Fourth Amendment, which protects against unreasonable searches and seizures by the government, according to the ruling. It also found violations with the 14th Amendment's equal protection clause.

Judge Scheindlin found that the city "adopted a policy of indirect racial profiling by targeting racially defined groups for stops based on local crime suspect data." She rejected the city's arguments that more stops happened in minority neighborhoods solely because those happened to have high-crime rates.

"I also conclude that the city's highest officials have turned a blind eye to the evidence that officers are conducting stops in a racially discriminatory manner," she wrote.

Noting that the Supreme Court had long ago ruled that stop-and-frisks were constitutionally permissible under certain conditions, the judge stressed that she was "not ordering an end to the practice of stop-and-frisk. The purpose of the remedies addressed in this opinion is to ensure that the practice is carried out in a manner that protects the rights and liberties of all New Yorkers, while still providing much needed police protection."

City officials did not immediately comment on the ruling, or on whether they planned to appeal. Mayor Michael R. Bloomberg scheduled a news conference at 1 p.m. to discuss the decision.

To fix the constitutional violations, the judge designated an outside lawyer, Peter L. Zimroth, to monitor the Police Department's compliance with the Constitution.

Judge Scheindlin also ordered a number of other remedies, including a pilot program in which officers in at least five precincts across the city will wear body-worn cameras in an effort to record street encounters. She also ordered a "joint remedial process"—in essence, a series of community meetings—to solicit public input on how to reform stop-and-frisk.

The decision to install Mr. Zimroth, a partner in the New York office of Arnold & Porter, LLP, and a former corporation counsel and prosecutor in the Manhattan district attorney's office, will leave the department under a degree of judicial control that is certain to shape the policing strategies under the next mayor.

Relying on a complex statistical analysis presented at trial, Judge Scheindlin found that the racial composition of a census tract played a role in predicting how many stops would occur.

She emphasized what she called the "human toll of unconstitutional stops," noting that some of the plaintiffs testified that their encounters with the police left them feeling that they did not belong in certain areas of the cities. She characterized each stop as "a demeaning and humiliating experience."

"No one should live in fear of being stopped whenever he leaves his home to go about the activities of daily life," the judge wrote. During police stops, she found, blacks and Hispanics "were more likely to be subjected to the use of force than whites, despite the fact that whites are more likely to be found with weapons or contraband."

The ruling, in *Floyd v. City of New York,* follows a two-month nonjury trial in Federal District Court in Manhattan earlier this year over the department's stop-and-frisk practices.

Judge Scheindlin heard testimony from about a dozen black or biracial men and a woman who described being stopped, and she heard from statistical experts who offered their conclusions based on police paperwork describing some 4.43 million stops between 2004 and mid-2012. Numerous police officers and commanders testified as well, typically defending the legality of stops and saying they were made only when officers reasonably suspected criminality was afoot.

While the Supreme Court has long recognized the right of police officers to briefly stop and investigate people who are behaving suspiciously, Judge Scheindlin found that the New York police had overstepped that authority. She found that officers were too quick to deem as suspicious behavior that was perfectly innocent, in effect watering down the legal standard required for a stop.

"Blacks are likely targeted for stops based on a lesser degree of objectively founded suspicion than whites," she wrote.

She noted that about 88 percent of the stops result in the police letting the person go without an arrest or ticket, a percentage so high, she said, that it suggests there was not a credible suspicion to suspect the person of criminality in the first place.

Critical Thinking

1. Do you agree with the judge's ruling?
2. Despite the fact that the court's decision has been overturned on appeal, do you believe the incoming mayor should follow the judge's ruling, as he has said he will?

Create Central

www.mhhe.com/createcentral

Internet References

American Civil Liberties Union
www.aclu.org/racial-justice/racial-profiling
Jurist
http://jurist.org/paperchase/2013/11/federal-appeals-court-upholds-stop-and-frisk-ruling.php

Article

Prepared by: Joanne Naughton

New ACLU Report Takes a Snapshot of Police Militarization in the United States

RADLEY BALKO

Learning Outcomes

After reading this article, you will be able to:

- State the findings of the ACLU's year-long study of police militarization regarding the circumstances under which police SWAT teams are used.

- Explain how the drug war justifies the use of military equipment by police departments.

T he American Civil Liberties Union has released the results of its year-long study of police militarization. The study looked at 800 deployments of SWAT teams among 20 local, state and federal police agencies in 2011–2012. Among the notable findings:

- 62 percent of the SWAT raids surveyed were to conduct searches for drugs.
- Just under 80 percent were to serve a search warrant, meaning eight in 10 SWAT raids were not initiated to apprehend a school shooter, hostage taker, or escaped felon (the common justification for these tactics), but to investigate someone still only suspected of committing a crime.
- In fact, just 7 percent of SWAT raids were "for hostage, barricade, or active shooter scenarios."
- In at least 36 percent of the SWAT raids studies, *no contraband of any kind* was found. The report notes that due to incomplete police reports on these raids this figure could be as high as 65 percent.
- SWAT tactics are disproportionately used on people of color.

- 65 percent of SWAT deployments resulted in some sort of forced entry into a private home, by way of a battering ram, boot, or some sort of explosive device. In over half those raids, the police failed to find any sort of weapon, the presence of which was cited as the reason for the violent tactics.
- Ironically (or perhaps not), searches to serve warrants on people suspected of drug crimes were more likely to result in forced entry than raids conducted for other purposes.
- Though often justified for rare incidents like school shootings or terrorist situations, the armored personnel vehicles police departments are getting from the Pentagon and through grants from the Department of Homeland Security are commonly used on drug raids.

In other words, where violent, volatile SWAT tactics were once used only in limited situations where someone was in the process of or about to commit a violent crime—where the police were using violence only to defuse an already violent situation—SWAT teams today are overwhelmingly used to investigate people who are still only suspected of committing nonviolent consensual crimes. And because these raids often involve forced entry into homes, often at night, they're actually *creating* violence and confrontation where there was none before.

When SWAT teams are used in a way that's consistent with their original purpose, they're used carefully and cautiously. The ACLU report finds that, "In nearly every deployment involving a barricade, hostage, or active shooter, the SWAT report provided specific facts that gave the SWAT team reason to believe there was an armed and often dangerous suspect." By contrast . . .

. . . incident reports for search warrant executions, especially in drug investigations, often contained no information about why the SWAT team was being sent in, other than to note that the warrant was "high risk," or else provided otherwise unsubstantiated information such as "suspect is believed to be armed." In case after case that the ACLU examined, when a SWAT team was deployed to search a person's home for drugs, officers determined that a person was "likely to be armed" on the basis of suspected but unfounded gang affiliations, past weapons convictions, or some other factor that did not truly indicate a basis for believing that the person in question was likely to be armed at the moment of the SWAT deployment. Of course, a reasonable belief that weapons are present should not by itself justify a SWAT deployment. Given that almost half of American households have guns, use of a SWAT team could almost always be justified if this were the sole factor.

But we've already seen cases in which the mere factor that the resident of a home was a *legal* gun owner—in some cases by virtue of the fact that the owner had obtained some sort of state license—was used as an excuse to execute a full-on SWAT raid to serve a warrant for an otherwise nonviolent crime. Of the SWAT raids the ACLU studied in which police cited the possibility of finding a weapon in the home, they actually found a weapon just 35 percent of the time.

A 2004 classified memo all but confirms the blurring of the lines between the drug war and the U.S. military by calling the Drug Enforcement Agency (DEA) the "other" warfighter and stating that the war on drugs "has all the risks, excitement, and dangers of conventional warfare."

—From the ACLU report on police militarization

The report also finds almost no outside oversight on the use of SWAT tactics. This is consistent with my own research and reporting. The decision to send the SWAT team is often made by the SWAT commander or by fairly low-ranking officials within a police agency. Consequently, factors such as using the minimum amount of force necessary or the civil rights of the people who may be affected by the raid often aren't taken into consideration. The ACLU, for example, found that although some police agencies in the survey were required to write after-action reports or present annual reports on the SWAT team, "internal reviews mostly pertain to proper weapons use and training and not to evaluating important civil rights implications of SWAT use."

The report also makes important contributions on other aspects of militarization that will be familiar to people who follow this issue, including the effect that militarization can have on the mindset of police officers, and the role that federal anti-drug grants have played in boosting this trend.

Finally, the ACLU concedes that its report is necessarily incomplete, because "[d]ata collecting and reporting in the context of SWAT was at best sporadic and at worst virtually nonexistent."

The ACLU filed public records requests with more than 255 law enforcement agencies during the course of this investigation. One hundred and fourteen of the agencies denied the ACLU's request, either in full or in part. Even if the ACLU had received and examined responsive documents from all 255 law enforcement agencies that received public records requests, this would represent only a sliver of the more than 17,000 law enforcement agencies that exist throughout the United States, and thus would shine only a dim light on the extent of police militarization throughout the country.

This, too, is consistent with my own experience. Among the excuses police agencies gave the ACLU for not turning over records were that the requested information "contained trade secrets," that turning over such information could affect the effectiveness of SWAT teams and that the information requested was too broad, would cost too much to produce or wasn't subject to open-records law. In short, we have police departments that are increasingly using violent, confrontational tactics to break into private homes for increasingly low-level crimes, and they seem to believe that the public has no right to know the specifics of when, how and why those tactics are being used.

This report is a valuable contribution to the public debate over police militarization. In some ways, it merely confirms what Eastern Kentucky University criminologist Peter Kraska already documented in the late 1990s (and what I documented in my book last year). But Kraska's last survey was in 2005, so this is an important new set of data conclusively demonstrating that the trends Kraska first documented nearly 20 years ago have only continued and have in some ways intensified. The most revealing part of the report, however, may be what *isn't* in it. That is, that police agencies are using these tactics with increasing frequency but are doing so with sloppy and incomplete record-keeping, little heed for the safety and civil rights of the people on the receiving end of these raids and are troublingly reluctant to share any information about the tactics.

I'm sure that the report will generate lots of media coverage, just as Kraska's studies did. The mass media seem to find renewed interest in this issue every 5 or 6 years. The problem, as the ACLU documents well, is that none of that coverage has generated any meaningful reform. And so the militarization continues. I'll have more on the ACLU's recommendations in a subsequent post. In the meantime, the ACLU has also released a series of videos with snippets of raid footage it obtained in its investigation. Here's one of them: https://www.youtube.com/watch?v=0QKBDT4UKTE&list=PLwfdTKcPlB5nTMaaoFgWHmx9KiBjnUZf3&index=1

Critical Thinking

1. Why is outside oversight on the use of SWAT important?
2. Why is the ACLU report incomplete?

Internet References

ACLU

https://www.aclu.org/sites/default/files/assets/jus14-warcomeshome-report-web-rel1.pdf

YouTube

https://www.youtube.com/watch?v=0QKBDT4UKTE&list=PLwfdTKcPlB5nTMaaoFgWHmx9KiBjnUZf3&index=1

RADLEY BALKO blogs about criminal justice, the drug war, and civil liberties for *The Washington Post*. He is the author of the book *Rise of the Warrior Cop: The Militarization of America's Police Forces.*

Article   Prepared by: Joanne Naughton

Understanding the Psychology of Police Misconduct

BRIAN D. FITCH

Learning Outcomes

After reading this article, you will be able to:

- Express your familiarity with the rationalizations that contribute to unethical behavior by police.

- Argue in favor of the importance of ethics training for law enforcement officers.

- Describe how police officers can reduce the psychological discomfort that might accompany their misconduct.

L aw enforcement is a unique profession, with officers experiencing a host of freedoms not available to the general public, including the application of deadly force, high-speed driving, and seizing personal property. While these liberties may be necessary, they also can create opportunities for wrongdoing, especially if such behavior is likely to go undetected because of poor supervision. The embarrassment caused by misconduct can damage the public trust, undermine officer morale, and expose agencies to unnecessary—and, in many cases, costly—litigation.[1] Consequently, a clear understanding of the psychology underlying unethical behavior is critical to every law enforcement supervisor and manager at every level of an organization, regardless of one's agency or mission.

Law enforcement agencies go to great lengths to recruit hire, and train only the most qualified applicants—candidates who have already demonstrated a track record of good moral values and ethical conduct. Similarly, most officers support the agency, its values, and its mission, performing their duties ethically while avoiding any misconduct or abuse of authority. Yet despite the best efforts of organizations everywhere, it seems that one does not have to look very far these days to find examples of police misconduct particularly in the popular press.[2] Even more disturbing, however, is that many of the officers engaged in immoral or unethical behavior previously demonstrated good service records, absent any of the "evil" typically associated with corruption or abuse.

While it is probably true that at least some of the officers who engage in illicit activities managed somehow to slip through the cracks in the hiring process and simply continued their unethical ways, this account fails to explain how otherwise good officers become involved in misconduct. The purpose of this article is to familiarize law enforcement managers and supervisors with the cognitive rationalizations that can contribute to unethical behavior. The article also offers strategies and suggestions intended to mitigate misconduct, before it actually occurs, by developing a culture of ethics.

Moral Responsibility and Disengagement

Most law enforcement professionals are, at their core, good, ethical, and caring people. Despite the overuse of a popular cliché, many officers do in fact enter law enforcement because they want to make a positive difference in their communities. Officers frequently espouse strong, positive moral values while working diligently—in many cases, at great personal risk—to bring dangerous criminals to justice. Doing so provides officers with a strong sense of personal satisfaction and self-worth. As a result, most officers do not—and in many cases cannot—engage in unethical conduct unless they can somehow justify to themselves the morality of their actions.[3]

Decades of empirical research have supported the idea that whenever a person's behaviors are inconsistent with their attitudes or beliefs, the individual will experience a state of psychological tension—a phenomenon referred to as cognitive dissonance.[4] Because this tension is uncomfortable, people will modify any contradictory beliefs or behaviors in ways intended to reduce or eliminate discomfort. Officers can reduce psychological tension by changing one or more of their cognitions—that is, by modifying how they think about their actions and the consequences of those behaviors—or by adjusting their activities, attitudes, or beliefs in ways that are consistent with their values and self-image. Generally speaking, an officer will modify the cognition that is least resistant to change, which, in most cases, tends to be the officer's attitudes, not behaviors.

One of the simplest ways that officers can reduce the psychological discomfort that accompanies misconduct is to cognitively restructure unethical behaviors in ways that make them seem personally and socially acceptable, thereby allowing officers to behave immorally while preserving their self-image as ethically good people. The following is a partial list of common rationalizations that officers can use to neutralize or excuse unethical conduct.[5]

Denial of victim. Officers who rely on this tactic argue that because no victim exists, no real harm has been done. It is probably safe to suggest that officers do not generally regard drug dealers, thieves, and sexual predators as bona fide victims, regardless of the nature of an officer's conduct. An officer, for instance, who takes money from a suspected drug dealer during the service of a search warrant might argue that because the dealer acquired the currency illegally, the dealer was never actually entitled to the proceeds. Rather, the money belongs to whoever possesses it at the time.

Victim of circumstance. Officers who utilize this method convince themselves that they behaved improperly only because they had no other choice. Officers may claim that they were the victims of peer pressure, an unethical supervisor, or an environment where "everyone else is doing it," so what else could they possibly have done? Regardless of the context, these officers excuse their conduct by alleging that they had no alternative but to act unethically.

Denial of injury. Using this form of rationalization, officers persuade themselves that because nobody was actually hurt by their actions, their behavior was not really immoral. This explanation is especially common in cases involving drugs, stolen property, or large amounts of untraceable cash where it can be difficult, if not impossible, to identify an injured party. Officers who use this tactic may further neutralize their deviant conduct by comparing it to the harm being done by the drug dealer from whom the money was stolen.

Advantageous comparisons. Officers who depend on this explanation rely on selective social comparisons to defend their conduct. Officers who falsify a police report to convict a suspected drug dealer, for example, might defend their actions by minimizing their participation or the frequency of their unethical behavior, while at the same time vilifying a coworker as someone who "lies all the time on reports." In comparison to an officer who routinely falsifies reports, the first officer's conduct can seem less egregious.

Higher cause. Officers who practice this type of cognitive restructuring argue that sometimes, it may be necessary to break certain rules to serve a higher calling or to achieve a more important goal. An officer who conducts an unlawful search to uncover evidence against a suspected pedophile might reason that the nature of the crime justifies breaking the rules. "The ends justify the means," officers might assert—suggesting that they did what was necessary, regardless of the legality or morality of their conduct, to put a dangerous criminal behind bars. This form of rationalization can be especially disturbing because it goes beyond merely excusing or justifying deviant behavior to the point of actually glorifying certain forms of wrongdoing in the name of "justice" or "the greater good."

Table 1   Rationalizing Misconduct

Strategy	Description
Denial of Victim	Alleging that because there is no legitimate victim, there is no misconduct.
Victim of Circumstance	Behaving improperly because the officer had no other choice, either because of peer pressure or unethical supervision.
Denial of Injury	Because nobody was hurt by the officer's action, no misconduct actually occurred.
Advantageous Comparisons	Minimizing or excusing one's own wrongdoing by comparing it to the more egregious behavior of others.
Higher Cause	Breaking the rules because of some higher calling—that is, removing a known felon from the streets.
Blame the Victim	The victim invited any suffering or misconduct by breaking the law in the first place.
Dehumanization	Using euphemistic language to dehumanize people, thereby making them easier to victimize.
Diffusion of Responsibility	Relying on the diffusion of responsibility among the involved parties to excuse misconduct.

Blame the victim. An officer who uses this form of justification blames the victim for any misconduct or abuse. If, for instance, officers use unreasonable force on a suspected drug dealer, they can simply argue that the victim brought on this suffering by violating the law. "If the dealer doesn't want to get beat up, the dealer should obey the law," the officer might reason. "I'm not using force on law-abiding citizens, only on drug dealers; they give up their rights when they break the rules." By assigning blame to the victim, the officer not only finds a way to excuse any wrongdoing, but also a way to feel sanctimonious about doing so.

Dehumanization. The amount of guilt or shame officers feel for behaving unethically depends, at least in part, on how they regard the person being abused. To avoid the feelings of self-censorship or guilt that often accompany misconduct, officers can employ euphemistic language to strip victims of their humanity. Using terms like "dirtbag" to describe law violators has the effect of dehumanizing intended targets, generally making it easier for officers to justify, ignore, or minimize the harmful effects of their actions, while at the same time reducing their personal responsibility for behaving in ways that they know are wrong.

Diffusion of responsibility. An officer who uses this excuse relies on the shared participation—and, by extension, the shared guilt—of everyone involved in an incident of misconduct to excuse or reduce any personal culpability. With each additional accomplice, every individual officer is seen as that much less responsible for any wrongdoing that might have occurred. If, for instance, money is stolen from an arrestee, officers might assert that there were many officers at the crime scene who could have done this, so an individual cannot be blamed. Similarly, if ten officers were involved in the service of a search warrant, then each officer is only one-tenth responsible for any misconduct that occurs.

Misconduct's Slippery Slope

It is important to note that most officers do not jump headfirst into large-scale misconduct—instead, they weigh in gradually in a process referred to as incrementalism.[6] The strength and ease with which officers can rationalize unethical behavior also depends, at least in part, on how they view their conduct, the people harmed by their actions, and the consequences that flow from their actions. An officer's initial slide down the slippery slope of misconduct can begin with nothing more than simple policy violations that, if left unchecked, generate a mild feeling of psychological tension or discomfort. However, by learning to rationalize wrongdoing in ways that make it psychologically and morally acceptable, officers are able to relieve any feelings of distress or discomfort, effectively disengaging their moral compasses.

Officers can employ cognitive rationalizations prospectively (before the corrupt act) to forestall guilt and resistance, or retrospectively (after the misconduct) to erase any regrets. In either case, the more frequently an officer rationalizes deviant behavior, the easier each subsequent instance of misconduct becomes.[7] This is because the more frequently officers employ rationalizations, the easier it becomes to activate similar thought patterns in the future. With time and repeated experience, rationalizations can eventually become part of the habitual, automatic, effortless ways that officers think about themselves, their duties, and the consequences of their actions, eventually allowing officers to engage in increasingly egregious acts of misconduct with little, if any, of the guilt or shame commonly associated with wrongdoing.

As officers learn to pay less attention to the morality of their actions, the ways they think about misconduct—that is, their attitudes, beliefs, and values—may begin to change as well. Officers can begin defining behaviors that were once seen as unethical or immoral as necessary parts of completing their assigned duties. Even more troubling, however, is that once rationalizations become part of an agency's dominant culture, they can alter the ways officers define misconduct, particularly if wrongdoings are rewarded either informally by an officer's peer group or formally by the organization.

Ethics Education

Law enforcement agencies throughout the United States, as well as abroad, have begun to recognize the importance of ethics training. While such attention represents a significant step in the right direction, ethical instruction is often limited to little more than the discussion and development of proper moral values—an approach commonly referred to as character education.[8] Proponents of this method suggest that officers who possess the right values—and, by extension, the right character—will always do the right thing, regardless of

the circumstances. Although few people would argue with the importance of good moral values and character, ethical decisions are not always simple.

Before officers can act ethically, they must recognize the moral nature of a situation; decide on a specific and, hopefully, ethical course of action; possess the requisite moral motivation to take action; and demonstrate the character necessary to follow through with their decisions.[9] To further complicate matters, even the best of intentions can be thwarted by peer pressure or fear of retaliation. For example, the 2003 National Business Ethics Survey found that approximately 40 percent of those surveyed would not report misconduct if they observed it because of fear of reprisal from management.[10]

This cloud does, however, contain a silver lining. Research has demonstrated that ethics education can assist officers in better navigating moral challenges by increasing ethical awareness and moral reasoning—two critical aspects of ethical decision making.[11] However, conducting meaningful ethics education requires more than lengthy philosophical lectures on the importance of character. Rather, instructors should focus on facilitating a dialogue that challenges officers on key moral issues and assumptions; tests their reasoning and decision-making skills; and allows them to share their experiences in a safe, supportive environment.[12]

For ethics education to be truly effective, organizations must make moral discussions a regular part of the agency's training program. In the same way that officers routinely train in defensive tactics, firearms, and law to better prime them for field duties, officers should prepare equally well for any ethical issues they might encounter.[13] Supervisors can stimulate ethical discussions with a video documentary, news clip, or fictional story. Regardless of the stimulus, however, the more frequently officers discuss ethics, the better able they will be to recognize a moral dilemma, make the appropriate ethical decision, and demonstrate the moral courage necessary to behave honorably.

Next, law enforcement agencies must establish a clear code of ethical conduct, including a set of core values and a mission statement. Merely establishing a code of ethical conduct is not enough, however; the department's top management must lead by example. It is important to remember that a code of conduct applies equally to employees at all levels of an organization.[14] As most leaders can confirm from experience, officers can be surprisingly quick to point out any inconsistencies between the organization's stated values and the conduct of senior management. If leaders expect officers to behave ethically, leaders must model the way.

Departments must also work to create systems that reward ethical conduct and punish unethical behavior.[15] Core values and codes of conduct are of little value if they are not supported by wider agency objectives that reward ethical actions. Not only should law enforcement organizations reward officers for behaving ethically, they must also seriously address officers' ethical concerns by thoroughly investigating any allegations, while protecting the confidentiality of those reporting such incidents. And, finally, agencies should strive to create an open environment where ethical issues can be discussed without fear of punishment or reprisal.

In the end, mitigating and, hopefully, eliminating misconduct require regular ethics training, high ethical standards, appropriate reward systems, and a culture in which ethical issues are discussed freely. While the responsibility for creating a culture of ethics rests with leadership, individual officers must do their part to behave ethically, support the moral conduct of others, and challenge misconduct in all its forms. Only by remaining vigilant to the psychology of misconduct can law enforcement professionals focus attention back on the positive aspects of their profession, while enjoying the high levels of public trust necessary to do their jobs.

Notes

1. For a more complete discussion on the impact of police misconduct see Adam Dunn and Patrick J. Caceres, "Constructing a Better Estimate of Police Misconduct," *Policy Matters Journal* (Spring 2010): 10–16.

2. For a more complete description of police misconduct, media coverage, and public attitudes toward law enforcement see Joel Miller and Robert C. Davis, "Unpacking Public Attitudes to the Police: Contrasting Perceptions of Misconduct with Traditional Measures of Satisfaction," *International Journal of Police Science and Management* 10, no. 1 (2008): 9–22.

3. For a more complete report on the frequency of police misconduct see Mathew R. Durose, Erica L. Smith, and Patrick A. Lanan, *Contacts Between Police and the Public, 2005,* NCJ 215243, Bureau of Justice Statistics, Office of Justice Programs, Special Report (April 2007), http://bjs.ojp.usdoj.gov/content/pub/pdf/cppOS.pdf (accessed November 22, 2010).

4. For a discussion of research on cognitive dissonance, see Joel Cooper, Robert Mirabile, and Steven J. Scher, "Actions and Attitudes: The Theory of Cognitive Dissonance," in *Persuasion: Psychological Insights and Perspectives,* ed. Timothy C. Brock and Melaine C. Green (Thousand Oaks, California: Sage Publications Inc., 2005), 63–80.

5. For a more complete list of cognitive rationalizations, see Albert Bandura et al., "Mechanisms of Moral Disengagement in the Exercise of Moral Agency," *Journal of Personality and Social Psychology* 71, no. 2 (1996): 364–374; John F. Veiga, Timothy D. Golden, and Kathleen Dechant, "A Survey of the Executive's Advisory Panel: Why Managers Bend Company Rules," *Academy of Management Executive* 18, no. 2 (May 2004): 84–90; and Celia Moore, "Moral Disengagement in Processes of Organizational Corruption," *Journal of Business Ethics* 80 (June 2008): 129–139.

6. For a complete discussion of incrementalism, see Ehud Sprinzak, "The Psychopolitical Formation of the Extreme Left in Democracy: The Case of the Weathermen," in *Origins of Terrorism: Psychologies, Ideologies, Theologies, States of Mind,* ed. Walter Reich and Walter Laqueur (Cambridge, England: Cambridge University Press, 1990), 65–85.

7. For a discussion of implicit decision making, see Daniel Kahneman and Shane Frederick, "Representativeness Revisited: Attribute Substitution in Intuitive Judgment" in *Heuristics and Biases: The Psychology of Intuitive Judgment,* ed. Thomas Gilovich, Dale Griffin, and Daniel Kahneman (New York: Cambridge University Press), 20(G), 49–81.

8. See for example, Michael Josephson, *Becoming an Examplary Peace Officer. The Guide to Ethical Decision Making* (Los Angeles: Josephson Institute, 2009).

9. For further discussion on ethical decision making, see Russell Haines, Marc D. Street, and Douglas Haines, "The Influence of Perceived Importance of an Ethical Issue on Moral Judgment, Moral Obligation, and Moral Intent" *Journal of Business Ethics* 81 (2008): 387–399.

10. Ethics Resource Center, *2003 National Business Ethics Survey (NBES)* (May 21, 2003), www.ethics.org/resource/2003-national-business-ethics-survey-nbes (accessed November 24, 2010).

11. See, for example, Cubie L. L. Lau, "A Step Forward: Ethics Education Matters," *Journal of Business Ethics* 92 (2010): 565–584.

12. For a more complete discussion on facilitation, see Peter Renner, *The Art of Teaching Adults: How to Become an Exceptional Instructor and Facilitator* (Vancouver, Canada: Training Associates, 2005).

13. For a more complete discussion of ethics training, see Brian Fitch, "Principle-Based Decision Making," *Law and Order* 56 (September 2008): 64–70.

14. See, for example, Simon Webley and Andrea Werner, "Corporate Codes of Ethics: Necessary but Not Sufficient," *Business Ethics: A European Review* 17, no. 4 (October 2008): 405–415.

15. For further discussion on ethics and supervisory influence, see James C. Wimbush and Jon M. Shepard, "Toward an Understanding of Ethical Climate: Its Relationship to Ethical Behavior and Supervisory Influence," *Journal of Business Ethics* 3, no. 8 (1994): 637–647.

Critical Thinking

1. How can a police officer reduce the psychological discomfort that accompanies misconduct?

2. Explain the slippery slope theory regarding misconduct.

3. What can law enforcement agencies do to make ethics education truly effective?

Create Central

www.mhhe.com/createcentral

Internet References

Applying Social Learning Theory to Police Misconduct
    http://ww2.odu.edu/~achappel/DB_article.pdf
Drury University
    www.drury.edu/ess/irconf/dmangan.html

Article Prepared by: Joanne Naughton

Behind the Smoking Guns: Inside NYPD's 21st Century Arsenal

GREG B. SMITH

Learning Outcomes

After reading this article, you will be able to:

- Describe some of the high-tech tools and massive databases of information available to the NYPD.

- Discuss some of the uses of CompStat.

Big Brother—With a Badge

In the early morning hours of last Sept. 25, a stocky young man bolted the Bora Bora Lounge in Highbridge, the Bronx, with a gun in his hand and squeezed off seven shots.

His target fell dead on the street as the shooter fled into the darkness, leaving little behind for police save a nearly useless description: "Unknown male Hispanic in 20s."

Enter Big Brother—with a badge.

With the aid of surveillance video at the club and facial recognition technology, cops tracked down a suspect and made an arrest.

To solve a Bronx street shooting in 21st century New York—and most other crimes committed citywide—the NYPD now employs a wide variety of high-tech tools and massive databases of information culled from an incredible array of sources.

The NYPD recently provided the Daily News with an unprecedented look at its 21st century arsenal, which includes:

- Thousands of security cameras scattered throughout the city linked together in a network called the Domain Awareness System (DAS).

- Records of hundreds of thousands of license plate numbers scanned and pinned to specific locations at specific times.

- Social media posts bragging about criminal behavior.

- Facial recognition technology that matches facial characteristics of potential suspects to images in a massive NYPD database.

- Improved ballistics capability that allows cops to quickly identify the source of a bullet.

- Prosecutors in Manhattan, Brooklyn, and Staten Island have created crime strategies units, using data to identify ties between crimes. Authorities can also map the crime to spot trends, quality of life issues, or gang activity.

- A system of sensors the NYPD plans to install that would detect gunshots—even when residents don't report the shootings. Cops can then sync the sensors with cameras to capture footage of the crime.

- Last week, a select group of cops answered calls with Microsoft tablet computers in hand that can instantly tap into the criminal history at an address—including residents with outstanding warrants.

"There's nothing that technology doesn't play a huge role in today," NYPD Deputy Commissioner John Miller told *The News.*

Harder to Get Away

The long arm of the law now spends a good amount of time with its fingers on a keyboard, downloading and Web-scraping.

The trend accelerated after the Sept. 11 attacks, with new antiterrorist tech advances morphing into all-purpose crime-fighting tools used to track down miscreants from car thieves to killers.

"So much of what has been acquired for terrorism purposes day to day, informs our crimes—with license plate scanners, the pinging capabilities we have on the phones," Police Commissioner Bill Bratton said. "And that's one of the great benefits New York gets out of being the most likely terrorist target in the world today is that the funds that come in help us on our more prevalent, consistent issue of day-to-day crime."

Of course, the nation's biggest police department continues to rely on the usual methods to crack cases—canvassing for witnesses, working informants, relying on analysis of ballistics, fingerprints, and autopsy reports.

But year by year, the NYPD has embraced the latest technology, starting perhaps most notably in 1994 with the advent of CompStat—precinct-by-precinct computerized analysis of nitty-gritty crime stats used to strategically target police activity. Bratton—who first introduced CompStat with the late Jack Maple—said current technology augments traditional police work in ways that he wouldn't have thought possible in the '90s.

"Every shell case and every piece of ballistic evidence we get, we're going to have the ability to analyze that in a very quick, timely fashion," Bratton said.

He recounted a recent CompStat session where bullet cartridges found at several crime scenes over the prior two months were matched to one gun. Surveillance cameras at multiple crime scenes revealed the same vehicle present at each scene. From there they tied the vehicle to an owner, and soon enough to a suspect.

All types of technology are now in play. In the last few years, the NYPD has discussed the introduction of infrared technology that can detect weapons on a person. They also bought two pairs of Google glasses—as yet unused.

The department also has set aside $1.5 million for a sound sensor system called Shotspot that captures gunshots at specific locations. That allows police to respond to shots even if no one calls 911.

The gunshot system has been used in Milwaukee, Oakland, Calif., and Yonkers. In 2011, the department launched a pilot program in Brownsville, Brooklyn, that was never expanded. The technology has since improved and is now considered much more reliable.

The age of social media provided police with another crime-fighting tool—tracking criminals as they brag about their misdeeds on Facebook or Twitter.

"You do a keyword search on 'capped him,' 'shot him,' 'popped him' and you bring up those pages that refer to those things that are . . . the slang words for a shooting," said Miller, the NYPD's counterterrorism chief.

Cameras, in particular, now play a huge crime-solving role. The number of NYPD and private cameras has multiplied radically over the years. Detectives now routinely track down tapes from cameras around a crime scene, and can also tap into a new $30 million network created 2 years ago with Microsoft and dubbed the Domain Awareness System.

Set up as an antiterror tool, the DAS allows the department to search images in real time from 7,000 active NYPD and private cameras, along with 400 special cameras—either at fixed locations or mounted on police cruisers that patrol the streets, collecting license plate numbers as vehicles pass by.

This puts vehicles in specific locations at specific times, useful information in corroborating a suspect's whereabouts at the time of a crime.

Cameras played a crucial role in generating an arrest in the Bora Bora shooting.

Homicide detectives started with seven bullet casings found on the street and vague witness descriptions about the shooter.

The club provided surveillance video that yielded a decent freeze frame with an image of the man witnesses believed was the shooter.

Here another crucial high-tech tool came into play—facial recognition software.

Initiated as a pilot program in Manhattan South in late 2011, the NYPD facial recognition unit works in a small windowless room at 1 Police Plaza.

Detectives there collect images of suspects and witnesses alike from Facebook, cell phones, and surveillance cameras across the city.

Since its inception, city detectives have sent more than 4,400 images to the facial recognition unit, said Inspector DeLayne Hurley, commanding officer of the NYPD's Real Time Crime Center.

Most were too blurry to be of use. But, as of last month, they'd matched more than 1,000 images to the department's database of 9 million mug shots. In the Bora Bora shooting, the club's cameras caught the alleged shooter at an angle.

Facial recognition technology requires a face-on image, so the unit used software to create a 3D, computer-generated image of the shooter's face.

With this usable image, the system brought up at least 200 mug shots deemed close matches. The unit then carefully examined each one, looking for physical similarities such as distance between the eyes, ear size, tattoos, scars, and other unique body tell-tales.

At the start of the facial recognition program, the software produced results that appeared to have misidentified five individuals. None were arrested.

"These were all in the beginning when we were all learning to use the system," Hurley said. "And people can look a lot alike."

The system has since improved dramatically, resulting in 450 arrests and the identification of 397 individuals helpful to investigators, including eyewitnesses.

The technology helped produce arrests in 11 homicides, 124 robberies, 111 larcenies, and 89 assaults or shootings.

In the Bora Bora case, detectives picked out a single likely mug shot and showed it to witnesses in the traditional photo array of similar mug shots. Witnesses all identified the same guy—Yeltsin Beltran, 22, a 5-foot-6, 150-pound Bronx man with prior arrests including false impersonation and drug possession.

Beltran was arrested Oct. 11 for second-degree murder. His lawyer, Paul Lieber, insists his client is innocent.

"My guy had nothing to do with this murder," he said, acknowledging that Beltran was identified by one eyewitness in an actual lineup.

A second witness, who identified Beltran in a photo array, picked a different man in a lineup.

Questions of Privacy

The growing use of technology to solve crimes has triggered increased concerns about the erosion of privacy rights.

In the past few years, the courts have been asked to address concerns about everything from police warehousing data on law-abiding citizens to cops surveilling individuals without judicial permission.

Just last month, the U.S. Supreme Court ruled cops must first obtain a warrant before searching through a person's smartphone.

Four years ago the New York Civil Liberties Union took issue when it learned the NYPD was storing tens of thousands of names, addresses, and birth dates of everyone stopped and questioned on the street.

Given that 95% of those stopped broke no laws, the NYCLU argued the NYPD was wrongfully keeping tabs on citizens without probable cause to do so. In 2011, New York passed a law prohibiting this practice. This personal information is no longer stored.

The latest concern involves the NYPD's increased use of license plate scanners that result in hundreds of thousands of plate numbers being stored in a massive data file.

Cops can run a plate and see where a vehicle has been in the past few months—all without a warrant. The problem, says the NYCLU's Chris Dunn, is that 99.9% of the stored numbers belong to law-abiding citizens.

Dunn says the license plate readers allow the NYPD to "just vacuum up information about everybody regardless of suspicion. Once we're there, that's where the privacy concerns come in." Privacy rights recently triumphed regarding another high-tech device—the GPS (Global Positioning System).

In New York, police now must obtain permission from a judge before slapping a GPS device on a suspect's vehicle to track his or her whereabouts. That's because an upstate burglar named Scott Weaver objected to police secretly attaching a GPS device to his van without obtaining a warrant.

A jury found him guilty, but in 2009 the Court of Appeals—the state's highest court—reversed the conviction, finding police had violated his constitutional rights via warrantless surveillance.

Critical Thinking

1. What are the constitutional issues to be concerned about with the use of these tools?

2. Are you confident that facial recognition software helped to correctly identify the killer in the Bora Bora case?

Internet References

NYPD
   http://www.nyc.gov/html/nypd/html/home/home.shtml
Police Foundation
   http://www.policefoundation.org/content/compstat-practice-depth-analysis-three-cities
The Police Chief
   http://www.policechiefmagazine.org/magazine/index.cfm?fuseaction=display&article_id=998&issue_id=92006

Article

Prepared by: Joanne Naughton

Excited Delirium and the Dual Response: Preventing In-Custody Deaths

BRIAN ROACH, KELSEY ECHOLS, AND AARON BURNETT

Learning Outcomes

After reading this article, you will be able to:

- Define excited delirium syndrome and show how it occurs.
- Specify the risk factors associated with ExDS.
- State the treatments to be used when the situation occurs.

Excited delirium syndrome (ExDS) is a serious and potentially deadly medical condition involving psychotic behavior, elevated temperature, and an extreme fight-or-flight response by the nervous system. Failure to recognize the symptoms and involve emergency medical services (EMS) to provide appropriate medical treatment may lead to death. Fatality rates of up to 10 percent in ExDS cases have been reported.[1] In addition to the significant morbidity and mortality associated with unrecognized ExDS, a substantial risk for litigation exists. These patients often die within 1 hour of police involvement. One study showed 75 percent of deaths from ExDS occurred at the scene or during transport.[2] Law enforcement organizations should take steps to increase officer awareness of ExDS and its symptoms and develop procedures to engage the medical community when identified. Without placing themselves or others at a greater risk for physical harm, officers must be able to rapidly detect symptoms of ExDS and immediately engage EMS for proper diagnosis and medical treatment. Failure to do so may prove fatal.

Historical Data and Cases Reviewed

Reports of presentations consistent with ExDS have occurred for more than 150 years. In 1849 Dr. Luther Bell, a psychiatrist in Massachusetts, described an acute exhaustive mania (Bell's Mania) in which patients developed hallucinations, profound agitation, and fever, which often were followed by death.[3] A decrease in reports occurred in the 1950s that coincided with the advent of antipsychotic medications and then an increase again in the 1980s likely secondary to widespread cocaine use. At that time, there were several reports in which an intoxicated person or an individual with mental illness exhibited aggression, hallucinations, and insensitivity to pain; was physically restrained (often in a prone position); and then died in custody.

In the last 20 years, law enforcement officers have seen this syndrome repeatedly. Several cases were outlined by a special panel review on ExDS at Penn State.[4]

Excited delirium-associated death after handcuffing/ Hog-tying. In October 2005 a West Palm Beach, Florida, police officer found a shirtless and distraught man stumbling on the road and attempting to stop vehicles. Told to relax, the man kept gesticulating wildly with vehicles stopping to avoid him. After a struggle the officer placed the man in a prone position and handcuffed him. Other officers arrived, helped move the man out of the street, and further restrained him by hog-tying his legs and hands. The man later became unconscious. Responding paramedics failed to resuscitate him. The chief medical examiner for Palm Beach County determined the cause of death was "sudden respiratory arrest following physical struggling restraint due to cocaine-induced ExDS."

Excited delirium-associated death after major physical struggle. A panel member who also serves as a Vancouver Police Department sergeant related the case of officers responding to a male subject who had a knife in a street confrontation. A foot chase ensued with police grounding the subject and multiple officers restraining him. The sergeant stated,

"The subject was so resistive and so strong that he lifted five officers off of him at one point." After a protracted struggle, the subject suddenly was quiet, went into cardiac arrest, and died at the scene. The subject suffered from mental illness and had alcohol and marijuana in his system. An autopsy concluded the subject died from choking due to the officer's restraint, and the coroner ruled the death accidental.

Excited delirium-associated death after TASER use. According to press reports, Dallas, Texas, police found a 23-year-old male subject in his underwear, screaming and holding a knife on a neighbor's porch on April 24, 2006. The man refused English and Spanish instructions and came at the officers with the knife. One officer fired a TASER, which failed to connect. A second shot did, causing electrical shock. A third was reportedly fired. After being handcuffed on an ambulance backboard, the subject stopped breathing and was pronounced dead at a hospital. The Dallas County medical examiner attributed the death to "excited delirium."

Excited delirium-associated death with no police presence. Certainly, the cases cited in the 1849 paper by Dr. Luther Bell in the *Journal of Insanity* had no police presence. Most recently, a case occurred involving an Anderson University basketball player. An Anderson County, Indiana, coroner "said [the man] had complained of cramps and vision problems just before he collapsed on a campus basketball court September 30 and had an 'extremely elevated body temperature' when he was rushed to the emergency room of AnMed Health Medical Center. The man's death days later was caused by 'acute drug toxicity with ExDS that led to multiple organ failure.'"[5]

Further, an expert panel convened by the American College of Emergency Physicians recognized ExDS as a unique clinical syndrome amenable to early therapeutic interventions.[6] This article provides a scientific background for ExDS, outlines risk factors, clarifies identification of the syndrome based on common signs and symptoms, and discusses control and sedation of affected individuals.

Medical Background

The mechanism in which ExDS occurs is complex and not fully understood; however, recent research has provided greater insight. Although cocaine use is associated with ExDS, postmortem cocaine levels in those who have died after ExDS are similar to those of recreational cocaine users and lower than individuals who have died from heart attacks or other non-ExDS causes after cocaine use.[7] These findings suggest that cocaine intoxication alone does not cause ExDS. Further, a degree of cellular or genetic susceptibility may exist that leads some cocaine users to develop ExDS while others do not.

Researchers began to explore other mechanisms for ExDS, and the central dopamine theory emerged as a leading hypothesis.

Dopamine is a neurotransmitter with many functions. It plays a role in the brain's perception of reward and temperature regulation. Increased dopamine levels result in fast heart rates, feelings of euphoria, and hallucinations. Highly addictive drugs, specifically cocaine and methamphetamine, increase the level of dopamine in the brain. Schizophrenia also results in elevated levels of dopamine in the brain, and antipsychotics work to treat hallucinations by blocking dopamine on a cellular level. In chronic cocaine abusers who have died of ExDS, research has shown a loss of a crucial protein that eliminates dopamine from the brain. This loss results in increased dopamine levels and chaotic signaling in the brain. The elevated dopamine levels help explain some of the similarities between ExDS and schizophrenia (e.g., hallucinations, paranoia), but they do not account for the high rates of sudden cardiac arrest seen in the former but not the latter.

Clinical Presentation

The clinical presentation of excited delirium has distinct and recognizable features. Much of what is used to identify excited delirium both on the street and in the hospital is based on case reports that have identified common clinical features, patient behaviors, and historical factors. In 2009, the American College of Emergency Physicians Task Force on Excited Delirium established that both delirium (e.g., acute confusion, hallucinations, and disorientation that is rapid in onset and may fluctuate in intensity) and an excited or agitated state must be present to consider ExDS.[8] Previously published cases identified common sequences of events, typically involving "acute drug intoxication or a history of mental illness, a struggle with law enforcement, physical or noxious chemical control measures or electrical control device (ECD) application, sudden and unexpected death, and an autopsy which fails to reveal a definite cause of death from trauma or natural disease."[9]

ExDS subjects typically are males around the age of 30, and most have a history of psychostimulant use or mental illness (see Table 1). Law enforcement agents or EMS personnel often are called to the scene because of public disturbances, agitation, or bizarre behaviors. Subjects are usually violent and combative with hallucinations, paranoia, or fear. Additionally, subjects may demonstrate profound levels of strength, resist painful stimuli or physical restraint, and seem impervious to self-inflicted injuries. This information becomes particularly important to law enforcement personnel who may use techniques intended to gain control and custody of subjects through physical means, chemical agents, or ECDs. During initial assessment patients often are noted to have elevated body temperatures, fast heart rates, rapid breathing, elevated blood pressures, and sweaty skin.

Risk Factors Associated with Excited Delirium Syndrome

Males (average age 36)
Stimulant drug use
- Cocaine and to a lesser extent methamphetamine, PCP, and LSD
  Chronic users after an acute binge
  Preexisting psychiatric disorder
- Schizophrenia, bipolar disorder

Certain medical conditions have presented similarly to ExDS, including low blood sugar, thyroid abnormalities, and decompensated psychiatric illness. Methamphetamine, cocaine, PCP, and bath salt intoxication are associated with ExDS, but not every intoxicated individual develops it. Intoxication without ExDS will lack elevated body temperatures and certain laboratory abnormalities, such as metabolic acidosis. Severe sweating, a clue that a patient has an elevated temperature, combined with hallucinations always should prompt a consideration of ExDS. Differentiating ExDS from other medical causes or uncomplicated intoxication can prove difficult, but a prudent course is to assume the worst and bring patients to the hospital via EMS for evaluation by a physician.

Treatments

When subjects are identified as potentially exhibiting excited delirium, rapid control of the situation, and timely execution of medical evaluation are important. Protocols vary by region according to local EMS policies and in many cases are driven by consensus opinions. Subjects with excited delirium often do not respond to verbal redirection. Additionally, attempts at physical control may not be as effective given extreme levels of strength and resistance to painful stimuli. Ongoing physical struggle can worsen a subject's innate fight-or-flight system, which can raise a patient's temperature, cause changes in the body's acid-base balance, and increase the risk of sudden death.

Medications are required to sedate ExDS patients to expedite the medical evaluation, decrease their fight-or-flight response, and avoid further harm to both the subject and those involved in the patient's care. Several classes of medications are available, as well as different routes of administration, including intranasal, intramuscular, and intravenous. Advanced life support EMS personnel capable of cardiac monitoring, advanced airway management, and medical resuscitation should be present

at the time of administration. Common medications include benzodiazepines (e.g., lorazepam, midazolam, and diazepam), antipsychotics (e.g., haloperidol, droperidol, olanzapine, and ziprasidone), and the dissociative agent ketamine. Benzodiazepines are very safe but are limited by varying dose requirements from patient to patient, as well as variable time until adequate sedation. Antipsychotics often are more useful in subjects presenting with acute exacerbations of psychiatric illness but are plagued by warnings about potential cardiac side effects and prolonged time until onset.

Ketamine is a unique medication that may play a larger role in the initial treatment of patients with excited delirium. It is characterized by a rapid onset of action (less than 5 minutes), stable effects on blood pressure, consistent ability to provide adequate sedation, and, in general, it maintains the subject's ability to breathe. Potential side effects include hallucinations and confusion as the medication wears off (10 to 20 percent of adults 30 to 120 minutes after administration), vocal cord spasm, and increased salivation. A recent study published by Regions Hospital EMS in St. Paul, Minnesota, reviewed 13 cases between April and December 2011 where ketamine was administered prior to hospital arrival for excited delirium.[10] This review further supports ketamine as an effective prehospital treatment of the ExDS patient. Peak sedation was achieved in less than 5 minutes in 11 of 13 cases. Moderate or deeper sedation was achieved in 12 of 13 patients. However, ketamine is a powerful medication, and ExDS is a life-threatening condition. Three patients developed low oxygen saturations. Two required endotracheal intubation, and one was assisted with a bag-valve mask. Three patients experienced emergent reactions, two of which were successfully treated with low doses of benzodiazepines. There were no deaths.

Conclusion

In summary, excited delirium is becoming increasingly recognized as an important medical emergency encountered in the prehospital environment. Law enforcement agencies should undertake a concerted effort to increase awareness among officers of ExDS to include information to help identify symptoms and to establish protocols to engage the medical community. Armed with this information, officers will be in a better position to engage EMS for an urgent evaluation, treatment, and transport to the hospital. Using teamwork to safely and efficiently control these patients will lead to improved outcomes. Promising research is being conducted regarding the underlying mechanisms of this disease, as well as new methods of treatment, including ketamine, which may improve the ability to care for these patients.

Notes

1. M.D. Sztajnkrycer and A.A. Baez, "Cocaine, Excited Delirium, and Sudden Unexpected Death," *EMS World,* April 2005 (updated January 11, 2011), http://www.emsworld.com/article/article.jsp?id51863 (accessed April 30, 2014).

2. D.L. Ross, "Factors Associated with Excited Delirium Deaths in Police Custody," *Modern Pathology* 11 (1998): 1127–1137.

3. L. Bell, "Acute Exhaustive Mania," *American Journal of Psychiatry* (October 1849).

4. Information regarding these cases is derived from the National Institute of Justice Weapons and Protective Systems Technologies Center, "Special Panel Review of Excited Delirium, December 2011," https://www.justnet.org/pdf/ExDS-Panel-Report-FINAL.pdf (accessed April 14, 2014).

5. As reported by N. Mayo, *Independent Mail* (November 15, 2011).

6. American College of Emergency Physicians Excited Delirium Task Force, "White Paper Report on Excited Delirium Syndrome, September, 10, 2009: Report to the Council and Board of Directors on Excited Delirium at the Direction of Amended Resolution 21(08)," http://www.fmhac.net/Assets/Documents/2012/Presentations/KrelsteinExcitedDelirium.pdf (accessed April 14, 2014).

7. D.C. Mash, L. Duque, J. Pablo, Y. Qin, N. Adi, W. Hearn, B. Hyma, S. Karch, H. Druid, and C. Wetli, "Brain Biomarkers for Identifying Excited Delirium as a Cause of Sudden Death," *Forensic Science International* 190 (2009): e13-e19.

8. American College of Emergency Physicians Excited Delirium Task Force.

9. American College of Emergency Physicians Excited Delirium Task Force.

10. A.M. Burnett, J.G. Salzman, K.R. Griffith, B. Kroeger, and R.J. Frascone, "The Emergency Department Experience with Prehospital Ketamine: A Case Series of 13 Patients," *Prehospital Emergency Care* 16 (2012):1–7.

Critical Thinking

1. Are there other medical conditions that appear to be similar to ExDS?

2. What types of situations will often result in law enforcement or EMS being called?

3. How should law enforcement agencies treat this issue?

Internet References

American College of Emergency Physicians Excited Delirium Task Force

http://www.fmhac.net/Assets/Documents/2012/Presentations/KrelsteinExcitedDelirium.pdf (accessed April 14, 2014).

EMS World

http://www.emsworld.com/article/10324064/cocaine-excited-delirium-and-sudden-unexpected-death

Unit 4

UNIT

Prepared by: Joanne Naughton

The Judicial System

The courts are an equal partner in the American justice system. Just as the police have the responsibility of guarding our liberties by enforcing the laws, and prosecutors have the obligation to do justice rather than merely win cases, the courts play an important role in defending these liberties by applying and interpreting these laws, with the goal of attaining justice. The courts are the battlegrounds where civilized "wars" are fought without bloodshed, to protect individual rights and to settle disputes.

Courts must be vigilant to guard against the use of improper evidence obtained from violations of Constitutional rights, such as a suspect's right to remain silent, to be free from illegal searches, or to have legal counsel. Today, DNA testing of evidence seems almost routine, and in some cases it is capable of providing foolproof evidence of a suspect's guilt or innocence. But DNA testing in old cases too often highlights the tragedy of defendants having been convicted of crimes they didn't commit.

Our judicial process is an adversary system of justice, where the state is always represented by counsel, and the defendant's need for counsel is recognized in the Constitution.

Article   Prepared by: Joanne Naughton

"I Did It"

Why Do People Confess to Crimes They Didn't Commit?

ROBERT KOLKER

Learning Outcomes

After reading this article, you will be able to:

• Explain what could motivate an innocent person to plead guilty.

• Argue that a criminal suspect should not agree to be interviewed by police.

The woman was naked from the waist down, her pants and underwear tossed into the weeds. Her down jacket was pulled to her chest, exposing her left breast to the autumn chill. Her head and face had been pummeled, and embedded in the blows were pellets from a BB gun; smashed shards of the gun were found nearby in the brush. Her hair was so gummed with blood that the hunter who stumbled on her body couldn't tell that it had once been all white.

By nightfall on November 29, 1988, the whole upstate village of Hilton was talking about Viola Manville—74 years old and a grandmother, a free spirit, outspoken, and now a homicide victim. Hilton is a small, blue-collar farm town on the edge of Lake Ontario west of Rochester where a good number of people once worked on the assembly lines at Kodak. The town can be rough—one neighbor from a wealthier suburb calls it "a little Appalachia here in New York"—but Hilton had never seen a murder like this. The Monroe County Sheriff's Office interviewed dozens of people: neighbors, family members, an ex-boyfriend, troubled teenagers. They learned that Manville often had been seen walking along the same set of abandoned railroad tracks where her body was found, even after having been the victim of an attempted rape there three years earlier. The man arrested in that attack, Glen Sterling, was still in prison.

Glen Sterling had a brother named Frank. He was tall but hunched and painfully shy. Frank Sterling grew up just 100 yards from the abandoned railroad tracks, a mile from the spot where the victim's body was found. Both his parents were janitors, and Frank was the middle child, a chain-smoker so lonely that as a teenager he'd do almost anything to make a friend. His classmates at Hilton Central High called him Bug Chower, after a story got around that he ate insects to get attention. The name stuck. "He was the kid in school that everybody berated," says a former classmate, Rob Cusenz. "An easy mark."

At the time of the murder, Frank was 25 and still living at home, working as a school-bus monitor. He had a clean criminal record, but to the police, he had the makings of a motive. What if Frank had been angry that his brother Glen was in jail? What if he'd been nursing a grudge against Manville ever since she accused his brother of trying to rape her? What if this wasn't a sex-related murder but revenge? It was all just speculation, and indeed when the police questioned Sterling, they found his alibi was solid—he'd been seen working on the school bus all morning, and he recited the plots of the *Smurfs* and *Chipmunks* episodes he'd watched that afternoon. There was no physical evidence linking him to the crime, and Sterling was not arrested. Within a few months, other leads also dried up, and the Manville murder went unsolved.

Almost three years later, on July 10, 1991, an unmarked police car with two plainclothes detectives pulled up to the Sterling family's house. This was the third time in four years that the police had come to see him. He was now almost 28. He had become a truck driver and moved to Alabama for a year, then came back when work dried up. That afternoon, he was tired; he'd just finished a job that took him through a half-dozen states over two days. The detectives said they'd been assigned to reinterview people of interest in the case, and they realized Sterling had never been polygraphed. They asked him to come with them to a Rochester police station. He agreed.

At 7 P.M., Sterling followed a polygraph technician, Mark Sennett, into a small room on the fourth floor, where he sat at a table and waited. Before hooking up Sterling to the lie detector, Sennett spent more than two hours asking him questions: Did he know why he was there? Why would the police think he might have killed Vi Manville? Early on, Sennett told him that Glen had told his fellow inmates that one of his brothers had killed Manville—a lie he'd made up on the spot to see how the suspect might react. Sterling was startled; he said (maybe a little too defensively, Sennett thought) that there was no way his brother would have said that. Sennett told Sterling he was in for a long night. When the polygraph man left the room at 10:45 P.M., Sterling began to panic. If he stayed, he feared, the police wouldn't stop—but asking to leave or for a lawyer, he thought, would be as good as admitting he was a murderer.

At 11:20 P.M., another interrogator came to see Sterling. Patrick Crough, a young, confident detective, had worked just two homicide cases before the Manville murder, but he had already shown a natural talent for bonding with suspects. Crough spoke softly and leaned in close to Sterling, taking his time explaining his theory of the case. He talked about the love Sterling must have had for his brother and the anger he must have felt about his not being home for Thanksgiving. He told Sterling he thought he might have bottled up his anger about Glen being in jail. Maybe, Crough said, it was the reason for his upset stomach, his bad teeth.

Sterling admitted to Crough that he was angry enough to have "killed the bitch"—and threw his lighter across the room, saying, "I didn't kill her, but I sure as hell could have." Still, as midnight approached, Sterling maintained his innocence—and even asked to be hypnotized to prove he wasn't hiding anything. At about 12:45 A.M., Sennett returned and suggested what he called a "relaxation technique." He had Sterling lie down on the floor and keep his feet elevated on his chair. He told him to take four deep breaths, then slid his own chair up to Sterling and held his hand. He asked Sterling if he could picture himself on those railroad tracks, running into a lady with white hair, arguing with her, seeing her lying naked in the bushes. He asked him how he felt about seeing her this way. "Happy," Sterling said.

Seconds later, Sterling jumped to his feet and snapped, "This is a bunch of bullshit! I didn't do nothing!"

"You're right, this is bullshit," Sennett said before walking out of the room. "I think you killed this lady, and I'm going to prove it."

Sterling was trembling now, verging on hysteria. He had been in the small room for close to eight hours. Crough came in again at 2:40 A.M. and started rubbing Sterling's back. "I was whispering," Crough said later, "simply that we would not dislike him, that we were here for him, we understood—we felt he should tell the truth to get it off his chest." Crough's partner, Thomas Vasile, held Sterling's other hand, and the two detectives huddled around him for a long time, gently reassuring him. Finally, according to the police report, Sterling blurted out, "I did it . . . I need help."

Just before dawn, at 5:22, Sterling made a videotaped statement. Onscreen for just over twenty minutes, Sterling can be seen speaking in a slow, defeated monotone, the ash of his cigarette burning to the nub. With Sennett working the camera, Sterling nods and agrees to every detail Crough and Vasile ask about—the BB gun, the naked body—breaking into sobs now and then as the two officers console him. He mentions the purple color of Manville's jacket—a crime-scene detail police said no one else could have known. Sterling's motive, he explains on the videotape, is exactly what Crough had said: "I was already upset about not having my brother home for Thanksgiving. Turned out later she was that one my brother was in prison for. She said the wrong thing at the wrong time. Things transpired . . . After she said, 'Your brother got what he deserved,' I hit her."

Without witnesses or physical evidence linking him to the crime scene, prosecutors made the videotaped confession the centerpiece of their case. On September 29, 1992, Frank Sterling was convicted of murder and later sentenced to 25 years to life in prison, and sent to the state prison in Elmira. And several days after the trial, when a number of people in Hilton came forward saying that a 19-year-old man named Mark Christie was telling everyone he knew that he'd just gotten away with murder, the police didn't pay them much attention. The killer, after all, had confessed.

In the criminal-justice system, nothing is more powerful than a confession. Decades of research on jury verdicts have demonstrated that no other form of evidence—not eyewitnesses, not a video record of the crime, not even DNA—is as convincing to a jury as a defendant who says "I did it." The police, of course, understand the power of confessions and rely on interrogation techniques to produce them quickly so they can clear their cases. This is the stuff of countless TV procedurals—the small interrogation room with a bare table and two-way mirror; the good-cop–bad-cop routine; the deployment of outright lies like "You failed the polygraph" or "Your prints are on the knife." As a society, we have come to view these as acceptable, if blunt, tools of justice. We count on the integrity of police and safeguards like Miranda rights to prevent abuses, and we take it on faith that innocent people would never confess to crimes they haven't committed.

But, of course, they do. In recent years, the use of DNA evidence has allowed experts to identify false confessions in unprecedented and disturbing numbers. In the past two decades, researchers have documented some 250 instances of false confessions, many resulting in life sentences and at least four in wrongful executions. Of the 259 DNA exonerations tracked by a major advocacy group, 63 of them—or one out of every four—was found to have involved a false confession. Counting just the homicide cases, the proportion shoots up to 58 percent of all exonerations. Even this number could be an underestimate. "Most of the documented false confessions have been in highly publicized murder cases," says Steven Drizin, of Northwestern Law School's Center on Wrongful Convictions. "There is no reason not to think the same tactics would be as effective if not more effective in lesser cases, where the punishment that could flow from a confession would be less." False confessions appear to be particularly common in New York State, in which twelve of the 27 DNA-based exonerations have turned out to be based on bogus admissions of guilt.

Researchers who study false confessions say the roots of the problem lie in the interrogation tactics themselves. The most influential such method is the Reid technique, a decades-old, nine-step procedure designed to isolate and persuade a suspect to reveal his deceptions. Virtually every police department in the country has been influenced, directly or indirectly, by the Reid technique. Its defenders see it as the cornerstone of good police work, but its detractors say it places too much power in the hands of interrogating officers. In light of the new research documenting the scope of the problem, reformers in New York and elsewhere are calling for a wholesale reevaluation of the way the police question suspects. Frank Sterling's story should help their cause; it demonstrates just what can go wrong with the science of interrogation.

In 1940, a burly, clean-cut, Irish Catholic cop named John E. Reid was thinking of quitting the Chicago police force. Reid was tough, a former guard on the DePaul University football team, but was never comfortable carrying a gun. At the last minute, he applied for a transfer to a desk job at the Chicago crime lab. He arrived in the midst of a technological revolution in police work. In 1931, a presidential panel known as the Wickersham Commission had exposed abuses brought by the "third degree," the use of force by police to extract confessions. Police across the country had held suspects' heads underwater, hung them out of windows, and beaten them. In 1936, the Supreme Court decision *Brown v. Mississippi*—the brutal case of three black men who were beaten and whipped until they confessed—effectively outlawed confessions brought by brute force. Crime labs like Chicago's began developing new, more scientific means to solve cases: ballistics, document examination, and lie detection.

As much as anyone, John Reid can be credited with leading American law enforcement into the modern age. Reid's advances began with the lie detector. In 1945, he designed a chair that used inflated rubber bladders to detect a subject's jitters. In 1947, he essentially created the modern polygraph procedure with the "control-question technique," a way of measuring a suspect's reaction to provocative questions. That same year, Reid left the crime lab and founded John E. Reid & Associates, which went on to train scores of polygraph analysts, including members of the CIA and the Mossad.

Reid's most influential work focused on the art of the interrogation. Soft-spoken and sincere, he had a knack for gently persuading suspects to confess. "It was almost a priestlike approach," says George Lindberg, who worked for Reid for thirteen years. "He'd hold your hand and say, 'You should really get this off your chest.'" Reid played an important role in a number of high-profile Chicago murder trials, and other cities shuttled him in as a closer for their most sensitive cases. He was credited with personally helping to solve some 300 murders and coaxing 5,000 thieves to confess. Some in law-enforcement circles called him the most famous name next to J. Edgar Hoover. Reid's aim wasn't always true—in 1955, he got a Nebraska man named Darrel Parker to admit to killing his wife, and the real killer confessed 33 years later—but his faith in his own ability, and in the professionalization of his craft, led him to believe interrogations could be systematized to the point of being foolproof. "It's almost as if every crook reads the same book on what to do and say to give themselves away," he liked to say.

In 1962, Reid and his mentor, a Northwestern Law professor named Fred Inbau, co-wrote the first edition of *Criminal Interrogation and Confessions.* Criminologists and law historians credit their method with defining the culture of police-interrogation training for the past half-century. The procedure basically involves three stages meant to break down a suspect's defenses and rebuild him as a confessor. First, the suspect is brought into custody and isolated from his familiar surroundings. This was the birth of the modern interrogation room. Next the interrogator lets the suspect know he's guilty—that he knows it, the cops know it, and the interrogator doesn't want to hear any lies. The interrogator then floats a theory of the case, which the manual calls a "theme." The theme can be supported by evidence or testimony the investigator doesn't really have. In

the final stage, the interrogator cozies up to the subject and provides a way out. This is when the interrogator uses the technique known as "minimization": telling the suspect he understands why he must have done it; that anyone else would understand, too; and that he will feel better if only he would confess. The interrogator is instructed to cut off all denials and instead float a menu of themes that explain why the suspect committed the crime—one bad, and one not so bad, but both incriminating, as in "Did you mean to do it, or was it an accident?"

Reid was hailed in his time as the man who made the third degree obsolete. But if his method wasn't physically coercive, it was certainly psychologically so. The Supreme Court's 1966 Miranda decision singled out the Reid method for creating a potentially coercive environment, citing it as one reason suspects needed to be informed of their right to remain silent. Reid and Inbau made minor modifications to the program, adding some language about Miranda to the 1967 edition of their manual, but they remained true believers. *Criminal Interrogation and Confessions* asserts that Reid investigators could judge truth and deception with 85 percent accuracy, a higher rate than anyone else has ever claimed to have achieved—or, as Reid once put it, "better results than a priest."

In Elmira, Frank Sterling kept to himself, spending most of his time in what was called the college block, where inmates can study toward degrees. His family visited for a time, but his father died in 1995, and his mother stopped coming to see him after she developed heart problems and moved to Texas to live with her son Gary. Sterling had his own health issues. The dust at Elmira made it difficult for him to breathe, and some of the prisoners referred to him as Shaky because he trembled. "Each time I'd see Frank upon coming back from being at another prison, I'd see he had aged more—his face, his eyes," says fellow inmate Jeff Deskovic.

Sterling had tried to recant his confession almost immediately after he gave it. He told his lawyer he was so worn down by the police that he didn't even remember what had happened that night. But the authorities weren't moved by that claim. Right after Sterling's trial, Sterling's lawyer filed to vacate the conviction on other grounds: He argued that the rumors surrounding Mark Christie, the man who had been heard bragging about killing Vi Manville after Sterling was convicted, provided sufficient justification to investigate whether he was the real killer. Christie, whose alibi fell apart under new scrutiny, was asked to take a polygraph and agreed. He fidgeted too much for the first test to be considered conclusive but took it again the next day and passed. On December 23, 1992, a judge refused to overturn Sterling's conviction. Christie, the judge said, was simply a young man who liked to brag.

In 1996, four years into Sterling's sentence, Mark Christie reentered the picture. If Sterling had been the weird kid in Hilton, Christie had a creepier reputation: He wore combat fatigues every day and took an eighteen-inch Bowie knife with him wherever he went. Now Christie had confessed to another murder, the brutal killing of a 4-year-old Rochester-area girl named Kali Ann Poulton. His confession prompted Sterling's appeals lawyer, Don Thompson, to file a new motion to overturn Sterling's conviction. If Christie were capable of killing Poulton, couldn't he have killed Vi Manville? A State Supreme

Court judge rejected the motion. "Only Sterling confessed to authorities," read the decision. "Only Sterling had a motive to kill Manville. Only Sterling knew facts that had not been publicized."

Sterling and Thompson filed a total of four motions to vacate Sterling's conviction over the next eight years, but all of them failed. Then, in 2004, Thompson sought the help of the Innocence Project—the Benjamin Cardozo School of Law–based group led by Barry Scheck and Peter Neufeld that has won wide acclaim for its work in freeing the wrongly convicted. The first time Neufeld watched Sterling's confession, even he thought he was guilty. But he soon came to see how everything pointed toward Christie. In 2005, Monroe County District Attorney Michael Green agreed to let the Innocence Project conduct DNA tests on some of Manville's clothing from the crime scene. In the fall of 2008, after three years of testing and legal maneuvering, word came back with what seemed like a match. The samples contained so-called touch DNA—a few skin cells—instead of the more definitive evidence found in blood and semen samples. Still, Neufeld says, "the profile had a very rare type. And Christie has that type."

In spite of the apparent match, a year passed, and the Monroe County D.A. still didn't take action. Last fall, an Innocence Project staff attorney named Vanessa Potkin personally visited Christie in prison to try to persuade him to own up to the murder. She spent part of two days talking to Christie, and while he almost seemed to acknowledge his role, and perhaps even to taunt her a bit, he admitted nothing. "His attitude was he's not responsible for Frank being there in prison," Potkin says. "Frank's the one who talked."

Sterling's team decided on a new tactic. On January 22, Potkin visited Christie again, this time with a polygraph and interrogation expert named Richard Byington who worked for the leading company in the field: John E. Reid & Associates. Neufeld had been waiting for the right case to ask the Reid people for pro bono help—a sort of Nixon-in-China move—and the company's president, Joseph Buckley, had agreed. The hope was that Byington, an experienced and highly regarded interrogator, could persuade Christie to confess.

At first, Christie appeared to relish the visit. He boasted to Byington that he had stolen a copy of the Reid-Inbau manual from the Hilton library to try to beat the polygraph he'd been asked to take after the Manville verdict. Of course, he'd aced it. Byington spent several hours trying to get Christie to warm up to him. Eventually, Christie seemed to grow impatient. "What do you want?" Byington remembers Christie saying.

Byington turned more aggressive. "I said, 'Listen, here's the deal. There's no doubt that you committed the Manville murder. The physical evidence says it, and the DNA basically says it. Now you need to do the right thing so Frank, who hasn't done anything, can go home.'" But Christie, who still harbored thoughts of getting out one day, still wasn't inclined to talk. "Why should I say anything?" he told Byington.

Then Byington played another card. In a strange coincidence, the detective who had procured Christie's confession in the Kali Ann Poulton case was Patrick Crough, the same man who had gotten Frank Sterling to confess. Byington pulled out a copy of a newly published memoir Crough had written about child-abduction cases called *The Serpents Among Us* and pointed to the page where Crough calls Christie not just a child-killer but, he believed, a child molester. Christie became furious. After thirteen years in prison, he had no real sense of how well he was remembered in the outside world, and he had hoped Kali Ann's murder, and his role in it, might have been forgotten. Now he saw that Crough was working to keep the case alive—and accusing him of raping the young victim as well. He knew he'd never lead a normal life outside of prison now.

"You know more about this than you're telling me," Byington said to Christie. And shortly after, Christie's confession began.

Earlier this year, on April 28, Frank Sterling was set free. He wept at the courthouse, hugged Don Thompson, and expressed disbelief. Peter Neufeld took a shot at the cops who interrogated Sterling eighteen years earlier. "There's no question that in this case," Neufeld said, "the police officers had tunnel vision."

In the early days of DNA exoneration, even the lawyers working the cases didn't know what to make of the surprising number of false confessions they came across. "It wasn't until the late nineties that we began to see patterns emerge," says Neufeld. "But still, it was running against 25 years of my own experience. Why would an innocent person confess?"

That question was eventually taken up by a handful of researchers, including the University of San Francisco School of Law's Richard Leo, Berkeley sociologist Richard Ofshe, John Jay College's Saul Kassin, and Northwestern Law School's Steven Drizin. False confessions now are generally understood to break down into three categories. There are voluntary false confessions, in which innocent people come forward on their own. Some, like John Mark Karr in the JonBenet Ramsey case, do it for the attention—others to self-punish or because they've lost touch with reality. Then there are what Leo calls "persuaded false confessions," in which people are convinced by the interrogator that they actually committed the crime. In New York, 17-year-old Marty Tankleff famously falsely confessed to killing his parents in 1988 after being convinced he must have blocked it out. Finally, there are compliant false confessions, in which the suspect is psychologically coerced to confess even while believing he's innocent. They do it, Kassin writes, "to escape a stressful situation, avoid punishment, or gain a promised or implied reward . . . often coming to believe that the short-term benefits of confession relative to denial outweigh the long-term costs." This appears to be what happened in the infamous Central Park jogger case. It also seems to explain Frank Sterling's confession.

Critics say the Reid technique is a major source of the problem. What was once seen as the vanguard of criminal science, they argue, is nothing more than a psychological version of the third degree. Even beyond the Reid method, the courts have given police "carte blanche in the interrogation room for any tactics shy of physical abuse," says Drizin. Others believe police shouldn't be able to mislead suspects with lies or manipulate them by suggesting that what they did isn't so bad. Great Britain's police aren't allowed to employ those tactics, and Kassin says the best available data suggest the efficacy with which they arrest and convict criminals isn't diminished by that.

Reid detractors also say that police often feed evidence to suspects, which accounts for why false confessors sometimes know details about a crime that they wouldn't otherwise know. In a recently published study, University of Virginia law professor Brandon Garrett found that in 97 percent of the false-confession cases he studied from the DNA era, the wrongly accused suspects were said to have supplied such telling details—facts either picked up elsewhere or provided by police. Interrogators also tend to be overconfident of their abilities to spot guilty suspects. No study so far (aside from Reid's own research) has shown the police to be any better than average at picking out liars. In fact, they're sometimes worse. In one 1987 study, police officers watched videotaped statements of witnesses, and their record at identifying deceptive testimony was no better than the average person's. Over confidence can blind investigators to evidence suggesting that the suspect is innocent. The pressure to resolve cases quickly and tidily can have a similar effect, especially in high-profile cases. Simply wearing suspects down is another issue: At some point, a given suspect will say anything just to make the immediate discomfort stop. "Why don't they beat people anymore?" asks Don Thompson. "It's not because they're particularly enlightened now. It's because the psychological coercion is so much more effective."

Frank Sterling's confession, Thompson believes, was marked by a number of these problems. After Sterling says he hit Vi Manville, Patrick Crough asks Sterling what he hit her with. Sterling says, "My hand." A moment later, Crough says, "Frank, as best as you can remember, and I know this is difficult for you, did something happen with that BB gun?" Only after being prompted that way does Sterling say, "Yeah, I started hitting her with it." Mark Sennett, the polygraph examiner, lied to Sterling about his brother Glen. Crough teased out the motive and alternately pressured and consoled Sterling. Sterling knew about the supposedly telling crime-scene detail of Manville's purple jacket, but Thompson says many people in Hilton would have seen her on her daily walks in that jacket. Finally, there was Sterling's state of mind. Having been held alone, without counsel, in a small interrogation room and questioned for twelve hours, he became isolated, exhausted, and vulnerable to manipulation. Over the years, Thompson and Crough had crossed paths in Rochester, running into each other around town or at the supermarket. "I'm never really comfortable when I'm talking to him," Thompson says. "He's an accomplished interrogator, which translates to being an accomplished manipulator."

Shortly after Sterling's release, I had dinner with Crough in Rochester. Calm and self-assured, he did what he could to sound gracious about Sterling's ordeal. But he couldn't help but also be defensive. He insisted he did good work that night in 1991. "His responses kept the interview going," he told me. "As a homicide detective, you don't walk out on an interview when the person's giving you a little something." Crough pointed out that he was the one who visited Christie in prison—he volunteered to do it and talked him into giving his DNA sample when Christie didn't have to do that—and it was his book that helped persuade Christie to confess. After a while, though, some contrition bled through. "Like that hasn't haunted me?" he told me. "I've been doing interrogations in major crimes for twenty

years. This is the first time I've ever had one go bad on me. That's not a bad statistic, you know."

The law-enforcement community insists current interrogation techniques are sound. The courts have upheld tactics like deceit and minimization, Reid president Joseph Buckley notes, and without such methods police would have a far more difficult time eliciting confessions from suspects who are, in fact, guilty. When false confessions do happen, Byington says it's not the Reid technique that's to blame but the misapplication of it. The police's main mistake with Frank Sterling, he says, was starting in on their suspect before they were reasonably sure he was guilty. Then, when Sterling gave Crough and the others questionable information, they blindly barreled ahead. "When they ask Frank what he was wearing, he says he thinks he was wearing a T-shirt and jeans," Byington says. "Well, if Frank was wearing a T-shirt and jeans, he'd have frozen to death." In Byington's opinion, Sterling had essentially been fed information over twelve long hours, then encouraged to spout it back over twenty minutes of video. In a good confession, Byington says, the suspect should do about 80 percent of the talking, narrating their experience for the benefit of the police, not saying yes and no to a series of prompts.

To prevent false confessions, interrogation critics say there's a solution so simple that it's remarkable it hasn't happened already: videotaping every minute of every police interrogation. Where the idea was once impractical, they note, the digital era changed that. Some law-enforcement officials fear that if juries see how the sausage is made, they might blanch at convicting even guilty suspects. In fact, Kassin's recent research indicates that when people see two versions of a false confession—one with just the confession and another that includes the entire interrogation—they become more effective jurors, correctly acquitting the innocent and convicting the guilty. Still, eighteen states and more than 800 jurisdictions have already started taping interrogations. New York has moved slowly—when they videotape at all, police tend to tape only confessions, not whole interrogations—but the New York State Bar Association has called for taping the full questioning session.

Earlier this year, the NYPD announced with some fanfare that it would test recording interrogations in two precincts. Last week, spokesman Paul Browne told me the bids have been selected, and that the 67th Precinct in Brooklyn and 48th Precinct in the Bronx will soon be outfitted with interrogation rooms ready for digital recording. Tests should start after the first of the year. Commissioner Ray Kelly "is open to seeing what we learn," Browne says, though in the spring, Kelly told me deploying such a system throughout the NYPD was a complicated endeavor, and that it wasn't clear to him yet that the effort would be worth the results.

One group solidly against tape-recording in New York is the Detectives' Endowment Association, whose president, Michael Palladino, holds on to the belief that what happens in an interrogation room is too messy for some jurors to tolerate. He also worries that juries won't be the only ones influenced. "Every taped interrogation can be used as a training film for criminals on what to expect from the police during an interrogation," he says. "Certainly, the element of surprise is gone."

Curiously enough, however, research shows that police and prosecutors forced to tape their interrogations often wind up supporting the practice. One Minnesota prosecutor famously called it "the best thing we've ever had rammed down our throats." A taped record can mean fewer motions to suppress and fewer claims that suspects were unduly deceived or abused. Joseph Buckley says the Reid method and taping can go hand in hand. "When somebody claims there was coercion, the record speaks for itself," he says. Even Patrick Crough says he believes in it, calling it "a tool to let the jury see what we see."

Don Thompson has thought a great deal about what would have happened in 1992 if the jury had been able to see the whole Sterling interrogation and not just the final twenty minutes. "You can't describe to a jury the effects of isolation over a twelve-hour period," he says. "I'd make them sit through the whole twelve hours. Because at that point, even for the jurors sitting in the jury box, it begins to feel like a hostage crisis."

Frank Sterling is standing on the railroad tracks in Hilton behind his old house—a small ranch-style building on a two-lane road, about a quarter-mile from the high school. "When we first moved here, the trains were still running through," he says, pointing at the tracks. "Then they disbanded it."

As we walk down the gravel path, Sterling points in the direction of the Big M supermarket he walked to on the afternoon Vi Manville was killed. To get to the store, he had to cross a train trestle over a creek and then leave the tracks, walking along the opposite creek bed. To get to where Manville was killed, Sterling would have had to continue on the tracks away from the market—"another mile and a half down the road," he says, laughing.

Sterling is heavier now than he was when he was sent to prison. His teeth were neglected for so long that a week before his release, he had nine of them pulled. At the time, he joked to his lawyers that he put them under his pillow for the Exoneration Fairy. He can't drive a truck because of medical issues, but he hopes to find computer work. For now, he is living with friends one town over from Hilton. He drives to Rochester when he needs to see his lawyers about finding health benefits, job training, and donated clothes. Sterling says he's angry, but he tries not to dwell on it. "I don't want it to tear me up." He hasn't decided whether to file a civil suit for wrongful conviction. The first night he was out, he says, he woke up in the middle of the night to the sound of rain on a windowpane. "It was something I couldn't hear for eighteen years," he says. "It's amazing. Something so simple that happens every day. Something everyone complains about."

Is it difficult being back here? "No," Sterling says. "I enjoyed growing up here." The creek is where he liked to fish for salmon. The train trestle is where kids liked to drink and where Frank walked his dogs Outlaw and Shebia. For a time, he says, he considered Vi Manville a friendly presence on the tracks. "She'd reach into her pocket and give the dogs a cookie."

When Crough and his partner first came to Sterling's house in 1991, he says, "they claimed they were looking at others. But I have a feeling they were focused on, 'Okay, we'll make it look like we're looking into others but he's the one who probably did it for revenge.'" He agreed to the polygraph he says "because I didn't do it. I thought, *Okay, well, I've got nothing to hide, so I should pass with flying colors.*"

So why did he confess? "They just wore me down," he says, shaking his head. "I was just so tired. Remember, I hadn't had any sleep since about 2:30 Tuesday night."

He tries to explain what it was like to spar with the police for twelve hours.

"It's like, 'Come on, guys, I'm tired—what do you want me to do, just confess to it?'

'No, we want the truth.'

'Well you're not fucking listening to the truth, I'm telling you. What more do you want me to say?'

'We want to know what happened.'"

Sterling says the police never asked him to say in his own words what happened. "'Yes' and grunts—that's basically what the whole confession is about." Regarding the color of Manville's coat, he says, "I knew in the fall she always wore her purple jacket."

I ask him what he thinks when he watches the twenty-minute confession video now. "When you look, you'll notice I shake a little bit," he says. "But to hold on to the whole cigarette and let the whole cigarette go to ash and never take a drag off of it? I'm a smoker. Normally, I would be sitting there dragging on it, not letting the whole cigarette just sit there burning down. Yeah, I was not in the right mind, looking back at it now."

He knows some people will never understand why he admitted to a crime he didn't commit. "They say, 'Why confess if you didn't do it?' But they don't have the whole understanding of what I was going through at the time. It's like, yeah—I wanted to get it over with, get home, and get some sleep."

He laughs softly. "Eighteen years and nine months later, I finally get to go home."

Critical Thinking

1. What is the Reid technique of interviewing?
2. What did the Supreme Court say about the Reid technique in *Miranda v. Arizona*?
3. What could be done to prevent false confessions?
4. Do you believe it is advisable for a criminal suspect to agree to speak to police?

Create Central

www.mhhe.com/createcentral

Internet References

Futurity
www.futurity.org/innocent-confess

PsychCentral
http://psychcentral.com/news/2013/09/12/why-people-confess-even-if-they-didnt-do-it/59450.html

Article

Prepared by: Joanne Naughton

In Miranda Case, Supreme Court Rules on the Limits of Silence

Justices uphold the murder conviction of a Texas man who refused to answer a question. The 5–4 ruling says suspects must invoke their legal rights.

DAVID G. SAVAGE

Learning Outcomes

After reading this article, you will be able to:

- Illustrate how the 5th Amendment didn't help Salinas.
- Discuss the Court's approach to the Miranda decision.

Crime suspects need to speak up if they want to invoke their legal right to remain silent, the Supreme Court said Monday in a ruling that highlights the limited reach of the famous Miranda decision.

The 5–4 ruling upheld the murder conviction of a Texas man who bit his lip and sat silently when a police officer asked him about the shotgun shells that were found at the scene of a double slaying. They had been traced to the suspect's shotgun.

At his trial, prosecutors pointed to the defendant's silence as evidence of his guilt. In affirming the conviction of Genovevo Salinas, the court's majority admitted that some suspects might think they had a right to say nothing.

"Popular misconceptions notwithstanding," the Constitution "does not establish an unqualified 'right to remain silent,'" said Justice Samuel A. Alito Jr.

Rather, he said, the 5th Amendment says no one may be "compelled in any criminal case to be witness against himself." Since the Miranda decision in 1966, the court has said police must warn suspects of their rights when they are taken into custody.

But the Miranda decision covers only suspects who are held in custody and are not free to leave.

In the Texas case, Salinas was asked to come to the police station, and he agreed to do so. "All agree that the interview was noncustodial," Alito said, so the police were not required to read him his rights under the Miranda decision.

And although Salinas had a qualified right to remain silent under the 5th Amendment, a suspect must invoke his rights and say he wants to remain silent, the court ruled Monday.

Salinas "alone knew why he did not answer the officer's question, and it was therefore his burden to make a timely assertion of the privilege," Alito said.

The decision is consistent with the high court's grudging approach to the Miranda decision and related 5th Amendment questions over recent decades. The court's conservative-leaning justices have not been willing to overturn the Miranda precedent, but they have repeatedly narrowed its scope.

Chief Justice John G. Roberts Jr. and Justices Antonin Scalia, Anthony M. Kennedy and Clarence Thomas voted with Alito to uphold the conviction in *Salinas vs. Texas.*

Alito noted that during a trial, defendants may refuse to testify, and prosecutors may not use their silence in court as evidence against them, citing the court's 1965 ruling in *Griffin vs. California.* In a concurring opinion, Thomas and Scalia said the Griffin case was mistaken and should be overruled.

Meanwhile, in another case, Thomas spoke for himself and four liberal justices to require a jury to find a defendant guilty of every facet of a crime that could lead to a mandatory prison term.

In *Alleyne vs. United States,* the court ruled that before a judge imposes an extra mandatory prison term on a defendant for conduct such as brandishing a firearm, a jury must find the defendant guilty of that offense. To do otherwise violates the defendant's basic right to a jury trial with his guilt proven beyond a reasonable doubt, Thomas said.

Thomas has long maintained that juries, not judges, must decide whether a defendant is guilty of all the elements of a crime that warrant extra punishment. And in a rare show of unity with the court's more liberal members, he overruled earlier decisions that left this power in the hands of a judge.

In the case before the court, Allen Alleyne was given four years in prison for helping his girlfriend rob the manager of a convenience store. Following the prosecution's recommendation, the judge gave him an extra seven years for having brandished a firearm. But Alleyne said he had not brandished a gun, and the jury had not convicted him of that extra offense.

The 5–4 ruling overturns the extra seven-year term. The dissenters faulted the majority for overruling a precedent from 2002 that allowed judges to make such decisions.

Critical Thinking

1. How does the 5th Amendment protect us?
2. Who does the 5th Amendment protect?
3. Why didn't the 5th Amendment protect Salinas?

Create Central

www.mhhe.com/createcentral

Internet References

Miranda Rights
www.mirandarights.org/righttoremainsilent.html
NWSidebar
http://nwsidebar.wsba.org/2013/06/26/salinas-v-texas-miranda-rights

Article　　　　　　　　　　　　　　　　Prepared by: Joanne Naughton

Neuroscience in the Courtroom

Brain scans and other types of neurological evidence are rarely a factor in trials today. Someday, however, they could transform judicial views of personal credibility and responsibility.

MICHAEL S. GAZZANIGA

Learning Outcomes

After reading this article, you will be able to:

- Be skeptical about reports of eye witness identification of a suspect.
- State why brain scans might be valuable in a criminal case.

By a strange coincidence, I was called to jury duty for my very first time shortly after I started as director of a new MacArthur Foundation project exploring the issues that neuroscience raises for the criminal justice system. Eighty of us showed up for selection in a case that involved a young woman charged with driving under the influence, but most of my fellow citizens were excused for various reasons, primarily their own DUI experiences. Finally, I was called to the judge. "Tell me what you do," he said.

"I am a neuroscientist," I answered, "and I have actually done work relevant to what goes on in a courtroom. For example, I have studied how false memories form, the nature of addiction, and how the brain regulates behavior."

The judge looked at me carefully and asked, "Do you think you could suspend all that you know about such matters for the course of this trial?" I said I could try. And with that, he said I was excused.

I was dismayed but should not have been. In the interest of fairness, judges and attorneys are supposed to seek jurors who will be guided solely by what they hear in the courtroom and to steer clear of those whose real or imagined outside expertise might unduly influence fellow jurors. Yet, in a way, the judge's dismissal of me also paralleled the legal system's wariness today of the tools and insights of neuroscience. Aided by sophisticated imaging techniques, neuroscientists can now peer into the living brain and are beginning to tease out patterns of brain activity that underlie behaviors or ways of thinking. Already attorneys are attempting to use brain scans as evidence in trials, and the courts are grappling with how to decide when such scans should be admissible. Down the road, an ability to

link patterns of brain activity with mental states could upend old rules for deciding whether a defendant had control over his or her actions and gauging to what extent that defendant should be punished. No one yet has a clear idea of how to guide the changes, but the legal system, the public and neuroscientists need to understand the issues to ensure that our society remains a just one, even as new insights rock old ideas of human nature.

Unacceptable Evidence (For Now)

With the growing availability of images that can describe the state of someone's brain, attorneys are increasingly asking judges to admit these scans into evidence, to demonstrate, say, that a defendant is not guilty by reason of insanity or that a witness is telling the truth. Judges might approve the request if they think the jury will consider the scans as one piece of data supporting an attorney's or a witness's assertion or if they think that seeing the images will give jurors a better understanding of some relevant issue. But judges will reject the request if they conclude that the scans will be too persuasive for the wrong reasons or will be given too much weight simply because they look so impressively scientific. In legal terms, judges need to decide whether the use of the scans will be "probative" (tending to support a proposition) or, alternatively, "prejudicial" (tending to favor preconceived ideas) and likely to confuse or mislead the jury. So far judges—in agreement with the conventional wisdom of most neuroscientists and legal scholars—have usually decided that brain scans will unfairly prejudice juries and provide little or no probative value.

Judges also routinely exclude brain scans on the grounds that the science does not support their use as evidence of any condition other than physical brain injury. Criminal defense attorneys may wish to introduce the scans to establish that defendants have a particular cognitive or emotional disorder (such as flawed judgment, morality or impulse control), but—for now at least—most judges and researchers agree that science is not yet advanced enough to allow those uses.

Functional magnetic resonance imaging (fMRI) offers an example of a process that can provide good scientific information, of which fairly little is legally admissible. This technology is a favorite of researchers who explore which parts of the brain are active during different processes, such as reading, speaking or day-dreaming. It does not, however, measure the firing of brain cells directly; it measures blood flow, which is thought to correlate to some extent with neuronal activity. Further, to define the imaging signal associated with a particular pattern of brain activity, researchers must usually average many scans from a group of test subjects, whose individual brain patterns may diverge widely. A defendants fMRI scan may appear to differ greatly from an average value presented in court but could still be within the statistical boundaries of the data set that defined that average.

Moreover, scientists simply do not always know the prevalence of normal variations in brain anatomy and activity in the population (or groups within it). Showing a defendant's brain scan without data from an appropriate comparison group might profoundly mislead a jury. Judges have already had a hard time evaluating whether to admit physical brain-scan evidence of neurological or psychiatric problems that might bear on a defendant's culpability; they may face more difficulty in the years ahead when deciding whether to allow brain images to serve as indicators for more complex mental states, such as a witness's credibility or truthfulness.

Since the early 20th century, when psychologist and inventor William Moulton Marston first claimed that a polygraph measuring blood pressure, pulse, skin conductivity and other physiological signs could determine whether someone is lying, lie detection has been a hot topic in legal circles. U.S. courts have largely dismissed polygraph results as inadmissible, but other technologies are being developed, and courts will surely be forced eventually to evaluate their admissibility as well. These tools include brain-imaging methods that aim to detect mental states reflective of truthful behavior.

Detecting Lies and Determining Credibility

Recent work by Anthony D. Wagner and his colleagues at Stanford University, for instance, has revealed that under controlled experimental conditions fMRI, combined with complex analytical algorithms called pattern classifiers, can accurately determine that a person is remembering something but not whether the content of the detected memory is real or imagined. In other words, we might be able to use fMRI to detect whether individuals believe that they are recalling something, but we cannot tell whether their beliefs are accurate. Wagner concludes that fMRI methods may eventually be effective in detecting lies but that additional studies are needed.

Other experiments help to expose the nature of honesty: Does honesty result from the absence of temptation or from the exercise of extra willpower to resist it? In 2009 Joshua D. Greene and Joseph M. Paxton of Harvard University gave test subjects placed in a scanner a financial incentive to overstate their accuracy in a coin toss; the researchers were able to obtain fMRI images of individuals deciding whether or not to lie. Dishonest behavior correlated with extra activity in certain brain regions involved in impulse control and decision making. Yet Greene and Paxton noted that some subjects who told the truth also exhibited that same brain activity, so the fMRI images may capture only their extra struggle to resist temptation, not their ultimate truthfulness. The researchers therefore urge judges to be cautious about allowing these kinds of data in today's courtroom.

Their view is not universal, however. Frederick Schauer, professor of law at the University of Virginia and an expert on legal evidence, points out that courts now routinely admit many types of evidence that are far more dubious than the lie-detection science that is being excluded. The current approach to assessing whether witnesses or others are telling the truth is inaccurate and based on misconceptions about dishonest behavior: demeanor, for example, does not always provide reliable clues to honesty. The law has its own standards for determining admissibility into a court, and those standards are more lenient than scientific standards. Schauer argues that jurors should be allowed to consider the result of a lie-detection test that has a 60 percent accuracy rate because it could provide reasonable doubt as to guilt or innocence.

One of the first cases to tackle the use of brain-scanning technology for lie detection recently ended in a federal district court in Tennessee. In *United States v. Semrau,* a magistrate judge found that the evidence offered by a commercial fMRI lie-detection company should be excluded in part because of Federal Rule of Evidence 403, which holds that evidence must be probative and not prejudicial.

Furthermore, the judge explained why he found that the unfair prejudicial influence of the technology in the case substantially outweighed its probative value. The magistrate's main objection was that the defense expert conducting the lie-detection test could not tell the court whether the answer to any particular question was true or false. In fact, the expert testified that he could tell only whether the defendant was answering the set of questions about the case truthfully overall.

The use of neuroscience to assess the character and overall honesty of defendants may eventually trump its use for probing their truthfulness on any one matter.

One must wonder: In future cases, might the results be admissible with the more limited goal of simply determining whether or not the defendant was being deceptive in general? The use of neuroscience to assess the character and overall honesty of defendants may eventually trump its use for probing their truthfulness on any one matter in the courtroom. Federal Rule 608(b) provides that once the character of a witness has been attacked, counsel can introduce as evidence opinions about the witness's "character for truthfulness or untruthfulness." Today this type of evidence consists simply of testimony by others about the character of the witness. But what about tomorrow? Will juries want to know how a witness scores on a test of probable dishonesty? Will the evidence that someone tends toward dishonesty be more prejudicial if it comes out of a fancy machine? My guess is that such evidence will eventually be used and that it will initially tend to be prejudicial but that as society acquires more experience with the technology, the prejudicial effect will diminish.

Scanning for Psychopaths

Judges and attorneys are already being forced to work out the role of brain scans in the courtroom. In the long run, however, the greatest impact of neuroscience on the legal system will surely come from deeper insights into how our brain shapes our behavior. Even in infancy humans manifest innate senses of fairness and reciprocity, as well as desires to comfort the mistreated and punish transgressors. We are judge and jury from birth. On top of these instincts we have built our enlightened view of how culture should regard and punish antisocial behavior. Someday neuroscience could well force the legal system to revise its rules for determining culpability and for meting out sentences. It could also shake up society's understanding of what it means to have "free will" and how best to decide when to hold someone accountable for antisocial actions.

Consider the psychiatric and legal standing of psychopaths, who constitute less than 1 percent of the general population but roughly 25 percent of those in prison. That label, though used popularly as a catchall for many violent and nonviolent criminals, is properly reserved for those with a well-defined psychiatric condition diagnosed through a test called the Hare Psychopathy Checklist—Revised (PCL-R).

Psychopaths often display superficial charm, egocentricity, grandiosity, deceitfulness, manipulativeness, and an absence of guilt or empathy, all of which the PCL-R can assess. Yet psychometric tests such as the PCL-R are only proxies for measuring the neurological dysfunctions underlying these people's disturbed mental lives. Neuroimaging measurements of brain processes should therefore, at least in theory, provide a much better way to identify psychopaths.

To date, numerous studies have associated psychopathy with unusual brain activity. Psychopaths seem to exhibit, for example, abnormal neurological responses to stimuli that demand close attention and to words with emotional, concrete or abstract meanings. But such responses may also be found in people who have suffered damage to an area known as the medial temporal lobe—meaning they cannot be used as definitive signs of psychopathy. Other studies suggest psychopaths may have damage to the deep-brain structures of the limbic system, which helps to give rise to emotions, but the finding is preliminary.

Scientists are also beginning to look for abnormal connections in psychopaths' brains. Marcus E. Raichle, Benjamin Shannon and their colleagues at Washington University in St. Louis, along with Kent Kiehl of the University of New Mexico, analyzed fMRI data from scans of adult inmates and of juvenile offenders, all of whom were also assessed for psychopathy with the PCL-R. The adults, they found, had a variety of unusual connections between regions in their brains, although no one alteration predominated. Striking differences appeared more consistently and exclusively in the young offenders—and the degree of those changes increased along with their individual levels of impulsivity. One interpretation is that the impulsive juveniles lack some of the normal neural constraints on their choices of actions. Perhaps among juveniles who go untreated a brain abnormality that promotes impulsiveness eventually becomes more widespread, resulting in the diverse neural abnormalities seen in adults. Such a difference may also help explain why psychiatric treatments for psychopathy in juveniles are more successful than in adults, who are largely unresponsive.

Controversially, psychopathy is not now a recognized basis for an insanity defense. Instead psychopaths are seen as more dangerous than offenders without the pathology, and they receive longer or harsher sentences. A neuroimaging tool or method that could reliably identify psychopaths would be useful at the sentencing phase of a trial because it could help determine whether the defendant might deserve medical confinement and treatment rather than punitive incarceration. Getting the public to accept that people identified in this way should be committed to a mental hospital instead of a prison may be a tough sell, but with enough evidence the practice could eventually become legal doctrine. By then, one hopes, neuroscience will also have come up with better ways to help rehabilitate or cure them.

Neuroscience and Criminal Defenses

Criminal law currently accepts only a short list of possible defenses—will modern neuroscience begin to add to it? For example, the courts have consistently refused to accept a formal "battered woman defense" from defendants who retaliated with lethal force against spouses who regularly and violently beat them. Nevertheless, in some states the courts do allow experts to testify that battered-woman syndrome is a type of post-traumatic stress disorder, which judges and juries can take into consideration when assessing the credibility of a woman's claim that she acted to protect herself. Such precedents open a door to wider judicial uses of neuroscience.

How one defines a defendant's *mens rea,* or mental state, in a given context has a major effect on how much responsibility to ascribe to him or her. In ongoing fMRI-based research, Read Montague of Baylor College of Medicine and Gideon Yaffe, a law professor at the University of Southern California, study whether certain addicted individuals suffer from a subtle form of "risk blindness." Reasonable people learn not to rob stores by realizing that committing the crime would jeopardize their ability to enjoy a life with friends and family, pursue rewarding careers, and so on. Montague and Yaffe see indications, however, that at least some addicts cannot think through the benefits of those alternative courses of action. Potentially their findings could justify modifying the "reasonable person" standard in criminal law so addicts could be judged against what a reasonable addict, rather than a reasonable nonaddict, would have done in a given situation; such a finding might then lead to acquittal or reduction in punishment for an addicted defendant.

When the foregoing examples are taken together, profound questions emerge about how our culture and the courts will manage antisocial behavior. As neuroscientist William T. Newsome of Stanford University has asked, Will each of us have a personalized "responsibility" ranking that may be called on should we break the law? If we soon all carry our personal medical histories on a memory stick for reference, as some experts predict, will we also perhaps include a profile derived from knowledge of our brain and behavior that captures our reasonableness and irresponsibility? Would this development be good for society and advance justice, or would it be counterproductive? Would it erode notions of free will and personal responsibility more broadly if all antisocial decisions could seemingly be attributed to some kind of neurological deviation?

> **Would it erode notions of free will and personal responsibility if all antisocial decisions could seemingly be attributed to some kind of neurological deviation?**

I feel it is important to keep scientific advances on how the brain enables mind separate from discussions of personal responsibility. People, not brains, commit crimes. As I have spelled out elsewhere, the concept of personal responsibility is something that arises out of social interactions. It is a part of the rules of social exchange, not a part of the brain.

Proceed with Caution

In spite of the many insights pouring forth from neuroscience, recent findings from research into the juvenile mind highlight the need to be cautious when incorporating such science into the law. In 2005 in the case *Roper v. Simmons,* the U.S. Supreme Court held that the execution of a defendant who committed a murder at age 17 or younger was cruel and unusual punishment. It based its opinion on three differences between juveniles and adults: juveniles suffer from an impetuous lack of maturity and responsibility; juveniles are more susceptible to negative influences and lack the independence to remove themselves from bad situations; and a juvenile's character is less formed than an adult's. Although the court realized it was drawing an arbitrary line, it ruled that no person who was younger than 18 at the time of a crime could receive the death penalty.

In May 2010 the court expanded that limitation. In *Graham v. Florida,* it held that for crimes other than homicide, a sentence of life without the possibility of parole for a person under the age of 18 violated the Constitution's prohibition of cruel and unusual punishment. Citing information provided by the American Medical Association, the court stated that "psychology and brain science continue to show fundamental differences between juvenile and adult minds."

But how consistently do neuroscience and psychology support that opinion? A study by Gregory S. Berns, Sara Moore and C. Monica Capra of Emory University explored whether the irrefutable tendency of juveniles to engage in risky behavior resulted from immaturity in the cognitive systems that regulate emotional responses. This team tested the theory using a technology called diffusion tensor imaging (DTI) to examine the tracts of white matter that connect different control regions of the cortex in 91 teenage subjects. Surprisingly, the juveniles who engaged in risky behavior had tracts that looked *more adult* than did those of their more risk-averse peers.

Advanced neuroimaging has thus presented a finding directly contrary to the conventional scientific and legal perspectives on the capacity of juveniles. If further research supports those conclusions, then the law, by its own logic, might need to hold juvenile delinquents to adult criminal standards. Alternatively, justice might require that convicted juveniles undergo DTI or a successor technology to determine whether their white matter structure is adultlike. The results of such a test could then provide guidance to the court on sentencing. The scope of these consequences highlights why the courts should not incorporate insights from neuroscience into the law until a substantial body of studies have confirmed them.

Exciting as the advances that neuroscience is making every day are, all of us should look with caution at how they may gradually come to be incorporated into our culture. The legal relevance of neuroscientific discoveries is only part of the picture. Might we someday want brain scans of our fiancées, business partners or politicians, even if the results could not stand up in court? As the scientific understanding of human nature continues to evolve, our moral stance on how we wish to manage a just society will shift as well. No one I know wants to rush into a new framework without extreme care being given to each new finding. Yet no one can ignore the changes on the horizon.

More to Explore

Patterns of Neural Activity Associated with Honest and Dishonest Moral Decisions. Joshua D. Greene and Joseph M. Paxton in *Proceedings of the National Academy of Sciences USA,* vol. 106, no. 30, pages 12,506–12,511; July 28, 2009.

Adolescent Engagement in Dangerous Behaviors Is Associated with Increased White Matter Maturity of Frontal Cortex. Gregory S. Berns, Sara Moore and C. Monica Capra in *PLoS ONE,* vol. 4, no. 8, e6773; August 26, 2009.

Altered Functional Connectivity in Adult and Juvenile Psychopathy: A Rest-State fMRI Analysis. Benjamin Shannon et al. Abstract from the 16th Annual Meeting of the Organization for Human Brain Mapping. Barcelona, 2010.

Detecting Individual Memories through the Neural Decoding of Memory States and Past Experience. Jesse Rissman, Henry T. Greely and Anthony D. Wagner in *Proceedings of the National Academy of Sciences USA* vol. 107, no. 21, pages 9,849–9,854; May 25, 2010.

Who's in Charge? Free Will and the Science of the Brain. Michael S. Gazzaniga. Ecco HarperColins, 2011.

The Law and Neuroscience Project: www.lawandneuroscience project.org.

Critical Thinking

1. How could brain scans assist criminal defendants?
2. Should courts allow brain scans into evidence?

Create Central

www.mhhe.com/createcentral

Internet References

Clinical Neurological Sciences
www.cnsuwo.ca/ebn
Frontiers
www.frontiersin.org/journal/10.3389/fpsyg.2012.00385/abstract

US Supreme Court to Police: To Search a Cell Phone, "Get a Warrant"

The US Supreme Court, ruling 9 to 0, invalidated the warrantless searches of cell phones, which hold "the privacies of life." Police have no right to "rummage at will," the justices said.

WARREN RICHEY

Learning Outcomes

After reading this article, you will be able to:

- State the relevant facts in *Wurie* and *Riley*.
- Present the Court's decisions in these cases.
- Explain the Court's reasoning.

Washington—In a major affirmation of privacy in the digital age, the US Supreme Court on Wednesday ruled that police must obtain a warrant before searching digital information on a cell phone seized from an individual who has been arrested.

The 9-to-0 decision marks a Fourth Amendment landmark of profound importance given the ubiquity of cell phones, tablets, and portable computers in public places throughout society.

"Modern cell phones are not just another technological convenience," Chief Justice John Roberts wrote for the court. "With all they contain and all they may reveal, they hold for many Americans the 'privacies of life,'" he said.

"The fact that technology now allows an individual to carry such information in his hand does not make the information any less worthy of the protection for which the Founders fought," the chief justice said.

"Our answer to the question of what police must do before searching a cell phone seized incident to an arrest is accordingly simple—get a warrant."

In an indication of how fundamental these protections are in the justices' view, the chief justice likened warrantless searches of cell phones to the "general warrants" and "writs of assistance" imposed during colonial America that allowed British troops to "rummage through homes in an unrestrained search for evidence of criminal activity."

"Opposition to such searches was in fact one of the driving forces behind the Revolution itself," Chief Justice Roberts said.

In reaching its decision, the justices rejected arguments by the Obama administration and the California attorney general that law enforcement officials must be able to immediately search the contents of a cell phone or other electronic device when the device was found on a person at the time of his or her lawful arrest.

The justices also rejected a suggested fallback position to allow police to conduct a limited search of a cell phone without a warrant whenever it was reasonable to believe the device contained evidence of the crime that prompted the arrest of the individual.

Roberts said that fallback position provided no practical limit because it would still give "police officers unbridled discretion to rummage at will among a person's private effects."

Instead, the court established a bright line rule that if police seize a cell phone during an arrest they must seek approval from a neutral judge before searching the phone for any evidence of crime.

Steps can be taken to secure the data on the phone to prevent destruction of potential evidence, he said. And the warrant process is becoming more efficient.

"We cannot deny that our decision today will have an impact on the ability of law enforcement to combat crime," Roberts said. "Cell phones have become important tools in facilitating coordination and communication among members of criminal enterprises, and can provide valuable incriminating information about dangerous criminals."

But the chief justice added: "Privacy comes at a cost."

Roberts said the court recognized that there might be instances when the government faces exigent circumstances that required swift and decisive action. In those cases, the courts have recognized an exception to the warrant requirement, an exception that must be later justified case by case to a judge.

The decision reflects a recognition by the high court of a growing threat to privacy in the digital age, with vast amounts of personal records, photos, video, and other intimate information readily accessible on smart phones and other electronic devices.

The government had argued that once an individual is placed under arrest, he or she has a diminished privacy interest and that diminished privacy protection does not extend to anything found in their pockets. Under this approach, searching the contents of a cell phone should be considered no different than searching inside a cigarette pack found in an arrestee's pocket, the government argued.

"This is like saying a ride on horseback is materially indistinguishable from a flight to the moon," Roberts said.

"Modern cell phones, as a category, implicate privacy concerns far beyond those implicated by the search of a cigarette pack, a wallet, or a purse," he said.

Cell phones are different, he said. Even the term cell phone doesn't accurately account for the full scope of their use.

"They could just as easily be called cameras, video players, rolodexes, calendars, tape recorders, libraries, diaries, albums, televisions, maps, or newspapers," Roberts said.

"Most people cannot lug around every piece of mail they have received for the past several months, every picture they have taken, or every book or article they have read—nor would they have reason to attempt to do so," he said.

He said to do so would require dragging a trunk around. The chief justice noted that under existing legal precedents, police would need a warrant to search such a trunk.

"Prior to the digital age, people did not typically carry a cache of sensitive personal information with them as they went about their day," he said. "Now it is the person who is not carrying a cell phone, with all that it contains, who is the exception."

Wednesday's decision stems from two cases in which police used information discovered during warrantless searches of cell phones being carried by individuals at the time of their arrest.

The phones contained images and other information that police used as evidence of criminal activity or to identify other evidence of crime.

One case involved a suspected drug dealer in Boston named Brima Wurie. Police used his cell phone to identify Mr. Wurie's home address. After obtaining a warrant they raided the home where they found drugs, cash, and a weapon.

Wurie was charged with possession with intent to distribute cocaine base, distributing cocaine base, and with being a felon in possession of a firearm.

Wurie's lawyers filed a motion to suppress the evidence that resulted from the warrantless search of his cell phone.

A federal judge denied the motion. At trial, Wurie was convicted and sentenced to nearly 22 years in prison.

On appeal, the First US Circuit Court of Appeals reversed the trial judge, ruling that the police should have obtained a warrant *before* accessing the information in Wurie's phone.

The other case involved a suspected criminal gang member in San Diego named David Riley.

Mr. Riley was pulled over in a traffic stop for driving with expired tags. After discovering that Riley's license had been suspended, the officer impounded Riley's car.

During a routine search of the car, police found two firearms under the car's hood. Riley was arrested.

As he was taken into custody, police seized Riley's smartphone. The arresting officer scrolled through the phone's text files and noticed notations that suggested that Riley was a gang member.

Two hours later, at the police department, the phone was turned over to a detective who specialized in gang crime investigations. The detective examined the contents of the phone and discovered images that allegedly linked the suspect to an earlier gang-related shooting. Police also used photos and video images found on the phone to connect the suspect to other gang-related activities.

Riley was charged with shooting at an occupied vehicle, use of a semiautomatic firearm, and attempted murder. He was also charged with involvement in a gang-related crime.

His lawyer argued that evidence obtained without a warrant from Riley's smartphone must be excluded from his trial. The judge rejected the motion, ruling that the action did not violate the Fourth Amendment.

Riley was convicted and sentenced to 15 years to life in prison. The California Court of Appeal upheld the conviction, noting that the California Supreme Court in 2011 had issued an opinion that police may search a smartphone without a warrant whenever the phone is being carried by an individual at the time of arrest.

In its ruling on Wednesday, the Supreme Court reversed the California Court of Appeal and affirmed the decision of the First Circuit in Boston.

The cases were *US v. Wurie* (13–212) and *Riley v. California* (13–132).

Critical Thinking

1. What were the "general warrants" and "writs of assistance" referred to in the Court's decision?

2. Why is searching a cell phone different from searching inside a cigarette pack found in an arrestee's pocket?

3. Is privacy worth the cost to law enforcement?

Internet References

Encyclopedia.com
  http://www.encyclopedia.com/topic/Writs_of_assistance.aspx

Findlaw
  http://criminal.findlaw.com/criminal-rights/search-and-seizure-and-the-fourth-amendment.html?DCMP=ADCCRIM_SearchSeizure-4thAmendment&& HBX_PK=fourth+amendment+regulation

The Christian Science Monitor
  http://www.csmonitor.com/Innovation/2013/0718/FISA-101-10-key-dates-in-the-evolution-of-NSA-surveillance/Before-the-September-11-attacks

By Warren Richey. Reprinted with permission from the June 25, 2014 issue of The Christian Science Monitor. © 2014 The Christian Science Monitor (www.CSMonitor.com).

Article   Prepared by: Joanne Naughton

One Simple Way to Improve How Cops and Prosecutors Do Their Jobs

MIKE RIGGS

Learning Outcomes

After reading this article, you will be able to:

- Set forth what Byrne Grants are.
- Describe how the bulk of Byrne Grants are primarily used.

Every year, the U.S. Justice Department sends hundreds of millions of dollars to states and municipalities via the Edward Byrne Memorial Justice Assistance Grant. Named for 22-year-old NYPD Officer Edward Byrne, who was murdered in 1988 while he sat in his patrol car, the JAG program provides "critical funding necessary to support a range of program areas, including law enforcement; prosecution, courts, and indigent defense; crime prevention and education; corrections and community corrections; drug treatment and enforcement; program planning, evaluation, and technology improvement; and crime victim and witness initiatives."

Despite what that long list suggests, the bulk of JAG funding ends up going toward fighting the drug war. "Historically," the Drug Policy Alliance noted in 2010, "Byrne Grants have been used primarily to finance drug task forces, which have a record of racially disproportionate low level drug arrests and increased local and state costs with no measurable impact on public safety." At the time, the group suggested that JAG funding be reallocated in favor of more drug treatment programs, rather than enforcement.

As it stands, 60 percent of JAG funding over the last 3 years—totaling more than half a billion dollars—has gone to law enforcement activities. In a new report, titled "Reforming Funding to Reduce Mass Incarceration" [PDF], the Brennan Center for Justice explains why: Because law enforcement agencies can do whatever they want with this money, and most of them think the best way to keep that money coming is to arrest as many people as possible.

This is no accident. The annual self-evaluation JAG recipients are required to complete measures performance in a way, says the Brennan Center report, that is "roughly analogous to a hospital counting the number of emergency room admissions, instead of considering the number of lives saved." Agencies are asked how many arrests they made, and prosecutors are asked how many cases they won. Not only is that data rather useless in terms of assessing the effectiveness of a given policy, it also says to the person answering the questions that their numbers should be really big.

JAG funding is only a slice of a law enforcement agency's budget, but it can still be a lot of money. Many cities receive JAG funding directly (L.A., New York, Chicago, Houston receive millions a year), and money also goes to states to dole out as they see fit. In 2013, Texas, California, Florida, New York, and Illinois received between $10 and $30 million in JAG grants. As a result of the perception that more arrests are better, the majority of JAG funding goes toward drug and gang enforcement. Programs that arguably should receive more funding in an age of overincarceration get far less: drug treatment programs receive only 5 percent of JAG funding, while on average .004 percent goes toward indigent defense.

Former and current law enforcement officials interviewed by the Brennan Center said that the DOJ's current JAG questionnaire encourages agencies to report "accomplishments that are easy to track but meaningless." To change that, says the Brennan Center, the Justice Department could do something awfully simple: ask a better set of questions when reviewing how agencies spent their grant money.

Is a new questionnaire going to "fix" over-policing of minor crimes and overincarceration of nonviolent offenders? No. But changing incentives is a first step in changing culture. "By signaling to recipients that effectiveness, proportionality, and fairness are DOJ priorities," the Brennan report suggests, "the proposed measures can help turn off the 'automatic pilot' of more punishment—and more incarceration."

Critical Thinking

1. What is the Brennan Center's main criticism of Byrne Grants?

2. Do you agree that too much emphasis is placed on enforcing drug and gang laws?

Internet References

Brennan Center for Justice
http://www.brennancenter.org/publication/reforming-funding-reduce-mass-incarceration

Bureau of Justice Assistance U.S. Department of Justice
https://www.bja.gov/Publications/JAG_LE_Grant_Activity_03-13.pdf

Drug Policy Alliance
http://www.drugpolicy.org/sites/default/files/FactSheet_ByrneJAG_Sept.%202010.pdf

Article   Prepared by: Joanne Naughton

U.S. Reviewing 27 Death Penalty Convictions for FBI Forensic Testimony Errors

SPENCER S. HSU

Learning Outcomes

After reading this article, you will be able to:

- Understand that any human endeavor is subject to the possibility of error, including forensic science.

- Comprehend the value of media scrutiny of government entities.

- Know that hair analysis cannot be used as positive identification, despite the fact that a prosecution witness may say it can.

- Discuss the death penalty as it relates to wrongful convictions.

An unprecedented federal review of old criminal cases has uncovered as many as 27 death penalty convictions in which FBI forensic experts may have mistakenly linked defendants to crimes with exaggerated scientific testimony, U.S. officials said.

The review led to an 11th-hour stay of execution in Mississippi in May.

It is not known how many of the cases involve errors, how many led to wrongful convictions or how many mistakes may now jeopardize valid convictions. Those questions will be explored as the review continues.

The discovery of the more than two dozen capital cases promises that the examination could become a factor in the debate over the death penalty. Some opponents have long held that the execution of a person confirmed to be innocent would crystallize doubts about capital punishment. But if DNA or other testing confirms all convictions, it would strengthen proponents' arguments that the system works.

FBI officials discussed the review's scope as they prepare to disclose its first results later this summer. The death row cases are among the first 120 convictions identified as potentially problematic among more than 21,700 FBI Laboratory files being examined. The review was announced last July by the FBI and the Justice Department, in consultation with the Innocence Project and the National Association of Criminal Defense Lawyers (NACDL).

The unusual collaboration came after *The Washington Post* reported last year that authorities had known for years that flawed forensic work by FBI hair examiners may have led to convictions of potentially innocent people, but officials had not aggressively investigated problems or notified defendants.

At issue is a once-widespread practice by which some FBI experts exaggerated the significance of "matches" drawn from microscopic analysis of hair found at crime scenes.

Since at least the 1970s, written FBI Laboratory reports typically stated that a hair association could not be used as positive identification. However, on the witness stand, several agents for years went beyond the science and testified that their hair analysis was a near-certain match.

The new review listed examples of scientifically invalid testimony, including claiming to associate a hair with a single person "to the exclusion of all others," or to state or suggest a probability for such a match from past casework.

Whatever the findings of the review, the initiative is pushing state and local labs to take similar measures.

For instance, the Texas Forensic Science Commission on Friday directed all labs under its jurisdiction to take the first step to scrutinize hair cases, in a state that has executed more defendants than any other since 1982.

Separately, FBI officials said their intention is to review and disclose problems in capital cases even after a defendant has been executed.

"We didn't do this to be a model for anyone—other than when there's a problem, you have to face it, and you have to figure how to fix it, move forward and make sure it doesn't happen again," FBI general counsel Andrew Weissmann said. "That tone and approach is set from the very top of this building," he said, referring to FBI Director Robert S. Mueller III.

David Christian "Chris" Hassell, director of the FBI Laboratory, said the review will be used to improve lab training, testimony, audit systems and research, as it has done when previous breakdowns were uncovered. The lab overhauled scientific practices when whistleblowers revealed problems in 1996 and again after an FBI fingerprint misidentification in a high-profile 2003 terrorism case, he said.

"One of the things good scientists do is question their assumptions. No matter what the field, what the discipline, those questions should be up for debate," Hassell said. "That's as true in forensics as anything else."

Advocates for defendants and the wrongly convicted called the undertaking a watershed moment in police and prosecutorial agencies' willingness to re-open old cases because of scientific errors uncovered by DNA testing.

Peter J. Neufeld, co-founder of the Innocence Project, which supports inmates who seek exoneration through DNA testing, applauded the FBI, calling the review historic and a "major step forward to improve the criminal justice system and the rigor of forensic science in the United States."

Norman L. Reimer, executive director of the NACDL, also praised the effort, predicting that it would have "an enormous impact on the states" and calling on the defense bar to represent indigent convicts.

"That's going to be a very big job as this unfolds," said Reimer, whose group has spent 1,500 hours identifying cases for the second round of review.

Under terms finalized with the groups last month, the Justice Department will notify prosecutors and convicted defendants or defense attorneys if an internal review panel or the two external groups find that FBI examiners "exceeded the limits of science" when they claimed to link crime scene hair to defendants in reports or testimony.

If so, the department will assist the class of prisoners in unprecedented ways, including waiving statutes of limitations and other federal rules that since 1996 have restricted post-conviction appeals. The FBI also will test DNA evidence if sought by a judge or prosecutor.

The review will prioritize capital cases, then cases in which defendants are imprisoned.

Unlike DNA analysis, there is no accepted research on how often hair from different people may appear the same.

The federal inquiry came after the Public Defender Service helped exonerate three D.C. men through DNA testing that showed that three FBI hair examiners contributed to their wrongful convictions for rape or murder in the early 1980s.

The response has been notable for the department and the FBI, which in the past has been accused of overprotecting its agents. Twice since 1996, authorities conducted case reviews largely in secret after the scientific integrity of the FBI Lab was faulted.

Weissmann said that although earlier reviews lawfully gave prosecutors discretion to decide when to turn over potentially exculpatory material to the defense, greater transparency will "lessen skepticism" about the government's motives. It also will be cheaper, faster and more effective because private parties can help track down decades-old cases.

Scientific errors "are not owned by one side," he said. "This gives the same information to both sides, and they can litigate it."

The review terms could have wide repercussions. The FBI is examining more than 21,000 federal and state cases referred to the FBI Lab's hair unit from 1982 through 1999—by which time DNA testing of hair was routine—and the bureau has asked for help in finding cases before lab files were computerized in 1985.

Of 15,000 files reviewed to date, the FBI said a hair association was declared in about 2,100 cases. Investigators have contacted police and prosecutors in more than 1,200 of those cases to find out whether hair evidence was used in a conviction, in which case trial transcripts will be sought. However, 400 of those cases have been closed because prosecutors did not respond.

On May 7, Mississippi's Supreme Court stayed the execution of Willie Jerome Manning for a 1992 double homicide hours before he was set to die by lethal injection.

FBI cases may represent only the tip of the problem.

While the FBI employed 27 hair examiners during the period under review, FBI officials confirmed for the first time this week that records indicate that about 500 people attended one-week hair comparison classes given by FBI examiners between 1979 and 2009. Nearly all of them came from state and local labs.

State and local prosecutors handle more than 95 percent of violent crimes.

In April, the accreditation arm of the American Society of Crime Laboratory Directors declined to order state and local labs to conduct reviews, but issued a public notice recommending that each laboratory evaluate the impact of improper statements on past convictions, reminding them of their ethical obligation to act in case of a potential miscarriage of justice.

FBI Lab officials say they have not been contacted by other labs about their review or who completed the FBI classes.

Critical Thinking

1. In light of what we now know about how these cases were prosecuted, do you think the death penalty remains an appropriate penalty in any case?

2. Why do you think these errors occurred?

3. Do you think we have ever executed innocent people?

Create Central

www.mhhe.com/createcentral

Internet References

Prison-Justice for America
    http://prison-justice.org

Think Progress
    http://thinkprogress.org/justice/2013/07/19/2330071/federal-forensics-investigation-calls-into-question-hundreds-of-convictions

Article

Prepared by: Joanne Naughton

Drug Defendants Are Being "Forced" to Plead Guilty, Report Claims

Saki Knafo

Learning Outcomes

After reading this article, you will be able to:

- Explain why almost all drug defendants in federal cases chose to plead guilty in 2012 rather than go to trial.

- Show the effect of mandatory-minimum sentencing laws on these cases.

Only 3 percent of U.S. drug defendants in federal cases chose to go to trial instead of pleading guilty in 2012, according to a new report from Human Rights Watch. The small number begins to make sense if you consider the consequences faced by drug defendants convicted in court, argues the report's author, Jamie Fellner.

"Prosecutors can say, 'Take these 10 years or, if you get a trial and are convicted, you're going to look at life,'" said Fellner, an attorney who specializes in criminal justice issues at Human Rights Watch. "That's a pretty amazing power that unfortunately they are more than willing to wield."

The effect, she argues, is that prosecutors essentially "force" defendants to plead guilty.

Last year, drug defendants in federal cases who went to trial and lost were sentenced to more than three times as many years in prison as those who took a plea, according to the report's analysis of data from the United States Sentencing Commission, a government agency.

And the majority of those who did go to trial—89 percent of them—lost.

The percentage of defendants in 2012 who fought their charges is likely an all-time low. In 1980, the first year for which the report reviewed the relevant data, the percentage of federal drug defendants who pleaded guilty was slightly more than 60 percent, and it has risen steadily since then.

The advent of mandatory-minimum sentencing laws in the mid-80s is largely responsible for the steady increase in guilty pleas, according to Fellner. Such laws required judges to impose harsh, predetermined sentences on people convicted of the distribution and, in some circumstances, possession of illicit drugs, while giving prosecutors the ability to offer defendants smaller sentences as part of a deal.

"If you can get someone to acknowledge guilt without the burden and expense of a trial, without having to marshal witnesses and line up witnesses, and without risking an acquittal, why not?" said Fellner. "You don't have the cost of a trial, it doesn't take the time and resources, and it increases the notches on your belt of how many convictions you've gotten."

But in reality, the government lacks the resources needed to try everyone who is charged with a drug offense, said Steven Jansen, the vice president and chief operating officer of the Association of Prosecuting Attorneys, a professional group based in Washington.

"Justice would almost stand still if we took the majority of our cases to trial," he said.

Jansen noted that efforts are underway to reform the nation's mandatory-minimum sentencing laws. Lawmakers from both parties have introduced bills that would scale back the reach of those laws, and U.S. Attorney General Eric Holder has directed federal prosecutors to shift their attention away from drug cases.

"Our system is looking at mandatory minimums and what we're going to either do or not do about them," Jansen said. "But a defendant is really not forced to accept a guilty plea. Obviously they have a right to go to trial no matter what the sentence is."

Critical Thinking

1. Do you believe defendants are really forced to plead guilty?
2. What are the incentives to a prosecutor to convince a defendant to plead guilty?

Internet References

The Huffington Post
http://www.huffingtonpost.com/2013/10/31/bipartisan-drug-war_n_4183221.html

Human Rights Watch
http://www.hrw.org/reports/2013/12/05/offer-you-can-t-refuse

Unit 5

UNIT

Prepared by: Joanne Naughton

Juvenile Justice

Although there were variations within specific offense categories, the overall arrest rate for juvenile violent crime remained relatively constant for several decades. Then, in the late 1980s, something changed: more and more juveniles charged with violent offenses were brought into the justice system. The juvenile justice system is a 20th-century response to the problems of dealing with children in trouble with the law, or children who need society's protection.

Juvenile court procedure differs from the procedure in adult courts because juvenile courts are based on the philosophy that their function is to treat and help, not to punish and abandon the offender. Recently, operations of juvenile courts have received criticism, and a number of significant Supreme Court decisions have changed the way that the courts must approach the rights of children. Despite a trend toward dealing more punitively with children who commit serious crimes, by treating them as if they were adults, the major thrust of the juvenile justice system remains one of diversion and treatment, rather than adjudication and incarceration.

Article

Prepared by: Joanne Naughton

Juveniles Facing Lifelong Terms Despite Rulings

ERIK ECKHOLM

Learning Outcomes

After reading this article, you will be able to:

- Relate the Supreme Court's decisions in *Miller* and *Graham*.

- Show how some states are responding to the Court's decisions regarding the use of mandatory life sentences for juveniles.

Jacksonville, FL—In decisions widely hailed as milestones, the United States Supreme Court in 2010 and 2012 acted to curtail the use of mandatory life sentences for juveniles, accepting the argument that children, even those who are convicted of murder, are less culpable than adults and usually deserve a chance at redemption.

But most states have taken half measures, at best, to carry out the rulings, which could affect more than 2,000 current inmates and countless more in years to come, according to many youth advocates and legal experts.

"States are going through the motions of compliance," said Cara H. Drinan, an associate professor of law at the Catholic University of America, "but in an anemic or hyper-technical way that flouts the spirit of the decisions."

Lawsuits now before Florida's highest court are among many across the country that demand more robust changes in juvenile justice. One of the Florida suits accuses the state of skirting the ban on life without parole in nonhomicide cases by meting out sentences so staggering that they amount to the same thing.

Other suits, such as one argued last week before the Illinois Supreme Court, ask for new sentencing hearings, at least, for inmates who received automatic life terms for murder before 2012—a retroactive application that several states have resisted.

The plaintiff in one of the Florida lawsuits, Shimeek Gridine, was 14 when he and a 12-year-old partner made a clumsy attempt to rob a man in 2009 here in Jacksonville. As the disbelieving victim turned away, Shimeek fired a shotgun, pelting the side of the man's head and shoulder.

The man was not seriously wounded, but Shimeek was prosecuted as an adult. He pleaded guilty to attempted murder and robbery, hoping for leniency as a young offender with no record of violence. The judge called his conduct "heinous" and sentenced him to 70 years without parole.

Under Florida law, he cannot be released until he turns 77, at least, several years beyond the life expectancy for a black man his age, noted his public defender, who called the sentence "de facto life without parole" in an appeal to Florida's high court.

"They sentenced him to death, that's how I see it," Shimeek's grandmother Wonona Graham said.

The Supreme Court decisions built on a 2005 ruling that banned the death penalty for juvenile offenders as cruel and unusual punishment, stating that offenders younger than 18 must be treated differently from adults.

The 2010 decision, *Graham v. Florida*, forbade sentences of life without parole for juveniles not convicted of murder and said offenders must be offered a "meaningful opportunity for release based on demonstrated maturity and rehabilitation." The ruling applied to those who had been previously sentenced.

Cases like Shimeek's aim to show that sentences of 70 years, 90 years or more violate that decision. Florida's defense was that Shimeek's sentence was not literally "life without parole" and that the life span of a young inmate could not be predicted.

Probably no more than 200 prisoners were affected nationally by the 2010 decision, and they were concentrated in Florida. So far, of 115 inmates in the state who had been sentenced to life for nonhomicide convictions, 75 have had new hearings, according to the Youth Defense Institute at the Barry University School of Law in Orlando. In 30 cases, the new sentences have been for 50 years or more. One inmate who had been convicted of gun robbery and rape has received consecutive sentences totaling 170 years.

In its 2012 decision, *Miller v. Alabama,* the Supreme Court declared that juveniles convicted of murder may not automatically be given life sentences. Life terms remain a possibility, but judges and juries must tailor the punishment to individual circumstances and consider mitigating factors.

The Supreme Court did not make it clear whether the 2012 ruling applied retroactively, and state courts have been divided, suggesting that this issue, as well as the question of de facto life sentences, may eventually return to the Supreme Court.

Advocates for victims have argued strongly against revisiting pre-2012 murder sentences or holding parole hearings for the convicts, saying it would inflict new suffering on the victims' families.

Pennsylvania has the most inmates serving automatic life sentences for murders committed when they were juveniles: more than 450, according to the Juvenile Law Center in Philadelphia. In October, the State Supreme Court found that the Miller ruling did not apply to these prior murder convictions, creating what the law center, a private advocacy group, called an "appallingly unjust situation" with radically different punishments depending on the timing of the trial.

Likewise, courts in Louisiana, with about 230 inmates serving mandatory life sentences for juvenile murders, refused to make the law retroactive. In Florida, with 198 such inmates, the issue is under consideration by the State Supreme Court, and on Wednesday it was argued before the top court of Illinois, where 100 inmates could be affected.

Misgivings about the federal Supreme Court decisions and efforts to restrict their application have come from some victim groups and legal scholars around the country.

"The Supreme Court has seriously overgeneralized about under-18 offenders," said Kent S. Scheidegger, the legal director of the Criminal Justice Legal Foundation, a conservative group in Sacramento, Calif. "There are some under 18 who are thoroughly incorrigible criminals."

Some legal experts who are otherwise sympathetic have suggested that the Supreme Court overreached, with decisions that "represent a dramatic judicial challenge to legislative authority," according to a new article in the *Missouri Law Review* by Frank O. Bowman III of the University of Missouri School of Law.

Among the handful of states with large numbers of juvenile offenders serving life terms, California is singled out by advocates for acting in the spirit of the Supreme Court rules.

"California has led the way in scaling back some of the extreme sentencing policies it imposed on children," said Jody Kent Lavy, the director of the Campaign for the Fair Sentencing of Youth, which has campaigned against juvenile life sentences and called on states to reconsider mandatory terms dispensed before the Miller ruling. Too many states, she said, are "reacting with knee-jerk, narrow efforts at compliance."

California is allowing juvenile offenders who were condemned to life without parole to seek a resentencing hearing. The State Supreme Court also addressed the issue of de facto life sentences, voiding a 110-year sentence that had been imposed for attempted murder.

Whether they alter past sentences or not, some states have adapted by imposing minimum mandatory terms for juvenile murderers of 25 or 35 years before parole can even be considered—far more flexible than mandatory life, but an approach that some experts say still fails to consider individual circumstances.

As Ms. Drinan of Catholic University wrote in a coming article in the Washington University Law Review, largely ignored is the mandate to offer young inmates a chance to "demonstrate growth and maturity," raising their chances of eventual release.

To give young offenders a real chance to mature and prepare for life outside prison, Ms. Drinan said, "states must overhaul juvenile incarceration altogether," rather than letting them languish for decades in adult prisons.

Shimeek Gridine, meanwhile, is pursuing a high school equivalency diploma in prison while awaiting a decision by the Florida Supreme Court that could alter his bleak prospects.

He has a supportive family: A dozen relatives, including his mother and grandparents and several aunts and uncles, testified at his sentencing in 2010, urging clemency for a child who played Pop Warner football and talked of becoming a merchant seaman, like his grandfather.

But the judge said the fact that Shimeek had a good family, and decent grades, only underscored that the boy knew right from wrong, and he issued a sentence 30 years longer than even the prosecution had asked for.

Now Florida's top court is pondering whether his sentence violates the federal Constitution.

"A 70-year sentence imposed upon a 14-year-old is just as cruel and unusual as a sentence of life without parole," Shimeek's public defender, Gail Anderson, argued before the Florida court in September. "Mr. Gridine will most likely die in prison."

Critical Thinking

1. Should juveniles be prosecuted as adults, even though they aren't adults?

2. Do the advocates for victims have a valid argument against making *Miller* retroactive?

3. Do you believe Shimeek Gridine's sentence violates the Supreme Court's decision in *Graham*?

Internet References

Sentencing Law and Policy
http://sentencing.typepad.com/sentencing_law_and_policy/assessing-graham-and-its-aftermath/

Social Science Research Network
http://papers.ssrn.com/sol3/papers.cfm?abstract_id=2350316

The Campaign for the Fair Sentencing of Youth
http://fairsentencingofyouth.org/2014/10/01/american-correctional-association-opposes-jlwop/

Article Prepared by: Joanne Naughton

U.S. Inquiry Finds a "Culture of Violence" Against Teenage Inmates at Rikers

BENJAMIN WEISER AND MICHAEL SCHWIRTZ

Learning Outcomes

After reading this article, you will be able to:

- Relate the essence of a report about conditions at Rikers Island Jail, prepared by the U.S. Attorney in Manhattan.

- Describe instances of violence against adolescent inmates by correction officers.

- Show that officers were rarely punished for violence against young inmates.

In an extraordinary rebuke of the New York City Department of Correction, the federal government said on Monday the department had systematically violated the civil rights of male teenagers at Rikers Island by failing to protect them from the rampant use of unnecessary and excessive force by correction officers.

The office of Preet Bharara, the United States attorney in Manhattan, released its findings in a graphic 79-page report that described a "deep-seated culture of violence" against youthful inmates at Rikers, perpetrated by guards who operated with little fear of punishment.

The report, addressed to Mayor Bill de Blasio and two other senior city officials, singled out for blame a "powerful code of silence" among jail staff, along with a virtually useless system for investigating attacks by guards. The result was a "staggering" number of injuries among youthful inmates, the report said.

The report also found the department relied to an "excessive and inappropriate" degree on solitary confinement to punish teenage inmates, placing them in punitive segregation, as the practice is known, for months at a time.

Although the federal investigation focused only on the three Rikers jails that house male inmates aged 16 to 18, the report said the systemic problems that were identified "may exist in equal measure at the other jails on Rikers."

Correction officers struck adolescents in the head and face at "an alarming rate" as punishment, even when inmates posed no threat; officers took inmates to isolated locations for beatings out of view of video cameras; and many inmates were so afraid of the violence that they asked, for their own protection, to be placed in solitary confinement, the report said.

Officers were rarely punished, the report said, even with strong evidence of egregious violations. Investigations, when they occurred, were often superficial, and incident reports were frequently incomplete, misleading, or intentionally falsified.

Among more than a dozen specific cases of brutality detailed in the report was one in which correction officers assaulted four inmates for several minutes, beating them with radios, batons, and broomsticks and slamming their heads against walls. Another inmate sustained a skull fracture and was left with the imprint of a boot on his back in an assault involving multiple officers. In another case, a young man was taken from a classroom after falling asleep during a lecture and beaten severely. Teachers heard him screaming and crying for his mother.

"For adolescent inmates, Rikers Island is broken," Mr. Bharara said at a news conference announcing the findings. "It is a place where brute force is the first impulse rather than the last resort, a place where verbal insults are repaid with physical injuries, where beatings are routine, while accountability is rare."

The federal investigation was not conducted as a criminal inquiry and no charges were announced against individuals. Officers involved in specific incidents were also not identified by name. But the report listed more than 10 pages of remedial measures, and it warned that if the city did not work cooperatively to develop new policies and procedures, the Justice Department could bring a federal lawsuit asking a judge to order the imposition of remedies. Mr. Bharara said the city had 49 days to respond to the findings.

Adolescents at Rikers were consigned to "a corrections crucible that seems more inspired by 'Lord of the Flies' than any legitimate philosophy of humane detention," Mr. Bharara said.

The report, which covered from 2011 through the end of 2013, touched on many of the same issues raised in an investigation by *The New York Times* into violence by guards at Rikers, particularly against inmates with mental illnesses, published last month.

The *Times* article documented 129 cases in which inmates of all ages were seriously injured last year in altercations with correction officers, including several attacks that were also singled out in the report.

New York is one of just two states in the country that automatically charges people aged 16 to 18 as adults. That population, which averages close to 500 inmates at Rikers Island, is among the most difficult at the jail complex, the report said. In the 2013 fiscal year, about 51 percent were diagnosed with a mental illness, compared with about 38 percent for the overall population. And nearly two-thirds were charged with felonies.

Even so, the report found that adolescents were overseen by the least experienced correctional staff, who, often out of frustration or malice, lashed out violently against them. In the 2013 fiscal year alone, inmates younger than 18 sustained 1,057 injuries in 565 reported uses of force by correctional staff members. In a tally of the adolescent population as of Oct. 30, 2012, nearly 44 percent had been subjected to a use of force by staff at least once. And the violence has steadily increased year by year, the report found.

Moreover, the report found, many violent episodes go unreported.

Assaults on Young Inmates

The report included detailed narratives on more than a dozen times in which correction officers assaulted adolescent inmates. Here are three of the most egregious assaults, which occurred last year.

The investigation found officers and supervisors used coded phrases like "hold it down" to pressure inmates into not reporting beatings. "Inmates who refuse to 'hold it down' risk retaliation from officers in the form of additional physical violence and disciplinary sanctions," the report said.

One inmate said that he was continually harassed by correctional staff after reporting that he was raped by a guard and that he was warned by guards not to speak about the episode in an interview with a consultant on the investigation.

The report also found that civilian staff members, including doctors and teachers, also failed to report abuse and faced retaliation when they did.

One teacher told an investigator that when abuse occurs, civilian employees know "they should turn their head away, so that they don't witness anything."

Even when abuse is reported, the report found, the investigations typically went nowhere. The federal inquiry was highly critical of the correction department's investigative division, which is overseen by Florence Finkle. The report described the investigative division as overwhelmed, understaffed and reliant on archaic paper-based record keeping. Investigations, which are supposed to take a maximum of five months to complete, often take more than a year.

There is also a substantial bias in favor of correction officer testimony even in cases when evidence clearly indicates a guard is lying, the investigation found. And when guards are disciplined, the punishment is rarely severe. Most are sent to counseling or "retraining," the report found. Sometimes, punishments recommended by supervisors are overruled by those higher in the chain of command.

In one January 2012 episode, a correction officer became incensed after an inmate splashed her with a liquid and began punching him in the face after he had been restrained by other guards. A captain ordered her to stop, and she punched another officer who tried to pull her off the inmate. An investigating captain later concluded that the officer's use of force was "not necessary, inappropriate and excessive." But a superior, backed by the investigative division, overruled the captain, concluding that the use of force was necessary. An investigator labeled the finding "astonishing."

The investigation found one officer who had been involved in 76 uses of force over a 6-year period and had been disciplined only once.

Because the correction department fails to conduct proper investigations and hold staff accountable, the report found, "a culture of excessive force persists, where correction officers physically abuse adolescent inmates with the expectation that they will face little or no consequences for their unlawful conduct."

The report noted that the city's new correction commissioner, Joseph Ponte, had only recently assumed his position and "was not present when the misconduct" found by the investigation had occurred. It also said the department had undertaken some steps to stem the violence like providing more programs for adolescents, adding staff and requiring young inmates to wear jail-issued uniforms and shoes. But none of these measures, the report said, address the core problem: abuse by correction officers and a lack of accountability.

In one case documented in the report, a correction officer wrapped metal handcuffs around her hand and punched an inmate who had fallen asleep during a class in the ribs, according to witnesses. The inmate told investigators that when he yelled an obscenity, the officer pulled him out of class and began to beat him. She was joined by other officers who proceeded to kick him while he was sprawled on the floor. The inmate said one officer sprayed pepper stray directly in his eye from about an inch away.

In their reports, the officers offered contradictory versions of what happened, the investigations found. But all concluded that the level of force that was used was appropriate.

One of the teachers interviewed said he heard "thumping" and "screaming" during the altercation and said he heard the inmate "crying and screaming for his mother."

When he looked out the door after the episode, the teacher reported that he "saw blood and saliva on the floor."

Critical Thinking

1. Do you believe it is necessary, in order to protect society, that 16-year-olds be considered adults under criminal law? Do you believe 16-year-olds are adults?

2. Isn't it necessary for correction officers to use force so that young inmates will respect them and obey the rules?

3. Why do you think officers were not punished for using unnecessary or excessive force?

Internet References

The New York Times
   http://www.nytimes.com/interactive/2014/08/05/nyregion/05rikers-report.html

The New York Times
   http://www.nytimes.com/2014/04/05/nyregion/joseph-ponte-new-yorks-new-corrections-commissioner-faces-challenge-at-rikers.html

Article   Prepared by: Joanne Naughton

Calculating "Return On Mission": Music as Medicine for Imprisoned Boys

How do we measure a return on human development? Genuine Voices, a non-profit working with detention centers in the US that leverages the determination of volunteers to help adolescent boys, set out to measure their impact. After encountering difficulties, they learned that some things are naturally unquantifiable, and that in lieu of ways to directly report a "return on mission", maybe emotional buzz is enough to support sustainability.

STEPHANIE ORMSTON

Learning Outcomes

After reading this article, you will be able to:

- Describe the effect Genuine Voices has had on some boys in juvenile detention centers.

- Demonstrate how some small non-traditional programs can help kids who have gotten into trouble.

In the Darwinian world of for-profits, only the strongest survive. We have countless ratios like return on investment, return on equity, return on sales, etc., to rate the performance and financial solvency of major companies. However, that isn't the case in the world of non-profits. Measuring success is an open-ended question where everyone has their own answer. In addition, success doesn't guarantee longevity in the life of a non-profit. Organizations with "trendy missions" continue to receive donations, despite gross mismanagement and lack of impact. Countless stories have broken in the last few years about mismanagement of non-profits, including Greg Mortenson's Central Asia Institute. Who could forget the United Way scandal of the early 90s, where CEO William Aramony was sentenced to prison for looting the organization of millions? And still we see countless worthy organizations floundering because they just can't gain momentum. How do we reward those organizations that don't have the political capital or scale to gain notoriety, have no clear way to report impact, but are still successful in executing their mission? How do you measure this "return on mission"?

Take Genuine Voices for example. Founded in 2002, Genuine Voices teaches music to boys committed to juvenile detention centers in the Boston, Massachusetts area. Boys take classes twice a week, and specialize in an area that comes natural to them—drums, guitar, lyric writing, or producing. Once

the boys are released, their involvement in the program ends. The boys' identities are kept confidential as they are minors, so it is impossible to reach out and track recidivism rates in alumni of the program. There are success stories of boys who have voluntarily kept in touch with Genuine Voices staff, like Dequan who was featured by Boston.com. But he represents a minority of the over 600 students who participates each year. Especially as an organization with a $14,000 operating budget, resources barely cover program costs, let alone monitoring and evaluation. Artistic director Juri Love has ambitious plans to turn that $14,000 into $50,000 this year and $100,000 in 2014. However, current priorities are paying instructors and increasing the size of the program, not tracking impact. She currently relies on no full-time employees but 30 volunteers who all already know the importance and impact of program. Their priority is to grow the reach of Genuine Voices. Unfortunately, securing funding proves to be a catch-22; to attract donors, Genuine Voices needs to prove it works.

I visited the Casa Isla detention facility with two instructors for a weekly lesson. We drove 15 minutes down a winding road past a security check point, to a remote island just south of Boston. It was fitting, that on this remote island was a population that most of society would rather pretend didn't exist at all. It's no doubt that Genuine Voices is making a difference in the lives of these boys. But like others who have experienced or seen the program firsthand, I cannot quantify the feeling I felt when I observed the lesson. The excitement when we walked into the center was palpable. For once, these boys had something to look forward to in an otherwise monotonous day at the detention center. The instructors adeptly customized the lesson to the needs of the boy that day, from lyric writing to an impromptu jam session. They are not just teachers, but positive role models who commit to the mission, and believe in the power of music to change lives. Love describes their work succinctly, "These boys have been taught that they are a burden on their families and on the system. We let them be something more."

The success of this program is contingent upon consistent and high-quality instructors. I was supposed to meet four teachers, but two were unable to attend because they had to work. It was evident that the two instructors I did meet, Steve Wilkinson and Wills McKenna, both professional musicians, have proven their worth to the boys by showing up and listening week after week. They've gained the trust of the boys—a crucial component in making the program work. But how is this model sustainable? You can't continue to depend on teachers whose only compensation is personal satisfaction. Love's goals for the program are ultimately to compensate her teachers $25 per hour. At two-hour lessons twice a week, this works out to only $5,000 a year to serve approximately 6–8 students. When it costs the Department of Youth Services and taxpayers $100,000 a year to care for one boy, the teacher's salary seems a pittance, especially given the life-long impact it could have on one boy.

There are programs that are beginning to address some of these issues. Non-profits are smaller, more innovative and agile than government programs. Social impact bonds (SIB), which ultimately reward non-profits for reducing the government's costs when dealing with an at risk population, are becoming a way to provide these non-profits the resources to operate on a larger scale. Essentially, the government contracts with an intermediary (like a large bank), who provides a loan to a non-profit. If the non-profit is successful in its initiatives (as rated by a third party rating agency), the state pays back the intermediary. This outsources the risk to for-profit organizations (the bank, in this case), and allows the government to take a chance on an innovative program that it is too sluggish to implement on its own. The first such program in the nation was announced in Massachusetts just last year, with the goal of dealing with juvenile justice and chronic homelessness. However, this initiative is in its infancy; only last year, McKinsey & Company issued a report about the potential of SIBs in the US. It certainly has a long way to go before it can widen its reach to be used with such tiny non-profits like Genuine Voices.

It is a common misconception that these boys have nothing to contribute to society. "These kids work. It's just not socially acceptable," Wilkinson told me, referring to theft, dealings and other unlawful actions that get the boys committed. "They deal to support a parent or younger sibling. We teach them to apply that effort to something positive." The most powerful initiative of Genuine Voices is their involvement with the "Music is Medicine" program. Boys in the centers are commissioned to create original songs for children dealing with terminal illnesses. The song "Believe In You", written by one of the boys I met that night at Casa Isla, will leave the listener with no doubt that these boys have good hearts. Unfortunately, we are still struggling with a system and a society that is reluctant to deal with cases like these and to provide substantial monetary support. Until we can begin to prove that initiatives like these do work, Juri Love and Genuine Voices will have to continue to believe, and do their best to convert others to believe as well.

Critical Thinking

1. What is Wilkinson's theory about the kids he deals with?
2. If Genuine Voices offers success in dealing with kids in trouble, what are the challenges to keeping it going?

Create Central

www.mhhe.com/createcentral

Internet References

Genuine Voices
   www.genuinevoices.com
Idealist
   www.idealist.org/info/Nonprofits/Wrong1

STEPHANIE ORMSTON is a writer for *Student Reporter*. We are a journalism incubator and online media outlet, providing media coverage of events and featuring current topics in management and economics around the world.

Article

Prepared by: Joanne Naughton

Juvenile Injustice: Truants Face Courts, Jailing without Legal Counsel to Aid Them

Tennessee court procedures highlight national debate over minor offenders' rights.

SUSAN FERRISS

Learning Outcomes

After reading this article, you will be able to:

- Describe "status offenses."

- Show the value of having legal counsel at a court appearance.

- State what the 1974 federal law provides, and what the 1980 amendment allows.

Knoxville, TN—She was barely 15 and scared at the prospect of being in court. She agreed to plead guilty to truancy. But when Judge Tim Irwin announced what he planned to do with her, the girl known as A.G. screamed in disbelief.

Guards forced the sobbing teen out of the Knox County Juvenile Court and clapped shackles on her legs. She had been struggling with crippling anxiety and what she said was relentless bullying at school. Now she was being led through a county juvenile detention center to a cell with a sliver of a window and a concrete slab with a mattress. For truancy.

"I cried all night long," A.G. said. "It seemed like everyone was against us in court."

Like tens of thousands of kids every year, A.G. was in court to answer for a noncriminal infraction that only a minor can commit. These infractions are called "status offenses," and they can include skipping school, running away, underage drinking or smoking or violating curfews. But since status offenses aren't technically crimes, indigent minors don't benefit from the constitutional right to the appointment of defense counsel before they plead guilty.

That meant A.G. whose family couldn't afford to hire a lawyer, was left with no trained defense counsel to argue that there might be justifiable reasons why she was having so much trouble going to school.

It also meant the girl had no counsel to object to her abrupt jailing in April 2008—a jailing that lawyers who reviewed A.G.'s file argue exceeded the court's statutory power during the teen's first appearance in court.

"A.G.'s incarceration immediately following her guilty plea for truancy, a status offense, was illegal under state and federal law," asserted Dean Rivkin, a law professor at the University of Tennessee who later represented A.G. and oversees the Knoxville campus' Education Law Practicum.

Due to litigation that's pending, Irwin declined repeated request to comment on A.G.'s case or those of other prosecuted truants, some of whom were also jailed.

A.G.'s lockup has never been investigated or reviewed on appeal. But it's the type of allegation that's put Tennessee at the center of a national debate over whether status offenders should be guaranteed immediate legal counsel once in court—to ensure minors' basic rights are respected—and under what conditions they can be incarcerated.

In late February, the nation's top juvenile justice official quietly asked the Justice Department's civil rights division to investigate whether Tennessee status offenders were wrongly deprived of legal counsel.

A.G., who was already in counseling, was so shattered by her shackling and detention that when she was released at 7 A.M. the next day her parents took her to a doctor rather than straight to school, as they said they were ordered to do. Their daughter had become suicidal, and she spent the next week in a psychiatric hospital.

Unraveling the Rules

Forty years ago, a federal law—the Juvenile Justice and Delinquency Prevention Act—actually *barred* states that receive federal juvenile-justice funds from sending status offenders into detention, reflecting the widespread belief that incarcerating these minors exposes them to danger and bad influences. In 1980, though, Congress amended the 1974 federal Act to allow judges a significant federal exception to the lockup ban. It's called the "valid court order" exception.

The exception permits jailing as a last resort to try to control status offenders once they've pleaded guilty and gone on to violate *instructions* from the court: the valid court order. But if states want federal funds, lockup as a punitive response is only supposed to occur after courts hold multiple formal proceedings, give children time to comply with instructions, consider alternatives to jail—and take great care to ensure kids benefit from full due process rights, including right to appointment of defense counsel for indigent children.

This chance to obtain defense counsel must be afforded *before* status offenders face formal accusations that they've disobeyed valid court orders and could potentially face jailing or removal from parents' custody.

This same federal law *does* allow status offenders to be held in detention before trial for less than 24 hours or over a weekend, but only under limited circumstances—such as credible concern that minors might not appear at a scheduled hearing or because police have found kids wandering on streets and no non-jail shelter space is available, or because parents are not immediately available to pick them up.

If states don't ensure courts follow these requirements to provide legal counsel and limits on detention, they can get their federal delinquency-prevention grants pulled.

In A.G.'s case, "nobody said anything about an attorney," said A.G.'s mother, who had no idea what her daughter's rights were before A.G. pleaded guilty and was taken away and put into detention.

The Knox County District Attorney's office, which prosecutes truants, said children's privacy rights prohibit staff from commenting on specific cases like A.G.'s.

A Continuing Controversy in Knox County

Since late last year, the Center for Public Integrity has been reviewing previously sealed documents that suggest a vigorous pattern of locking up status offenders in Knox County. Families and attorneys here have also alleged that accused truants with diagnosed mental-health and other difficulties were shackled and jailed straight from court.

Children whose only infraction was struggling with a loathing for school were pulled into the criminal-justice system, branded with permanent delinquency records and jailed with kids who had actually committed crimes, parents complained. All this happened without their kids having lawyers, some parents said, and some children dropped out rather than getting back to an education.

Patricia Puritz, executive director of the nonprofit National Juvenile Defender Center in Washington, DC, said that across the country there is a disturbing shortage of timely legal representation to ensure kids' rights are respected when they're pulled into courts for crimes and for status offenses.

"Little people, little justice," Puritz said.

In Knox County, a behind-the-scenes disagreement over providing access to counsel continues.

Judge Irwin, the county's elected and sole juvenile court judge, has refused to allow volunteer lawyers to set up a project at the courthouse to offer free counsel to accused truants as they arrive with their parents for hearings, according to Harry Ogden, a Knoxville business attorney who wants to participate in such pro bono representation.

"This project can be a 'win-win' for the court, the school system, the D.A.'s office . . . and—most of all—at-risk children and youth," wrote Rivkin, the University of Tennessee law professor, in a December 2012 letter to Judge Irwin.

Irwin did not respond to Rivkin's plea, and has also declined to speak to the Center about his decision not to endorse the pro bono idea, which remains in limbo.

On the court's behalf, Knox County Law Director Richard Armstrong sent a letter to the Center for Public Integrity that said: "Children and their families are welcomed and encouraged to retain counsel in all matters brought before the juvenile courts of this state."

But in March of last year, "know your rights" brochures that the volunteer lawyers had left in the court lobby for families of accused truants were removed, according to an email that Rivkin wrote to Irwin and sent to him via the judge's administrative assistant.

"Needless to say," Rivkin wrote, "we were surprised to learn that the brochures had been removed from the rack shortly after they were placed there." Irwin did not respond to Rivkin's email and an offer to meet to talk about the brochures.

In February, Rivkin also requested that the Tennessee Supreme Court review an appeal of one truant's conviction; for the last 2 years, as part of a series of appeals, Rivkin has also been trying, so far in vain, to convince a state court to issue an opinion that would guarantee faster appointment of defense for accused truants.

Heavy Penalties, Confusing Courts

Whether all kids in courts, including status offenders, should automatically benefit from defense counsel is part of a broader national debate over just what legal rights children have, and whether the country's confusing patchwork of state and local regulations is enough to ensure children are treated fairly.

The National Juvenile Defender Center is leading an ongoing project that dispatches observers to juvenile courts, so they can recommend, state by state, measures to improve proceedings that are supposed to be primarily rehabilitative.

Puritz said observers have witnessed kids facing serious repercussions with no lawyers to advise them, either because they were not afforded counsel, or because they waived rights with a casual shrug that belied their confusion over what was at stake. In 2006, observers reported that half the kids they saw in Indiana courts waived counsel even though the minors were accused of misdemeanors or felonies.

Agitated parents, Puritz added, sometimes hope a rough court experience will scare a kid straight. But parents often fail to grasp, Puritz said, how pleading guilty even to a status offense can lead to penalties that could bedevil minors for years.

In Texas, teen Elizabeth Diaz spent 18 days in an adult county jail when a judge in Hidalgo County began a campaign in 2009 to collect old truancy fines. The judge issued warrants to arrest minors once they turned 17 and force them to pay—or get thrown in jail.

Elizabeth's $1,600 in fines had been imposed in a court where she had no counsel. She missed her high school exit exam while jailed, the American Civil Liberties Union said, and was traumatized by harassment in jail. A federal court in 2012 ruled that her detention for failing to pay fines she couldn't afford was an unconstitutional violation of due process.

In Knox County, A.G. was required to return to court a month after being jailed and hospitalized, but she was still not afforded an attorney. Another five months went by before, on her third court appearance, as was then the practice, A.G. was appointed a public defender, for a fee of $100. After several more months, with A.G. continuing to miss school and warned she'd be jailed again, the family was referred to Rivkin at the University of Tennessee campus in Knoxville.

Rivkin was able to put a hold on the teen's ongoing prosecution and began representing her in negotiations with her school.

A.G.'s case, her lawyers said, illustrates why they believe timely, trained counsel is in the child's best interest: In spite of increasing difficulties at school, A.G. was not tested for special needs or offered an alternative education plan before her name was turned over for truancy prosecution. Instead, A.G.'s parents said, school staff advised them to ask police to force A.G. out of the house and into the school building. Reluctantly, they followed that advice, but it only deepened the family's crisis.

School district staff said privacy rules prohibit them from discussing students' histories. But Melissa Massie, executive director of student support services for the Knox County School District, said that she had not heard of staff advising parents to call police. She did say, though, that she was critical of some past antitruancy efforts.

In 2010, approximately 137,000 status offenders like A.G. were "petitioned," or sent into courts nationwide, more than a third for truancy, according to statistics cited by the Vera Institute of Justice. In Tennessee alone in 2012, more than 9,600 minors were taken to court for truancy.

The Education Law Practicum Rivkin supervises offers pro bono help to Knoxville area families seeking special-education services. Like the Vera Institute, Rivkin favors a "counter-narrative" on truancy: When counselors take the time, they find that most chronic truants are struggling with learning disabilities, emotional distress or mental-health illness, bullying, violence, or financial or other crises.

Few of these kids or their parents, Rivkin said, can be expected to understand that kids have more options than just pleading guilty in court.

In Tennessee, as in many states, statutes theoretically limit juvenile courts to initially responding to truants who plead guilty by issuing them monetary fines, ordering them to perform community service and putting them on probation, with instructions to follow, and initiating the valid court order process.

States are also expected to conduct audits to monitor how well courts are complying with the limits on putting status offenders in detention. Periodically, federal justice authorities review these state audits to look for patterns of violations.

Last November, Rivkin wrote to Robert Listenbee, the head of the Justice Department's Office of Juvenile Justice and Delinquency Prevention, suggesting a hard look at the lockups of status offenders in Knox County and the rest of Tennessee.

He suspected federal officials—while signing off on grants to the state—were not getting the full story.

In a reply to Rivkin dated Feb. 28 of this year, Listenbee explained that he had asked the Justice Department's Civil Rights Division for an "investigation."

Failure to provide counsel to kids potentially facing incarceration, Listenbee wrote to Rivkin, if true, "would be of great concern to all of us here . . . and is not in keeping with the best practices outlined by this office."

Appealing to Higher Courts

In 2011, Rivkin began a prolonged and complex attempt to overturn convictions of four students' truancy convictions, in an attempt to clarify some of these issues.

He first lost before Irwin, then before the state's Fourth Circuit and then before a state Court of Appeals panel. He submitted a final appeal this year to the Tennessee Supreme Court on behalf of only one plaintiff. As of May, his review request was still pending.

Along the way, the battle has revealed that judges, lawyers and other officers of juvenile courts can have strikingly different interpretations of laws that can end up critical to a child's life: Do indigent status offenders have a right to appointed counsel before valid court orders are issued to them, or only after they are accused of violating orders and are thus vulnerable to judges legally jailing them or removing them from their parents' custody?

In essence, Rivkin has argued that accused truants have the constitutional right of appointment of counsel if not before pleading guilty, then before judges begin imposing court orders that could pave the way to incarceration.

"There may be compelling reasons why the [valid court order] is not warranted due to the juvenile's mental health condition, due to educational disabilities, due to family circumstances such as lack of transportation, etc.," Rivkin wrote in his appeal to the Fourth Circuit.

"Without an attorney it is unrealistic to expect a juvenile to make these arguments," he wrote. Waiting to afford children attorneys until they face imminent potential jailing, Rivkin wrote, is "too little, too late."

The four original plaintiffs were Knox County students who, like A.G., suffered from significant mental-health stress and had no legal counsel at their side when they pleaded guilty. None could afford to hire attorneys, and some parents said they didn't dream they would need legal counsel.

None were jailed the same day they pleaded guilty, but they were threatened with jailing, Rivkin's appeal alleged, if they violated any of a litany of instructions given to them under the label of probation or, in some cases, valid court orders.

The plaintiffs were admonished not to miss another day of school, unexcused, or face jail. They were also told not to get into any trouble at school, and to pay for and attend court-selected counseling programs. They were also ordered to submit to and pay for random, mandatory drug testing, although none faced drug charges.

One plaintiff, a 13-year-old middle school student identified as T.W., was jailed twice, without the benefit of legal counsel first appointed to represent him, according to the appeal.

On a February 2009 mandatory return to court after pleading guilty, T.W. was jailed overnight directly from court because his school reported he had accumulated more unexcused absences after pleading guilty. During another return to court in January 2010, T.W. was given a drug screen that registered positive for marijuana and he was immediately taken into juvenile detention again for several days.

Some kids Rivkin eventually represented at the Practicum were appointed public defenders during their third visit to court.

But Rivkin argued that there was nothing in T.W. or the other plaintiffs' files proving in writing, as required by state regulation, that they'd agreed to waive the right to defense. Like other parents, T.W.'s mother, Debbie Jones, submitted an affidavit declaring that her son was not informed of his full rights to counsel.

As his appeal moved through courts, Rivkin submitted an affidavit signed by Knox County Public Defender Mark Stephens in 2012 noting that the public defender's office had no record of a single request from the court between 2010 and fall of 2012 to represent a truant before valid court orders were imposed.

In some cases, including T.W.'s, the court assigned truants lawyers known as guardians ad litem, who advise judges on what they believe is best for children, including removal from the home. But these lawyers are distinct from defense counsel. Minors interviewed by the Center said that their guardians ad litem didn't object to them being jailed or drug tested, and didn't raise questions about their schools' responsibility to evaluate them for special needs—issues Rivkin later raised for truants after he began representing them.

Setbacks

In 2011, in his rejection of Rivkin's appeal, Judge Irwin upheld his own convictions. In a written order, he said that the four truants entered court and after being advised of "the right to remain silent, the right to confront witnesses against them, and the right to an attorney, chose to enter a plea immediately, without the advice of counsel and offered no justification for . . . excessive absences."

But, again, while truants in Tennessee must be informed of the rights that Irwin recited, indigent status offenders don't have the right to the *appointment* of a defense attorney if they decide not to plead guilty and want a trial.

After Irwin's initial ruling, the state of Tennessee and the Knox County D.A.'s office took on the defense of the juvenile court's practices.

As part of that defense, the state argued that the juvenile court had adhered to proper procedure, including by jailing T.W., and that T.W. had missed a 10-day deadline for appealing his 2009 detention order. The state's lawyers submitted forms identified as court notes with identical language on them declaring that T.W., during each of his court appearances, was "advised of rights."

But as Rivkin noted in a filing, the state didn't challenge the argument that there were no signed waivers in the files of his plaintiffs.

In 2012, in a second rejection for Rivkin, Judge Bill Swann of the Fourth Circuit found that the juvenile court's actions were generally proper. He didn't opine on whether he thought T.W. had been appropriately afforded an opportunity for appointed counsel before he was jailed. But Swann did reject Rivkin's interpretation of federal law, arguing that existing law requires appointment of counsel only *after* indigent truants have already violated valid court orders and face possible incarceration.

"The constitutional right to counsel only attaches at that point, and not before," Swann wrote. But he added that the plaintiffs "laudably urge the advancement of a social policy" that only the state's legislators could change.

Last December, when a Court of Appeals panel also rejected Rivkin's arguments, the judges found that the plaintiffs didn't meet the burden of new evidence to justify a review of their convictions.

Knox County District Attorney Special Counsel John Gill told the Center for Public Integrity that the D.A.'s office acknowledges that state and federal law do not permit jailing truants except when valid court orders are issued and kids are informed that they have a right to the appointment of an attorney.

Asked about general allegations that kids were put into detention frequently in recent past years perhaps without understanding their rights, Gill did say: "There were some practices that hadn't been scrutinized."

"I'm not saying it hasn't happened," Gill said, referring to truants being jailed.

He said that he doesn't believe that valid court orders are currently being issued in the court to handle truants or that they are being jailed. The D.A.'s interest, he said, is "getting kids back to school, not convictions and not in locking them up."

How Many Were Shackled, Handcuffed, and Jailed?

In his appeal filings, Rivkin noted that by Knox County's own count, more than 600 accused truants were called to the juvenile court between 2008 and 2012. But it's hard to determine who among them was locked up because the court refuses to release detailed detention data that could include reasons for jailing, and whether detention was pretrial or posttrial and if the kids had counsel.

Without transparent data, Rivkin said, "there is no way of knowing how many children and youth have suffered the consequences our clients did before we began representing them."

In 2011, Rivkin filed public record act requests asking for lockup information, with juveniles' names redacted. Irwin declined the request. The judge retained a lawyer for himself, Robert Watson of Knoxville, who has since died. Watson argued in a letter that the records were "confidential and inspection is allowed only if the judge so chooses."

A Center associate in Tennessee filed a request for redacted juvenile detention records and was told in January that she would have to provide $17,500 in processing costs to Knox County first.

In the meantime, Rivkin was able to obtain, though an unofficial channel, an internal Knox court compilation tracing status offender histories over several years; the document contains no information about whether lawyers were appointed. But it is illuminating nonetheless.

The Center reviewed the compilation, which was submitted to the Fourth Circuit Court. The review found that in 2009 alone more than 50 status offenders identified only by "client" numbers were put into detention. The only charge listed in connection with some lockups was truancy. Most followed a succession of prior appearances and prior detentions for a mix of infractions no greater than truancy, running away, cigarette possession, curfew violation and probation revocation or valid court order violations.

One minor, the records show, appeared in court twice for truancy in 2006 and 2007, and then had probation revoked in 2008 and was put into detention that same year. The same minor was back in court again for tobacco possession in 2008, followed by revocation of probation again and detention again. In 2009, the minor was in court again for revocation of probation and again put into detention.

A young woman who asked to be identified as K.P. also has a history of cycling through court in Knox County during this time frame.

In February 2008, when she was 15, she pleaded guilty to truancy, without the benefit of an attorney. She was arrested twice later that year and put into detention both times. She was accused of disobeying truancy probation, but she had no valid court order in her file, lawyers at the Practicum who later represented her said.

In September 2008, K.P. was held for several days in detention. There was nothing in her file to indicate that she was being held to ensure she would appear for a court hearing that had been scheduled. In December 2008, K.P. was arrested by police again, this time in front of classmates, while she was attending classes at the same school she was accused of failing to attend.

"Defendant was picked up at [redacted] High School on an outstanding petition for revocation of probation. She was transported to Knox County Juvenile Center," an arrest report says.

In an interview, K.P. said that being put into handcuffs, shackles and prison garb "only made me want to rebel more."

She said she originally began refusing to go to classes because of sexual harassment—she was attacked on the school bus she rode daily—and because she had developed anxiety and bladder problems at school. She said her complaints were not addressed at school, and she was not offered an alternative learning option.

"These are not all kids with chains hanging off their belts, in gangs," said attorney Brenda McGee, who is Rivkin's wife and collaborates with the Education Practicum, and much later represented K.P.

State Proposal to Ensure Truants Get Counsel Fails

In 2012, a fledgling attempt to pass state legislation establishing an immediate right to appointment of counsel for truants quickly died.

The measure failed to get out of a subcommittee after it was estimated the state indigent defense fund would require an additional half a million dollars a year; that sounds modest, said its sponsor, former Sen. Andy Berke, now mayor of Chattanooga. But the increase was too much for some legislators, Berke said, given that less than $2 million out $37 million spent from the fund in 2010 went to juvenile defense.

Because of this failure, Rivkin believes it's more important than ever to provide pro bono counsel to accused truants.

States' rules and statutes all vary, and there's virtually no formal data on the issue, but Rivkin estimates based on his own research that 33 states now ensure a relatively early right to counsel for truants during court proceedings.

In some states, such as Pennsylvania, counsel is automatic and can only be waived after multiple steps to ensure children grasp what they are doing. Pennsylvania was rocked by a scandal a couple of years ago when two juvenile court judges in Wilkes-Barre were found guilty of taking bribes for sending kids who had waived counsel to do time at private detention camps.

Puritz of the National Juvenile Defender Center remains concerned that minors, who are being processed through crowded courts, too frequently waive rights even in states with expansive rights to counsel on paper.

The idea to offer pro bono counsel to accused truants in Knox County is modeled after a similar project in Atlanta. Judge Irwin privately confided to lawyers that he didn't think accused truants had extensive unmet legal needs, according to Harry Ogden of Knoxville's prominent Baker Donelson firm, one of those attorneys who tried to personally persuade the judge to support the project.

"He's a great guy," Ogden said of the judge, "but when you're 14 years old, and standing in front of the juvenile judge, then you are probably about as tongue-tied as I was as a third-year law student in front of a judge."

Unnecessary Drug Rehab, Diagnoses Ignored

Irwin, 55, is a 6-foot-7 former University of Tennessee football hero who went on to a more than 14-year-pro-football career, 13 of those years as a tackle for the Minnesota Vikings. He has plenty of fans in Knoxville who admire his strong support for the local Boys and Girls Club, and gestures like passing out stuffed animals to small kids in court who could be taken from parents due to neglect.

But A.G. and other truants said that the judge, who's been on the bench since 2005, was intimidating. A.G. said that when she returned to court after her stay in a psychiatric hospital, she tried to tell him about a diagnosis she was given of "school phobia" and bipolar disorder.

"He said, 'I have a phobia, too. It's a phobia of kids not going to school,'" according to A.G.

K.P. and her mother today believe that a hostile court environment forced the family into a decision they regret and believe could have been avoided if they'd had legal counsel.

When K.P. tested positive for marijuana while on truancy probation, her mother feared the court would take her child into state custody and foster care. The mother panicked, and scrambled to find space in a secure drug and behavior rehab facility—for nine months—even though she didn't believe K.P. required such treatment. The move satisfied the court, K.P.'s mother said, but "nearly tore us apart."

"They walked all over us because we didn't have a representative," said K.P.'s mom.

K.P. said, "I lost a year of my life. Being at that rehab center didn't help at all. It was awful. I felt like I didn't belong there."

Debbie Jones, T.W.'s mom and a daycare worker, has stuck with Rivkin's appeal because she feels the court's treatment of her son made his problems worse.

Jones told the Center that T.W. loved school as a young boy. "I couldn't pay him to stay home when he was sick," she said. But at 13, he became reclusive, and struggled with classroom learning. He pretended to board his school bus and hid out instead of going to classes.

"He said he felt smothered at school," Jones said.

For all the punitive treatment he received, T.W. never graduated and now he's too old to be prosecuted. Rivkin is looking for a suitable adult school for T.W., whose phobias make it difficult for him to sit among large groups.

John Gill, the D.A.'s special counsel, said that office has been working more diligently with educators and social workers to address roots of truancy and avoid putting kids into court.

About 80 percent of initial truancy complaints the D.A. gets are resolved now, he said, after families attend the mass meetings warning them to straighten out problems. New petitions—not including ongoing petitions—to prosecute these kids declined to 65 in 2012 compared to 76 in 2011.

Knox County Assistant Public Defender Christina Kleiser said the court's reaction to truancy seems to have softened. But not long ago, when police were referring to truancy as a "gateway crime," Kleiser said many truants were getting locked up over weekends to show toughness.

Massie, who leads the school district's student support services, admits to inconsistent intervention in the past to help struggling students who were frequently absent. Educators, she said, are now required to follow an intervention checklist and convene meetings more promptly with parents so specialists can evaluate students and plan targeted support.

"I think the truancy program is much better than it was before," she said.

But she said that by statute, the district is still required to provide the D.A.'s office with names of students when they reach more than 10 unexcused absences.

Although his pro bono services remain little known, Rivkin said, two parents did contact him this year complaining that children with emotional problems were threatened at school with jailing if they missed more school. Last fall, Rivkin also met, by chance, Carla Staley, a mom who received a warning letter from the D.A. accusing her son Lowell, 13, who has cerebral palsy, with excessive absences that could land them in court.

National Trends, Federal Teeth

Knox County isn't the only region where truancy has galvanized community crackdowns.

Communities want to increase graduation rates, boost collection of attendance-based funding schools lose when kids are absent, and keep kids off the streets. But aggressive campaigns involving prosecution are attracting scrutiny, especially when minors are not afforded counsel.

In Washington state, another lawsuit over truants' right to counsel led—briefly—to expansion of that right. In the state's Bellevue School District, a 13-year-old girl, a Bosnian refugee, appeared at an initial truancy hearing in 2006 with no counsel and signed a promise to attend school or face penalties ranging from community service to "house arrest, work crew and possibly detention," according to the American Civil Liberties Union.

The girl was appointed an attorney only when found in contempt because her absences continued and she then faced imminent punishment.

Asked to weigh in, that state's Courts of Appeals found that all accused truants had a constitutional right to counsel from the onset of hearings that could lead to penalties. The Washington State Supreme Court overturned that ruling in 2011, favoring the state's argument that truancy statutes protect a child's right to education, so no counsel is initially required.

Last December, the board of trustees of the National Council of Juvenile and Family Court Judges took another approach by urging Congress to eliminate the valid court order exception as part of a long-overdue reauthorization of the 1974 federal juvenile justice act. Back in 1980, it was this same judges' group that urged Congress to include the valid court order exception.

In 2009, Sen. Patrick Leahy, D-Vt., proposed eliminating this exception in the reauthorization of the act—which Congress has still failed to do. And in March of this year, Rep. Tony Cardenas, Democrat from California's San Fernando Valley, also introduced legislation to get rid of the valid court order.

Federal official Listenbee, a former defense attorney, is also starting to speak out more in his new role as the nation's top juvenile-justice official.

In a speech he gave last August, he warned that detention should not be taken lightly. "Research has . . . shown," Listenbee said, "that the minute a youth sets foot in detention or lockup, he or she has a 50 percent chance of entering the criminal justice system as an adult."

In March, Listenbee responded to Center for Public Integrity's inquiries about when his office believes status offenders' right to appointment of counsel begins.

Language in the federal regulations does not specifically address whether judges must afford appointment of counsel to kids before they are issued valid court orders, Listenbee acknowledged. But he believes that this is the intent. He also said he doesn't believe states can claim they're following the rules unless they ensure that courts provide counsel before valid court orders are meted out.

"Attorneys should be appointed in advance so they can have an opportunity to meet with their clients and properly prepare for the hearings," Listenbee said. "We make this clear in our training [for state officials] and do our best to emphasize this expectation in communicating with states around compliance matters."

In January, auditors on a visit from Listenbee's office found that Tennessee must "prioritize training and technical assistance" to ensure respect for due process and the valid court order process. But auditors only examined 2012 data.

As for A.G. and K.P., they're both 20 now. It was only last summer, after both young women turned 19, that Rivkin and McGee were legally able to request that Irwin expunge delinquency records the young women said they didn't even know the judge had given them back when they were teens. The judge granted the requests to expunge the records.

Delinquency records equate status offenders with kids who've committed crimes. And they remain on file, if they aren't expunged. A delinquency record can follow a youth, surfacing to jeopardize job, college, and other applications, lawyers warn.

After the Practicum began to represent A.G., more than a year after she was jailed, A.G.'s school finally designed a learning plan that shielded her from crowds of students and bullying and enabled her to graduate in 2011.

Looking back, K.P. said the adults who ultimately helped her finish high school in 2011 were the lawyers at the Practicum, who pushed for the school district to evaluate her for special needs and provide her a special-education plan—after she was twice jailed and put into unnecessary rehab for nine months.

With lawyers' help, she said, "I actually graduated a year early. So much for being the bad kid."

Critical Thinking

1. Should minors be able to waive their rights in court without a lawyer to advise them about what, exactly, those rights are?

2. Should Congress eliminate the "valid court order exception" to the 1974 federal juvenile justice act?

3. Does incarcerating young people have risks for their future adult lives?

Internet References

Center for Public Integrity
https://www.documentcloud.org/documents/1156538-knox-truant-found-guilty-jailed-same-day.html

Create Central
www.mhhe.com/createcentral

National Juvenile Defender Center
http://www.njdc.info/pdf/Indiana%20Assessment.pdf

Article   Prepared by: Joanne Naughton

Why Jonathan McClard Still Matters

Excerpted from a speech given by Gabrielle Horowitz-Prisco, director of the CA's Juvenile Justice Project, during the Raise the Age – NY! campaign launch press conference on July 11, 2013.

Learning Outcomes

After reading this article, you will be able to:

- Explain the fears a parent might have whose child is incarcerated.

- Show the harmful effects of putting teenagers in adult facilities.

About a year ago, I was writing a piece on youth in adult jails and prisons and I wanted to write about Jonathan McClard, a seventeen year old boy in Missouri who committed suicide by hanging in an adult facility as he was awaiting transfer to a notoriously abusive adult prison.

I had met Jonathan's mother, Tracy, at a youth justice event—after Jonathan's death, she quit her job as a school teacher to devote herself to getting kids out of adult jails and prisons. Over dinner, Tracy described to me the marked changes she observed in Jonathan's appearance as he spent time in adult facilities—the hardening and shutting down, the fighting he was forced to do, and his fear. She described her powerlessness as a mother to get her son out of what she knew was a life-threatening situation. How Jonathan had been placed in solitary confinement as punishment for putting his hands in his lap during their visit. The impact of solitary on his mind and spirit.

How she believed that it was his fear of being raped in prison that led him to take his own life.

I wanted to make sure that Tracy was okay with me writing these details down, with their potential publication. So I called her at home one night and asked.

I remember this moment—she said "let me check something with my husband" and she put the phone down and I could hear through the distance. She said: "Do you think it is accurate to say that it seems like Jonathan killed himself because he was afraid of being raped?" Her husband said yes. She got back on the phone and said: "if it helps another parent not go through what we have gone through, you can talk about that—you can share whatever part of his life will help."

Do you know those moments where the world sort of stops, time slows down, and you feel things deep, deep in your belly? It was one of those moments. I felt the presence of my own partner one room away from me. We were newly engaged and our whole lives together seemed spread out before us—full of joy and promise.

I remembered that Tracy's husband and son both tried to commit suicide themselves as they grappled with the pain of losing Jonathan. Her daughter had been hospitalized with severe anxiety. And I thought about how when our conversation was over, I would go into the living room and have a light-hearted normal night at home with the person I love so much, but Tracy and her husband may never again have that kind of night.

I thought about what I want you to know: Jonathan's death is not unique—children in adult jails are 36 times more likely to commit suicide than children in adult detention facilities, and the National Prison Rape Elimination Commission stated that "more than any other group of incarcerated persons, youth incarcerated with adults are probably at the highest risk for sexual abuse."

And children in adult jails and prisons are often placed in solitary confinement for up to 23 hours a day—where they are fed through a small slot in the door so that the only contact they have is a hand coming through a slot in the door. Can you imagine that: just an arm coming through a slot to push food in to a child. Children in solitary do not leave their cells to go to school or programs, and can stay for months and even years at a time.

This all happens in New York State, and it happens because we prosecute 16- and 17-year olds as adults and confine them in adult jails and prisons. This practice causes children immeasurable physical, emotional and sexual trauma.

And it is bad for public safety—children prosecuted as adults are far more likely to commit crime and violence in the future than youth prosecuted in the youth justice system.

Finally, it is bad for taxpayers. Not only does prosecuting children as adults keep many young people from lifelong education and employment opportunities—nearby Connecticut is spending approximately 2 million dollars less on youth justice than it was 10 years ago—despite having raised the age and adding millions of dollars to community services.

Most importantly, now is the time to act, so that the next time we are here at a press conference, you do not hear from another mother who lost her son or daughter while we were waiting for the law to change.

Critical Thinking

1. Do you believe teenagers should be considered adults in the criminal justice system?
2. Is it a good idea to prosecute children as adults when they commit very violent crimes?
3. Should the violence an inmate faces in prison be part of the punishment, or do inmates have a right to be incarcerated in a safe environment?

Create Central

www.mhhe.com/createcentral

Internet References

Correctional Association of New York
www.correctionalassociation.org/campaigns/raise-the-age

Justice Policy Institute
www.justicepolicy.org/images/upload/97-02_rep_riskjuvenilesface_jj.pdf

Article   Prepared by: Joanne Naughton

No Remorse

Should a teenager be given a life sentence?

RACHEL AVIV

Learning Outcomes

After reading this article, you will be able to:

- Show the long-term effects for the public of prosecuting teenagers as adults and confining them in adult facilities.

- Describe the fears felt by a teenager facing confinement in an adult facility.

Shortly after midnight on March 6, 2010, Dakotah Eliason sat in a chair in his bedroom with a .38-calibre pistol in his hands, thinking about what the world would be like if he didn't exist. One of his friends had recently killed himself, and his girlfriend had dumped him. Earlier that night, Dakotah, who was fourteen, had taken his grandfather's loaded gun off the coatrack. The breakup felt like a sign that he would always be a failure, and he figured no one would miss him after a few days. He got a pencil and tried to compose a suicide note, but he didn't know what he should say.

Dakotah wondered if he was ready to die, and contemplated taking someone else's life instead. He thought about how people have good and evil sides, and how the good doesn't always win. It was the theme of an adventure story he was writing. He drank a can of Mountain Dew, then went to the bathroom and looked at himself in the mirror. He was pale and lanky, with sandy bangs swept to the side. "What am I doing?" he said to himself. "Why? Why do I have the gun? I know better than this."

He walked into the living room and stared at his grandfather, Jesse Miles, who was sleeping on the couch. A retired machinist and an avid hunter, Jesse often fell asleep while watching the Discovery Channel, and stayed on the couch all night so his smoker's cough wouldn't wake his wife. For forty-five minutes, Dakotah sat on a wooden chair, three feet from his grandfather, and talked to himself quietly, debating what to do next. If he got hand towels from the bathroom, he could gag his grandpa. If he used a steak knife, the whole thing might be quieter. He figured he'd use the cordless phone on his bed to report the crime. He felt as if he were watching a movie about himself. Finally, at just after three in the morning, he raised the handgun, his arms trembling, and shot his grandfather in the head.

"Man, I shot Papa!" he shouted. He put the gun on the floor and rushed into his grandmother Jean's bedroom. She yelled for Dakotah to call 911, and he followed her orders "like a little puppy," she said later. When officers from the police department in Niles, a rural town in southeast Michigan, arrived, seven minutes later, Dakotah was waiting outside next to his grandmother, who was in her pajamas and frantically waving her hands. Jean explained that Dakotah had shot Jesse. "This is my grandson," she said, placing her hand on his shoulder.

A trooper named Brenda Kiefer handcuffed Dakotah, read him his Miranda rights, and told him that she needed to know what had happened but that she "was not here to judge." She asked if he wanted a parent there and heard him say no. (Dakotah insists that he said "Uh-huh," indicating that he did want a parent present, and that he rarely says "yes" or "no," a habit for which his father scolds him.) Dakotah had always admired police officers, and he responded politely to Kiefer's questions, as his grandfather, unconscious and bleeding heavily, was loaded into an ambulance. Dakotah told Kiefer that he had a loving relationship with his grandparents and often spent the weekends at their home, where he had his own room. He didn't know why he'd picked up the gun, but he guessed that it was "sadness and pent-up anger."

After talking to Kiefer for fifteen minutes, Dakotah was put in a patrol car, which was parked at the bottom of the driveway. The officer who sat up front, Eugene Castro, asked Dakotah his name, and then realized he had gone to high school with Dakotah's father, Steve. "So was he good at sports?" Dakotah asked. Castro said that Steve had played hockey and tried to end the conversation cordially, but Dakotah updated him on his father's path since graduation: after losing his job as a construction worker, he'd begun an associate's-degree program in criminal justice. Dakotah added that it would be nice to be on the police force, because of the job security.

Several times, Castro stepped outside the cruiser to answer phone calls. When Dakotah was alone in the car, which had a video camera running, his breathing became heavy and rapid, and he coughed and made retching noises. Then an Avril Lavigne song, "My Happy Ending," came on the radio. "Ugh, why does this song have to play!" he said. He began singing along with the chorus: "So much for my happy ending / Oh oh, oh oh."

Out the window, Dakotah could see the flash of cameras inside his grandparents' home, a two-story farmhouse that the couple had lived in for thirty-five years. "It looks like forensics is doing their thing," Dakotah said when Castro returned. "So what do you predict will happen to me? I mean, murder charge—that's big. I'm still a minor, but . . ." Castro said he didn't know, and explained that a judge, not the police, would decide. "My life just turned into 'Law & Order,'" Dakotah said. "But with no commercials."

When the officer didn't respond, Dakotah began breathing heavily again. "I wish I could take it back, but now I understand the feeling people get when they do that," he said, drawing out his words slowly. "You feel like nothing could ever hurt you— just for that split second, once you realize what you've done."

Steve Eliason had been asleep for only a few hours when a detective knocked at his door and told him that his stepfather, who had raised him, was in the hospital in critical condition and that his son had been arrested. Still groggy from a night of drinking with his wife, Lisa, and out-of-town guests, Steve expected that there would be some reasonable explanation. Dakotah's only previous encounter with the police involved a missing backpack, and he had quickly been absolved of blame. He was an honor-roll student with a close group of friends who called themselves the Randoms, because, unlike the jocks and the preps who occupied the upper tier of their school's social hierarchy, their hobbies were varied: video games, fan fiction, classic rock, anime.

The detective, Fabian Suarez, drove Steve to the police station and, just before five in the morning, led him into a windowless, fluorescent-lit room with a Formica table and three chairs. Dakotah sat alone at the table, and Steve stared at his son, shook his head, and then pulled up a chair next to him. For the second time that morning, Dakotah heard his Miranda rights—Suarez went through the litany rapidly, in a dispassionate monotone.

"Are you angry with me?" Steve asked Dakotah, his voice shaking. "Is it something I did?" He told Suarez that a family doctor had once suggested that Dakotah see a therapist, because Dakotah was upset that nothing he did could ever please his dad. Dakotah didn't play sports—he preferred singing, drawing, and writing stories—which meant that he didn't have to maintain his grade-point average for a team. "So I try to push him," Steve explained.

Detective Suarez asked if he could have a private conversation with Dakotah, whose focus had drifted; he was shaking his wrists, blowing on the skin where the handcuffs had been. Steve agreed and told Dakotah, "We are trying to get to the bottom of this. Please, please answer."

Alone with the detective, Dakotah was initially sluggish, as if humoring a concerned teacher. But when Suarez asked what made him angriest in life he said that he was mad at his mother, Mary, who had abandoned him when he was a baby and dropped in and out of his life, depending on whether or not she was with a new man.

Dakotah said it had never occurred to him to hurt his grandfather, but "something overcame me." It had been a typically boring Saturday: he played racing and fighting games on his PlayStation console for four hours, and watched part of "Terminator 3" and a few shows on Comedy Central. Then he had a brief, pleasant conversation with his grandmother before she went to sleep. Later that night, he started thinking about how his family and friends were too distant; it felt like everyone he loved was drifting away. For about two hours, the "main argument was homicide or suicide," he told Suarez. "You ever hear people talk about having voices in their head? Well, it's not so much that as multiple personalities. One is like the good guy and the other is essentially the bad guy."

"The thing is when you actually do kill somebody, whether you have an emotional attachment or not, you get about five seconds," Dakotah said. "All the tension goes away." He propped his elbows on the table and rested his head in his hands, rubbing his face. "It's just that initial feeling," he continued. "It's an overwhelming feeling—I'm not really sure how to explain it."

After ten minutes, Steve demanded to be let back into the room. He had spoken with his brother, who was at the hospital, and learned that their father had died. By the time he returned, the interview was over. Steve was aggressive and agitated, and told Dakotah he couldn't make sense of what had happened. "Help me understand," he pleaded. "You always seemed happy."

Dakotah looked up at him blankly, his hands folded on the table.

"You're not showing any remorse, Dakotah. I'm not saying it in a bad way, but is something wrong with your head? Do you have problems with thinking? I mean, because you're a very intelligent young man." Steve told him to imagine what would happen "if you weren't my kid, and I was in this room with the person that shot my dad." He raised his voice: "This is the shit they talk about. Kids get into these goddamn video games and they don't pull their head out of the fucking game. They think they can just go"—he pressed his finger into Dakotah's biceps—"hit the re-start button!" He said he couldn't accept "I don't know" as an answer. "Why would you shoot Papa, D.? Papa loved you."

Dakotah's face had turned deep red, and he hung his head a couple of inches from the table. He wiped his eyes with his sleeve.

"Don't hold it in. Let it out," Steve said. He put his arms around Dakotah, who had begun sobbing, and pulled him toward his chest. Dakotah circled his arms around his father, letting his weight collapse into him. "You've got to be strong for me, O.K.?" Steve whispered, rubbing Dakotah's back and staring at the wall with a bewildered expression. "You're my little boy."

Watching the local news the next day, Steve learned that Dakotah would be tried as an adult for first-degree homicide, which in Michigan carries a mandatory sentence of life imprisonment without the possibility of parole. The county's prosecuting attorney, Arthur Cotter, a towering man with white hair who was elected to office in 2008, had reviewed videotapes of Dakotah's statements to the police and concluded that Dakotah didn't belong in the juvenile justice system, which releases offenders from custody when they turn twenty-one. Cotter said that the decision was easy, because Dakotah had shown "an utter lack of remorse." "Even his father noticed it," he told me.

In Michigan, as in many states, prosecutors can try defendants older than fourteen in adult court without a hearing, a statement of reasons, or an investigation into the adolescent's background. The decision cannot be reviewed or appealed. This allows prosecutors to bypass the juvenile justice system, which was built upon the premise that youths are still malleable, in need of the state's protection, and uniquely capable of rehabilitation.

The first juvenile courts, which emerged at the turn of the twentieth century, aimed to treat criminal behavior, not punish it, by intervening in the domestic lives of children whose parents had failed them. The establishment of a separate court system for youths followed other progressive reforms, like compulsory education and child-labor laws, which extended the boundary of childhood. The psychologist G. Stanley Hall lent scientific legitimacy to the concept of adolescence, describing it, in 1904, as a "genetic period of storm and stress," with a "curve of despondency" that rises at the age of eleven and falls by twenty-three. Juvenile hearings were sealed to the public and focussed on the personal history of the offender rather than on the offense. Judges designed individualized treatment plans to address whatever had thwarted the child's development: neglect, abuse, a poor education, an overcrowded home, unrestricted exposure to books about bandits. In 1910, Benjamin Lindsey, one of the first juvenile-court judges in the country, wrote that "our laws against crime are as inapplicable to children as they would be to idiots."

The juvenile justice system quickly became a model for courts throughout the world—the judicial scholar Francis Allen called it the "greatest legal institution invented in the United States"—but the system's paternalistic outlook often led to capricious rulings. In the sixties, a new generation of children's advocates tried to redefine the "best interests of the child," focussing on liberating rather than protecting youths. In 1967, the Supreme Court reviewed the case of a fifteen-year-old who had been committed to a detention home for six years for making a lewd phone call, and ruled that the "condition of being a boy does not justify a Kangaroo Court." The decision established that juveniles deserve many of the same due-process rights as adults, including the right to a lawyer and the right against self-incrimination.

Once hearings became adversarial (resembling "junior varsity criminal trials," as one court decision put it), the system's original mission was gradually obscured. In the eighties, when youth crime rates began to rise, most visibly in gang-related violence, reformers argued that modern adolescents were more sophisticated than the youths of earlier eras. In 1985, Alfred Regnery, the head of the Justice Department's Office of Juvenile Justice and Delinquency Prevention, accused the juvenile courts of naïvely adopting Rousseau's theory that youths are "incapable of evil unless they are corrupted" and of listening to the "psychobabble of social workers." In the following decade,

juvenile gun homicides more than tripled, leading to widespread hysteria, promoted by sensational news reports, about a rising generation of juvenile "super-predators." They are "doing homicidal violence in 'wolf packs,'" wrote John DiIulio, then a professor of politics and public affairs at Princeton, who helped popularize the idea of a "demographic crime bomb." (He has since expressed regret, acknowledging that the prediction was never fulfilled.) Juvenile courts became increasingly punitive, and by the late nineties nearly half of committed juveniles were behind bars, rather than in community-supervision or treatment programs, and a quarter of them were locked up because of misdemeanors or probation violations. Forty-six states rewrote their laws to make it easier for minors to be tried as adults.

Although judges have long been attuned to the difficulty of trying mentally ill defendants, there is little recognition that people may be incompetent to stand trial because of their age. Each year, more than two hundred thousand offenders younger than eighteen are tried as adults, yet only about half of them understand the Miranda warning. According to studies of delinquent adolescents, they have trouble grasping that a "right" is an absolute privilege that they may exercise without penalty. Defendants fifteen and younger are particularly impaired, and waive their rights much more frequently than do adults. The vast majority misinterpret at least one of the four statements that make up the Miranda warning, stumbling on terms like "consult," "interrogation," "appoint," and "entitled," which may be above their reading level.

At a hearing to determine whether Dakotah's confessions were made voluntarily and could be used at trial, Dakotah maintained that he didn't realize that he was free to stop talking to the police once he had already started. The prosecutor, Arthur Cotter, broke down the Miranda warning and asked Dakotah which sentences he couldn't comprehend. Dakotah conceded that he understood the language ("Yeah, I know what a lawyer is"), but not its implications. He explained, "I just felt I had no choice but to answer the questions."

The judge, Scott Schofield, was not persuaded and ruled that all Dakotah's statements could be admitted as evidence. He pointed out that Dakotah watched "Law & Order," had proofread one of his father's papers for a criminology class, and used big words. (The trooper, Brenda Kiefer, testified that Dakotah, when describing his grandparents' property, had used the word "elevation" and warned that frozen ruts on the driveway were "treacherous.") Schofield dismissed the claim that Dakotah was in a psychotic or altered state of mind. He interpreted Dakotah's reference to hearing voices as an externalization of his own conscience, "a debate that he was having with himself—should I do the right thing, or should I not do the right thing?"

Dakotah often talked of becoming a writer. Throughout his freshman year, he wrote fantasy stories and shared them with his friends, who critiqued the plots and gave him tips for improvement. Tashawn Reese, who collaborated with him, said that Dakotah's stories were about underdogs who faced emotional challenges—the hero falls in love with an irresistible girl who's unavailable, or his parents die, or his school morphs into a crater—and usually the "theme was the eternal struggle between good and evil." The last story Dakotah brought to school was about two boys, one of whom develops demonic powers while the other acquires angelic ones; at the end, both soar into the sky.

Kelsey Crago, who dated Dakotah briefly, couldn't recall his doing anything unusual in the weeks before the murder. She knew that he was disappointed by his recent breakup—his girlfriend had broken things off by text message—but he didn't talk about it, because he didn't like drama. Kelsey described Dakotah as a "great listener, the main person I trusted if I needed advice," but he rarely shared his own problems. In letters to Dakotah, she repeatedly asked him why he had killed his grandfather, but never felt satisfied by his answers. "I wasn't thinking," he told her, and wrote that maybe he had watched too many crime shows.

At the Berrien County Juvenile Center, fifteen miles from his home, Dakotah complained that every time he closed his eyes he saw his grandfather's death, "like a movie." He told a caseworker that he was still trying to figure out what had happened and that he wished he had killed himself instead. He was forced to wear suicide garb, clothes too stiff to be torn, and was unable to sleep. His grandmother Jean, a petite, well-dressed woman with short white hair, wrote him a letter telling him that she forgave him, and visited him at the center after two weeks. "It was hard for him to look at me, with him knowing what he'd done," she told me. "He'd look up and then look away. Mostly, he just held my hand and rubbed it."

Steve berated himself for acting like a "maniac drill instructor" and losing his temper over anything his son did wrong. He also blamed Dakotah's "bio-mom," as he called her. In her statement to the police, Mary explained that she'd never intended to have a child with Steve. "I had a party at my apt.," she wrote. "We got drunk, we got pregnant." (Mary would not talk to me, explaining, "I have nothing to say.") She was rarely involved in Dakotah's life until he was seven; then she went to court to obtain joint custody. When Dakotah was twelve, she changed her mind and relinquished all her rights as a parent. Steve remembers Dakotah coming home from a visit and "brushing his hands like he'd just had crackers and was getting rid of the crumbs. He said, 'Mom finally washed her hands clean of me.' "

For Steve and his wife, the fact that Dakotah had killed his grandfather, a man he had loved, was proof that he'd been temporarily insane. A week after Dakotah was arrested, Steve hired Lanny Fisher, a local attorney who had gone to the same high school, was "great at sports but humble about it," and had been practicing law for three years. (Fisher offered to charge a fraction of his normal fee, since Steve and Lisa were living on her hourly wages from Subway.) Fisher, assuming that the trial would be a battle between mental-health experts, said he was "devastated" when he received the results of Dakotah's psychiatric report. The examiner, who interviewed Dakotah for a little more than three hours, noted that Dakotah preferred his own fantasies to reality, but he did not think his imaginary life had ever reached psychotic proportions.

Two more psychiatric reports were done, and neither found that Dakotah met the criteria for legal insanity, which would

have meant that he could not appreciate the wrongfulness of his crime or conform his behavior to meet the requirements of the law. No history of physical or sexual abuse was uncovered. Fisher and Arthur Cotter had been discussing a possible plea bargain—fourteen years to life for second-degree murder—but after reading the psychiatric reports Cotter chose to go to trial, a decision that several family members endorsed. Jesse Miles's forty-seven-year-old daughter, Vickie Hartz, Steve's stepsister, told me that she was disappointed that Michigan doesn't have the death penalty. "My dad was an easygoing, mellow guy who did everything for that kid," Hartz said. "And Dakotah killed him with as much emotion as if he were moving a chair."

The murder trial began on August 17th, less than six months after Jesse Miles's death. Judge Scott Schofield, who presides over all the criminal trials in Niles, is known for running a "rocket docket" when his cases get local media attention. He set brisk deadlines for motions and hearings, saying, "It's a cliché, I know," but "justice delayed is justice denied." The courtroom was filled to capacity, with reporters from four local TV stations. Schofield referred to the microphone as an ice-cream cone and encouraged jurors to hold it close to their mouths so they wouldn't make a mess.

At the juvenile center, where residents spend six hours a day in school and attend workshops on risk and anger management, Dakotah was "student of the week" three times, and received awards for "social skills," "fabulous achievement and effort," and "making a difference." Still, Cotter requested that Dakotah's legs be shackled during the trial, saying that he might pose a security risk because of "his feelings of power." "When he shot his grandfather, he felt for fifteen seconds that nothing in the world could hurt him," Cotter told the court. Judge Schofield acknowledged that defendants have the right to be free of restraint but concluded that in this case the shackles were warranted, since "the Court has some concerns about Mr. Eliason being psychologically conflicted."

Cotter, in his opening statement, portrayed Dakotah as a sociopath so callous he was capable of "chitchat" and making a "whooey sound" in the patrol car just moments after shooting his grandfather. Dakotah was fascinated by death, he said, and would have killed his grandmother, too, if she hadn't woken up. Cotter cautioned the jury that when they viewed the videotape of Dakotah's interview at the police station they might be moved by the sight of Steve Eliason, "in a true test of the unlimitedness of a parent's love," embracing his son. "Do not confuse the emotions you're going to feel—the empathy that you are going to feel when you watch that point with his father—with any sadness that that young man felt remorse," Cotter said.

Lanny Fisher, unassuming and amiable, opened with a speech that laid bare his own confusion. "Most cases, most stories, they have the who, the what, the where, the when, and the why," he said. "The reason that we're all here today is the why." After months of research, he could find no coherent motive, so he presented the crime's incomprehensibility as proof that it couldn't have been deliberate. Cotter referred to Dakotah as a "young man"; Fisher called him a "boy." He emphasized that in the past year Dakotah had endured a series of losses: his cousin had been in a fatal car crash, his father had told him they were losing their house because he could not pay the mortgage, a friend had committed suicide, and his dog, Bam-Bam, had died of old age.

Fisher's other line of defense was to urge the jury to recall how it felt to be fourteen. "You can't drink," he said. "You have to be twenty-one to do that. You can't smoke, or vote, or join the armed services. You have to be eighteen to do that. Can't even drive a car . . . That's the person that's on trial, ladies and gentlemen."

The trial lasted two and a half days, and much of it focussed on testimony from police officers and forensic technicians who established details about the crime that were not contested by the defense. Fisher chose not to have Dakotah testify, since juveniles tend to make poor witnesses—they are easily misled or intimidated and often give inconsistent, idealized accounts of their own actions. For character witnesses, Fisher called Dakotah's high-school principal, who said that Dakotah was never sent to his office and was "probably not the top student, but pretty good," and a family friend who described him as "very mild-mannered, kind." Since Fisher was not advancing any theory about the crime, his conversations with the witnesses for the defense lacked direction and at times helped the prosecutor's argument as much as his own. When Jean Miles, weeping, took the stand, Fisher helped her paint an image of domestic normalcy:

Fisher: Your house was kind of a getaway for him, wasn't it?

Miles: Yes.

Fisher: It would be you, and Jesse, and Dakotah, and he could kind of play video games, watch movies?

Miles: Yes.

Fisher: And you guys gave him attention?

Miles: Yes.

Fisher: O.K. He had fun over at your house?

Miles: Yes. I hope so.

Cotter concluded the trial by describing Dakotah as a young man incapable of reciprocating his family's love. He argued that the crime exemplified premeditation, since Dakotah "considered the pros and cons of killing" for more than two hours. "It's almost like he was building up the courage to do it," Cotter said, before acting out Dakotah's interior monologue: "Are you going to do it? Do it. Do it! Shoot him." Cotter described Dakotah's reaction to the shooting as "just bizarre": there was "not a tear, not a sob," no "ounce of emotion." He dwelled on Dakotah's remark that the "tension goes away" after murdering someone. "That's when it *starts*, that's when the conscience kicks in," Cotter said. "He's got the emotional curve all wrong."

The expectation that defendants will display remorse either shortly after their crimes or never is generally accepted as common sense. In a *Columbia Law Review* study of cases of juveniles charged with violent crimes, the Emory law professor Martha Grace Duncan found that youths who failed to express their contrition promptly and appropriately, as adults would, were often penalized for showing "less grief than the system demands." In many cases, she writes, the juveniles appeared to be in shock or in a kind of dissociative state and failed to appreciate the permanence of what they had done. "Less under the sway of the reality principle," they were more prone than adults to engage in forms of denial. But prosecutors and judges interpreted their strange reactions—falling asleep after the crime, giggling, rapping—as signs of irreparable depravity. Duncan found that courts looked for remorse in "psychologically naïve ways, without regard for defense mechanisms, developmental stages, or the ambiguity that inheres in human behavior."

One of Dakotah's closest friends, Christina Wardlaw, who sat through the trial, told me that she had to suppress the urge to laugh as she listened to Dakotah's recorded conversations with the police. "He still saw himself as the same old Dakotah, jabbering and singing and making jokes," she said. "He had no idea what he'd become."

Dakotah's reaction, with its apparent remorselessness, less than three hours after shooting his grandfather, was discussed by three witnesses for the prosecution. It also figured in the jurors' deliberations. They asked to view Dakotah's videotaped conversation with the detective again, and an hour after watching the tape, and just three hours after beginning deliberations, they announced that Dakotah was guilty of first-degree homicide.

One juror told me that several people on the jury were troubled by Dakotah's youth, but they'd been instructed that if the evidence indicated that the offense was premeditated and deliberate the crime was first-degree murder. Age had no place in that calculus. As is required under Michigan law, the jury was not informed that the conviction carried the automatic penalty of life imprisonment without the possibility of parole.

Before the sentencing hearing, Lanny Fisher filed a brief asserting that the punishment violated the Eighth Amendment, which prohibits sentences that are cruel and unusual, based on the "evolving standards of decency in our maturing society." Life imprisonment for juveniles is forbidden by the United Nations Convention on the Rights of the Child, a treaty ratified by every country in the world except the United States and Somalia. In his brief, Fisher relied heavily on two recent Supreme Court cases, which, he maintained, suggest that the U.S. is increasingly recognizing the "distinct emotional, psychological and neurological status of youth."

In a 2005 case, *Roper v. Simmons,* the United States became the last Western country to abolish the death penalty for juveniles. The decision drew on a growing body of scientific research that reaffirmed what, a hundred years earlier, passed for common sense: "the personality traits of juveniles are more transitory, less fixed." Anthony Kennedy, in his opinion, pointed out that the *Diagnostic and Statistical Manual of Mental Disorders* explicitly prohibits psychiatrists from giving people under eighteen a diagnosis of antisocial disorder (a euphemism for sociopathy), since many signs of the disorder—egocentricity, failure to accept responsibility, impulsiveness, proneness to boredom—are natural aspects of adolescence. Kennedy noted that "adolescents are overrepresented statistically in virtually every category of reckless behavior."

The Court extended the reasoning it had used three years earlier when it outlawed capital punishment for defendants with I.Q.s below seventy. But the four dissenting Justices in *Roper* rejected the idea that the same claim of diminished culpability could be made for all juveniles, since the Court's analysis had been based on aggregate differences between youths and adults, which may have little bearing on the sophistication of individual defendants, particularly those at the "margins between adolescence and adulthood." Antonin Scalia criticized the American Psychological Association, which submitted a brief in favor of abolition, for taking a conflicting stance on teen maturity in an earlier case regarding the rights of juveniles to get abortions. The large body of research on adolescent cognition, Scalia wrote, had allowed the Court to "look over the heads of the crowd and pick out its friends," finding empirical support for previously held opinions.

Five years later, in *Graham v. Florida,* the Court again pointed to "developments in psychology and brain science [that] continue to show fundamental differences between juvenile and adult minds," and, for the first time in a quarter century, invalidated a sentence other than capital punishment. Now the Court ruled that for juveniles—but only those whose crimes did not result in death—a sentence that offers "no chance for reconciliation with society, no hope" is cruel and unusual. Life-without-parole sentences have tripled since the early nineties, both because the punishment offers an alternative to death and because of crime policies that emphasize retribution and incapacitation rather than rehabilitation. The ruling did not guarantee young prisoners eventual release, only the possibility of it. In the decision, Justice Kennedy alluded to studies, outlined in a brief submitted by the American Medical Association, showing that the prefrontal cortex, which is associated with behavioral control, does not fully develop until people reach their twenties. Kennedy noted that in many states inmates who are ineligible for parole are denied access to educational programs, leading to the "perverse consequence in which the lack of maturity that led to an offender's crime is reinforced by the prison term."

Judge Schofield gave Cotter a week to submit a written response to Fisher's constitutional challenge and scheduled his own ruling and sentencing for the following week. At the hearing, on October 25th, Schofield gave a rhapsodic speech about how the legislative branch of government makes the law, and how the judicial branch has "nothing to do with that. And that's the way it should be." He called the case a "textbook example of our separation of powers" and denied Fisher's motion. He noted that the punishment wasn't unusual; thirty-nine states allow fourteen-year-olds to be sentenced to life without parole. No appellate or trial court has held that *Graham* applies to those convicted of homicide. Currently, there are some twenty-five hundred American inmates who were given life sentences for killing someone before their eighteenth birthday; for more than half of them, it was their first crime.

During the sentencing, Dakotah, who had just turned fifteen, periodically grasped at his chest and bent over, as if struggling to take in air. He wore a green prison jumpsuit, he had a new military buzz cut, and he showed early signs of a weak beard.

At the end of the hearing, he was given an opportunity to speak before the court for the first time. He stood up and said that his heart was pounding so hard that he thought he was going to die, and he was trying not to pee in his pants. "If I don't regret this every day, then I truly am less than human," he said. "Then I do deserve to die in prison."

He began crying and apologized to his aunt and his cousins, who were sitting on the prosecutor's side of the courtroom and had publicly expressed their wish that he never reenter society. "No matter how much anyone hates me—it doesn't make a difference—I will still love you all because you're my family," Dakotah said. "I never finished that statement at the courthouse or at the station. The tension, it goes away, but it comes back tenfold. You deal with it on a scale that can never be measured."

Nine days after his sentencing, Dakotah was transferred to Thumb Correctional Facility, a medium-security prison on the eastern edge of the state, two hundred miles from his home and sixty miles from Detroit. The forty-acre prison complex, which is a half mile from Interstate 69, is surrounded by three sets of twelve-foot fences, edged with coils of razor-ribbon wire. Although the law mandates that incarcerated juveniles have no contact with adult prisoners, the same protections do not apply to youths who have been prosecuted as adults. The prison has six squat beige brick units, two of which house four hundred and thirty inmates who are under twenty-one years old. They cross paths with the Old Heads, as they are called, during visits to the library, church, and the segregation unit, where prisoners of all ages are punished with solitary confinement.

The prison rarely permits media visits, and, last January, the warden denied my request, citing Dakotah's age and "health-related" concerns. Journalists are subject to the same admission requirements as the general public, so I waited six months, until Dakotah was eligible to update his list of ten visitors who are not immediate family, and visited him for the first time last June, eight months after he had arrived at the prison.

The prison's visiting room has an atmosphere of casual boredom, like the waiting room of a doctor's office. About fifty upholstered metal chairs are arrayed around coffee tables, and inmates and their visitors pass time by playing Uno or checkers, drifting to the vending machines and back, or holding each other subtly enough to escape the guards' scrutiny. Two kisses are permitted, one at the beginning of the visit and one at the end.

I got a Coke for Dakotah, who had been assigned a seat near the guard's podium, and he quietly thanked me, then took a dramatic swig. "If I drink Coke like I'm drinking beer, it's because I've had a few beers before," he said nervously. He admitted that he didn't consider himself cool in other respects. "I was the smiley wannabe emo kid," he said. The only physical activity he excelled at was dodgeball. He had also taken karate, when he was nine, and was grateful to his dad for enrolling him in the class, because "it could definitely be helpful, if I have to protect myself."

At the juvenile center, Dakotah had developed a close relationship with a pastor and been born again. For several months, his mind had been on the afterlife. Since he'd been in prison, though, the spiritual world seemed less relevant. "No two ways about it, I ain't worth shit religiously," he said tentatively, as if testing the sound of the phrase. When I asked why, he explained that he talked like a sailor and was getting to be racist. Black inmates who didn't even know him would tell him to "shut your white ass up," and refer to him as "white bitch," "snowflake," and "cracker," a term he didn't fully understand until he checked out a book on the Civil War from the prison library.

At the prison's health-care center, Dakotah had received a diagnosis of bipolar disorder, and he now took a heavy daily dose of an antidepressant and a sedative. The drugs had removed "this great weight, this nervous energy pouring off me," but they had also made him less creative. He rarely wrote stories anymore, and even letters to friends felt like an exertion. Though the medications helped, he wasn't convinced that the diagnosis was right; he still wished "someone could pinpoint what's wrong with me." He said that every time he hears a loud noise, like a door slam, "my mind goes right back to the incident, and all I hear is white noise."

Initially, other inmates wanted to know what he was in for (he kept his answer brief: "I shot someone"), but no one asked about his background anymore. Conversations rarely went much deeper than "What's for chow?" He scored well on the G.E.D. exam after taking the prison's prep class, but it was just a review of things he learned freshman year or picked up from the books he used to read secretly when classes were boring. "All I've learned in prison is some better ways to work out," he told me. He earned $1.14 a day mowing the grounds at the prison, and he figured that he would become a professional landscaper. He spoke casually of things he planned to do when he got out of prison, only occasionally catching himself to add "*if* I get out." He cheerily informed me that the prison has a policy whereby "guards will take you cuffed and shackled to your own funeral," before becoming flustered and correcting himself, explaining that he might get to attend the service when his grandmother dies.

Dakotah dreamed of becoming a country or rock singer, though he considered the goal cheesy. His first demo would be called "Generation Millennials." He spent most of his time listening to his MP3 player, purchased from the prison commissary, and singing along in his eight-by-eleven-foot cell. Depending on how much money his dad put into his account, he could buy about a dozen new songs a month, and he tried to memorize the lyrics to each one. The other day, his crew yard boss had referred to him as "the kid who sings," which he liked, since he'd become accustomed to responding to "white boy."

Dakotah quizzed me on the songs I knew, and each time I failed to recognize a hit he laughed and sang it for me in a whispery, high-pitched voice. As soon as he finished one song, he tried to find another, searching for anything I might know. "The only thing I really need is my music," he said, tapping his foot. "If I've got music, I'm straight—I can do my time. You won't hear a peep out of me."

Three months after the trial, Dakotah's case was assigned to the state appellate defender's office, which represents indigent clients who can't afford private counsel. His lawyer, the office's deputy director, has contested his sentence on the ground that Dakotah received ineffective counsel, in part because Lanny Fisher never brought in an expert to explain why Dakotah failed to show "stereotypical signs of adult-like remorse." A new medical evaluation characterized Dakotah as a "traumatized youth without access to his emotions in the moment." An evidentiary hearing will be held in February to determine whether Dakotah deserves a new trial.

Dakotah's sentence may also be affected by two cases that will be argued before the Supreme Court next term. Both cases, which will be heard in tandem, challenge the constitutionality of life-without-parole sentences for juveniles fourteen and younger. The two defendants maintain that early adolescence is a distinct developmental period during which susceptibility to influence reaches its peak. "Relative to the cognition of adults and even older adolescents, young teenage judgment is handicapped in nearly every conceivable way," one petition reads.

But pegging legal protections to age markers also invites the escalating possibility of further dividing populations. It is well documented, for instance, that girls mature faster than boys, both physically and psychologically. (At a teen-ager's recent murder trial, a University of Pennsylvania neuropsychologist testified that "biology would say" that boys should be held accountable for their crimes at a later age than girls.) Terry Maroney, a Vanderbilt law professor, said that legal arguments based on developmental research, which have become more prevalent since *Roper v. Simmons,* could be used to challenge children's autonomy rights and create an "unduly complicated system with different rules for each potential subgroup." Deborah LaBelle, a lawyer and the author of a report on Michigan inmates sentenced to life for crimes they committed before the age of eighteen, said that she doesn't want to redraw a boundary that, for more than a century, has reflected the fact that "society has a different kind of responsibility to youth."

In *Roper,* the dissenting Justices argued that judgments about a defendant's maturity and culpability should be left to juries. But, in the new cases before the Supreme Court, both fourteen-year-olds were tried in states with mandatory sentencing for murder, so jurors couldn't take their age into account. One of the petitioners was physically abused by his alcoholic father, had attempted suicide six times, and was drunk and high on the night of the crime. His lawyer has argued that his mandatory penalty is cruel and unusual and violates the Fourteenth Amendment, which protects defendants' rights to due process. In death-penalty cases, trial procedure requires that juries consider mitigating factors, such as youth, mental health, and prior record, but there are no parallel safeguards in place for the penultimate punishment.

In Michigan, several judges have described their discomfort with sentencing an adolescent to die in prison, but the state's automatic-sentencing laws leave them no choice. In July, a federal district court ruled that the American Civil Liberties Union can proceed with a lawsuit challenging the state's mandatory-sentencing scheme for juveniles. Michigan has the second-highest number of juveniles sentenced to life without parole, and in 2008 the state's House of Representatives voted to abolish the practice, but the bill never passed in the state Senate; the issue is politically unpopular.

Prosecutors, who are elected officials, are also subject to political pressures, yet they have unfettered discretion to set the terms of a juvenile's charge. LaBelle told me, "I can't think of anywhere else in the world where the state can change the legal status of an individual—'Yes, I know you are a child, but now I will make you an adult'—so rapidly and in a factual vacuum." She continued, "We are telling these kids there is no such thing as redemption. They can never make amends."

For many juveniles, it is several years before they grasp the gravity of their crime and the permanence of the penalty. Joshua Miller, a twenty-nine-year-old inmate at the Wilkinson County Correctional Facility, in Mississippi, told me that it wasn't until he reached his mid-twenties that the "'without parole' part of my sentence finally dawned on me." After killing his girlfriend when he was fourteen—she rejected him, and he wanted to stage a "'Romeo and Juliet' kind of thing"—Miller was placed in an adult prison, where older inmates "treated me like the weak coward that I was," he said.

During his first few years of imprisonment, Miller tried to stay abreast of new albums, movies, and fashions, but eventually he realized there was no point in "keeping tabs on a structure I could never be part of." He stopped reading fiction, because it was too painful to "journey into the free world." He said that he has never had sex. He considers his girlfriend, who was thirteen when he murdered her, the love of his life. Although he looks back longingly on his childhood, he doesn't like to hear stories about what became of his peers. "I can't ruin a memory, or I'll lose another attachment to that life," he said. "I refuse to believe that my friends aren't still children."

When I visited the Eliason family in June, Steve, Lisa, and their nine-year-old daughter had moved into Jean Miles's house, in order to save money. They had got a new couch and rearranged the living room, but the rest of the downstairs looked the same as it had in the police photographs. On top of the television was a framed photograph of Dakotah and his family standing in front of a pastoral autumn scene painted on a cinder-block wall in the prison's visiting room. Steve and Jean both told me with pride that Dakotah was learning to be a model inmate. He had called home, upset, the night before because the toilet in his cell had overflowed, and, when the guards wouldn't respond to his calls for help, he stayed composed and mopped up the sewage with his own clothes. "I tell him that if we go through the appeals process and nothing changes, then he can get as wild and crazy as he wants," Steve said. He has noticed Dakotah's language becoming foul, which "eats me up—he was a soft boy."

Steve and I had spoken on the phone several times before, and, in each conversation, he offered new theories about his stepfather's death and the ways it could have been prevented. At the house, he reenacted the crime as his mother sat in a rocking chair beside us. With his thumb and index finger extended like an imaginary handgun, he stood where he assumed Dakotah had been when he pulled the trigger. "If he had just missed by an inch, the bullet would have hit the glass cabinet over there and woken my father, who would have whupped Dakotah's ass," he said. "Then we would have gotten him some help."

Jean cried quietly throughout the demonstration, and added that Dakotah was a "loving grandson up until that moment." "I would bring him home tonight," she said. "I know the person he is." She often thought about what would have happened if she had forced her husband to hide his gun—it was kept by the door in case of intruders—or had sat down with Dakotah for dinner that night. All he ate was three cupcakes. "But I had all kinds of stuff for him in the freezer," she said under her breath.

The family talked about Dakotah's diagnosis of bipolar disorder, though it won't be relevant for the appeal—the legal bar for insanity is higher than simply having a psychiatric diagnosis. Since Dakotah's arrest, Steve had discovered a history of bipolar disorder in his family, and he, too, received a diagnosis of the illness. He often repackages lessons from his own therapy sessions for his son, who calls home every day. The family talks to him on a speakerphone until the prison phone service cuts them off, after fifteen minutes. When Dakotah complains of feeling homesick, Steve jokes with him, "Grow your beard a little thicker, and I'll shave my hair like you. You'll sneak out, and I'll take your place."

By September, Dakotah had spent nearly three months in solitary confinement. In April, 2011, after six months in prison, he got his first ticket for a rule violation, Threatening Behavior, which resulted in the standard punishment: thirty days in segregation. Dakotah had told a boy in his unit that he'd kill him if he kept prying into his case. The boy had been joking around, saying, "Who'd you kill? Who'd you kill?" Two months later, Dakotah received another ticket, for Sexual Misconduct, after a female guard accused him of exposing his penis through the vertical window on his steel door. According to Dakotah, he was sleeping at the time. He told the guard that it must have been his cellmate, but she said the skin she saw looked light, and his cellmate was black. Dakotah confronted his cellmate, a fifteen-year-old convicted of sexual assault, "but he just laughs about it," he said. "He giggles about all sorts of childish shit."

Two weeks after his punishment ended, he and his cellmate got into a fistfight, and, at the end of August, both boys were transferred to the segregation unit. His cinder-block cell had one barred window, a bed, a stainless-steel desk and stool that were attached to the floor, a toilet, a sink, and a mirror. All his meals were delivered to him through a metal flap on his door, starting with breakfast, at 4 A.M. The only time he could leave his cell was to shower, three times a week; he was handcuffed on the way there and locked into the shower stall.

When I visited Dakotah in September, it was the first time in nearly three weeks that he'd had an extended conversation with another person. We sat in a narrow cinder-block room, divided in half by shatterproof glass, and spoke to each other using rotary telephones whose dial pads had been removed. Dakotah had been animated in our previous conversations, but now he spoke in a dull, listless tone and sat slouched in his chair, his head resting against the wall of the cubicle. His eyes were dilated, and his lips were so chapped they looked bruised.

He told me that he was disgusted with himself for ruining his chance to see his family, who, for more than a month, had planned to visit on the second Sunday in September. It was the second time they'd had to cancel their plans at the last minute because he'd been placed in seclusion. (After a week without calls or letters from Dakotah, Steve had called the prison, and a phone operator told him that Dakotah was in the segregation unit, where visiting hours are restricted to Friday mornings.) Dakotah spent his first few nights in the segregation cell lying underneath his steel-framed bed, on the concrete floor, wearing nothing but shorts. "Oh, man, I was going off the deep end, like, living below the water," he said, jiggling the phone cord. "The little flame lighting my candle of sanity just blew out."

The effects of the sedative he'd been prescribed seemed to have worn off, and he struggled to sleep through the night. He woke up in cold sweats, with such vivid, violent dreams that he examined his body to see if he'd somehow been injured. "I don't understand sleep anymore," he told me. He had developed a theory, adapted from "The Matrix," which he had watched countless times, that maybe life is an illusion, a kind of thought experiment, and dreams are the true reality.

Dakotah began talking to himself in his cell, little comments and reminders at first, and then, as the days passed, full conversations. "I go into this other mode," he said, blowing air out of his mouth. "I can have all these conversations crisscrossing the room; there's a version of me on the bed, at the desk, at the sink."

At the end of my previous visits, Dakotah had chattered rapidly, nearly free-associating, occasionally singing, as if he would lose his visitor as soon as he paused. I had found myself coming to visiting hours later, to avoid prolonging the drama of separating. He would pick lint or stray hairs off my shirt or touch a scab on my hand, assuring me that it would fall off soon—any excuse for physical contact. But this time, our first visit with glass between us, he was the one to end the conversation. "I'm worn out," he told me. "My mind is kind of dead."

His sixteenth birthday was the next week, and I wished him happy birthday. "Yeah, I'm alive," he said, rolling his eyes. "Whoopdefuckingwhoo."

The day before Dakotah's birthday, September 23rd, Steve drove four hours to the prison to surprise him. Dakotah had recently been transferred to the Behavioral Modification Unit, where he had contact with other prisoners, but most of his privileges, including use of the phone, were still suspended. In the partitioned cubicle, Steve and Dakotah pressed their knuckles against the glass, as if they were touching. It had been three months since they'd seen each other. "You look pasty, son," Steve said tenderly. Dakotah, smiling broadly, smoothed the collar of his prison jumpsuit and confessed, "I don't feel like I look so good."

Steve updated Dakotah on developments in the lives of neighbors, relatives, and their pets, and then spoke at length about the mood-stabilizing medication he'd been taking. He said that he no longer acted like a tyrant at home, high-strung and aggressive. "That's one of our traits—not knowing how to express our emotions," he told Dakotah. The more Steve talked about their matching diagnoses, the more he seemed to convince himself that he was complicit in Dakotah's crime. He couldn't forgive himself for yelling at his children, which he now saw as a form of abuse. Dakotah, quiet and deferential, deflected his father's comments with reassuring jokes. (At an earlier visit, he described his dad as his role model, except for his domineering manner: "He was Sgt. Pepper, and I was the Lonely Heart Band.")

Steve wore an oversized tank top, which revealed a tattoo on his right shoulder in memory of his stepfather: "J.E.M., 1940–2010." Dakotah had wept when he first saw the tattoo, more than a year earlier, and now he intended to get one, too. He also wanted the name of his dead dog tattooed on his biceps, his dead cat on his forearm, and his great-grandmother's initials on his chest. At his father's request, he planned to wait until he got to the adult side of the prison, since the Old Heads were more likely to clean their needles.

Both father and son vaguely hoped that other problems, too, would be resolved on the adult side of prison: the units might be less chaotic and noisy, the inmates calmer and more responsible. Steve had reconciled himself to the possibility that Dakotah would eventually get affiliated—with the Aryan Brotherhood, he guessed—because he would need that protection. At the end of the visit, Steve reassured Dakotah that he would find mentors when he moved to the adult population. "Not someone who will take advantage of you but a man who was locked away from his own kids," Steve said. "I want a father in there watching over you."

Critical Thinking

1. Do you think a teenager who commits murder should receive a life sentence?

2. Should a teenager who commits murder be tried as if he were an adult?

3. If Dakotah Eliason should ever be released from prison, do you believe he will be a danger to society?

4. What do you think of the arguments made in the two cases that will soon go to the U.S. Supreme Court?

Create Central

www.mhhe.com/createcentral

Internet References

National Criminal Justice Reference Service
   www.ncjrs.gov/pdffiles1/ojjdp/232434.pdf
Teen Advocates USA
   http://teenadvocatesusa.homestead.com/innocencebetrayed_commentary.html

Unit 6

UNIT

Prepared by: Joanne Naughton

Punishment and Corrections

In the 1950s and 1960s the term *corrections* came to replace *penology,* reflecting a new philosophy that emphasized rehabilitation. But this philosophical view of offenders' treatment took an opposite turn in the 1980s when today's "get tough" policies were instituted. Corrections refers to programs and agencies that have legal authority over the custody or supervision of people who have been convicted of violating criminal law.

The correctional process begins with the sentencing of the convicted offender. The predominant sentencing pattern in the United States encourages maximum judicial discretion and offers a range of alternatives, from probation—supervised, conditional freedom within the community—through imprisonment, to the death penalty.

The current condition of the American penal system and the effects that sentencing, probation, imprisonment, and parole have on the convicted offender should receive serious consideration, because most people who have been sentenced to incarceration are eventually released back into their communities.

Article   Prepared by: Joanne Naughton

Oklahoma's Botched Lethal Injection Marks New Front in Battle Over Executions

CNN's original series "Death Row Stories" explores America's capital punishment system.

Josh Levs, Ed Payne, and Greg Botelho

Learning Outcomes

After reading this article, you will be able to:

- Describe what happened when Oklahoma executed Clayton Lockett.

- Relate the reason states with capital punishment have been forced to find new drugs to use.

- Explain some of the issues that arise regarding the drugs that are used in executions.

- See that not every state has the death penalty.

(CNN)—A botched lethal injection in Oklahoma has catapulted the issue of U.S. capital punishment back into the international spotlight, raising new questions about the drugs being used, and the constitutional protection against cruel and unusual punishment.

"We have a fundamental standard in this country that even when the death penalty is justified, it must be carried out humanely—and I think everyone would recognize that this case fell short of that standard," White House spokesman Jay Carney said Wednesday.

What went wrong Tuesday in Oklahoma "will not only cause officials in that state to review carefully their execution

procedures and methods," said Richard W. Garnett, a former Supreme Court law clerk who now teaches criminal and constitutional law at the University of Notre Dame, "it will also almost prompt many Americans across the country to rethink the wisdom, and the morality, of capital punishment."

"The Constitution allows capital punishment in some cases, and so the decision whether to use it or abandon it, and the moral responsibility for its use and misuse, are in our hands," he said.

Precisely what happened during the execution of convicted murderer and rapist Clayton Lockett remains unclear. Witnesses described the man convulsing and writhing on the gurney, as well as struggling to speak, before officials blocked the witnesses' view.

It was the state's first time using a new, three-drug cocktail for an execution.

Oklahoma halted the execution of another convicted murderer and rapist, Charles Warner, which was scheduled for later in the day.

Thirty-two U.S. states have the death penalty, as does the U.S. government and the U.S. military. Since 2009, three states—New Mexico, Connecticut, and Maryland—have voted to abolish it.

States that have capital punishment have been forced to find new drugs to use since European-based manufacturers banned U.S. prisons from using theirs for executions. One of those manufacturers is the Danish company Lundbeck, maker of pentobarbital.

Carney, speaking to reporters at a daily briefing, said he had not discussed the Oklahoma case with President Barack Obama.

"He has long said that while the evidence suggests that the death penalty does little to deter crime, he believes there are some crimes that are so heinous that the death penalty is merited." The crimes committed by the two men in Oklahoma "are indisputably horrific and heinous," Carney said.

"There Was Chaos"

Lockett lived for 43 minutes after being administered the first drug, CNN affiliate KFOR reported. He got out the words "Man," "I'm not," and "something's wrong," reporter Courtney Francisco of KFOR said. Then the blinds were closed.

Other reporters, including Cary Aspinwall of the Tulsa World newspaper, also said Lockett was still alive and lifted his head while prison officials lowered the blinds so onlookers couldn't see what was going on.

Dean Sanderford, Lockett's attorney, said his client's body "started to twitch," and then "the convulsing got worse. It looked like his whole upper body was trying to lift off the gurney. For a minute, there was chaos."

Sanderford said guards ordered him out of the witness area, and he was never told what had happened to Lockett, who was convicted in 2000 of first-degree murder, rape, kidnapping, and robbery.

After administering the first drug, "We began pushing the second and third drugs in the protocol," said Oklahoma Department of Corrections Director Robert Patton. "There was some concern at that time that the drugs were not having the effect. So the doctor observed the line and determined that the line had blown." He said that Lockett's vein had "exploded." The execution process was halted, but Lockett died of a heart attack, Patton said.

"I notified the attorney general's office, the governor's office of my intent to stop the execution and requested a stay for 14 days," said Patton.

Gov. Mary Fallin issued a statement saying that "execution officials said Lockett remained unconscious after the lethal injection drugs were administered."

Another State, Another Botched Execution

Earlier this year, a convicted murderer and rapist in Ohio, Dennis McGuire, appeared to gasp and convulse for at least 10 minutes before dying from the drug cocktail used in his execution.

Ohio used the sedative midazolam and the painkiller hydromorphone in McGuire's January execution, the state said.

Louisiana announced later that month that it would use the same two-drug cocktail.

Oklahoma had announced the drugs it planned to use: midazolam; vecuronium bromide to stop respiration; and potassium chloride to stop the heart. "Two intravenous lines are inserted, one in each arm. The drugs are injected by hand-held syringes simultaneously into the two intravenous lines. The sequence is in the order that the drugs are listed above. Three executioners are utilized, with each one injecting one of the drugs."

The execution was the first time Oklahoma had used midazolam as the first element in its three-drug cocktail. The drug is generally used for children "before medical procedures or before anesthesia for surgery to cause drowsiness, relieve anxiety, and prevent any memory of the event," the U.S. National Library of Medicine says. "It works by slowing activity in the brain to allow relaxation and sleep."

The drug "may cause serious or life-threatening breathing problems," so a child should only receive it "in a hospital or doctor's office that has the equipment that is needed to monitor his or her heart and lungs and to provide life-saving medical treatment quickly if his or her breathing slows or stops."

Cruel and Unusual?

The question for courts is whether using such drugs in executions constitutes "cruel and unusual" punishment, in violation of the Eighth Amendment to the U.S. Constitution.

After his execution, McGuire's family filed a lawsuit seeking an injunction of the execution protocol the state used.

"The lawsuit alleges that when Mr. McGuire's Ohio execution was carried out on January 16th, he did endure frequent episodes of air hunger and suffocation, as predicted," the office of the family's attorney Richard Schulte said in a statement. "Following administration of the execution protocol, the decedent experienced 'repeated cycles of snorting, gurgling and arching his back, appearing to writhe in pain,' and 'looked and sounded as though he was suffocating.' This continued for 19 minutes."

In Oklahoma, attorneys for both Lockett and Warner have been engaged in a court fight over the drugs used in the state's executions.

They'd initially challenged the state Department of Corrections' unwillingness to divulge which drugs would be used. The department finally disclosed the substances.

Lockett and Warner also took issue with the state's so-called secrecy provision forbidding it from disclosing the identities of anyone involved in the execution process or suppliers of any drugs or medical equipment. The Oklahoma Supreme

Court rejected that complaint, saying such secrecy does not prevent the prisoners from challenging their executions as unconstitutional.

After Lockett's execution, Adam Leathers, cochairman of the Oklahoma Coalition to Abolish the Death Penalty, accused the state of having "tortured a human being in an unconstitutional experimental act of evil."

"Medical and legal experts from around the country had repeatedly warned Oklahoma's governor, courts and Department of Corrections about the likelihood that the protocol intended for use . . . would be highly problematic," said Deborah Denno, death penalty expert at Fordham Law School.

"This botch was foreseeable and the state (was) ill prepared to deal with the circumstances despite knowing that the entire world was watching. Lethal injection botches have existed for decades but never have they been riskier or more irresponsible than they are in 2014. This outcome is a disgrace," Denno said.

Amnesty International USA called the botched execution "one of the starkest examples yet of why the death penalty must be abolished."

"Last night the state of Oklahoma proved that justice can never be carried out from a death chamber," Executive Director Steven W. Hawkins said in a statement.

Investigation

The Oklahoma attorney general's office is "gathering information on what happened in order to evaluate," said spokeswoman Dianne Clay.

Fallin ordered an independent review of the state's execution procedures and issued an executive order granting a two-week delay in executions.

"I believe the legal process worked. I believe the death penalty is an appropriate response and punishment to those who commit heinous crimes against their fellow men and women. However, I also believe the state needs to be certain of its protocols and its procedures for executions and that they work," she told reporters Wednesday.

Fallin gave no deadline for the review, which will be led by Department of Public Safety Commissioner Michael Thompson. If it is not done within the 14-day period, the governor said she would issue an additional stay for Warner.

Lockett's attorney slammed the announcement and called for a "truly" independent investigation.

"The DPS is a state agency, and its Commissioner reports to the Governor. As such, the review proposed by Governor Fallin would not be conducted by a neutral, independent entity.

"In order to understand exactly what went wrong in last night's horrific execution, and restore any confidence in the execution process, the death of Clayton Lockett must be investigated by a truly independent organization, not a state employee or agency," Dean Sanderford said in a statement.

Lockett was convicted in 2000 of a bevy of crimes that left Stephanie Nieman dead and two people injured.

Nieman's parents released a statement Tuesday prior to Lockett's scheduled execution.

"God blessed us with our precious daughter, Stephanie for 19 years," it read. "She was the joy of our life. We are thankful this day has finally arrived and justice will finally be served."

Warner, who now awaits execution, was convicted in 2003 for the first-degree rape and murder 6 years earlier of his then-girlfriend's 11-month-old daughter, Adrianna Waller.

His attorney, Madeline Cohen, said further legal action can be expected given that "something went horribly awry" in Lockett's execution Tuesday.

"Oklahoma cannot carry out further executions until there's transparency in this process," Cohen said. ". . . Oklahoma needs to take a step back."

In a CNN/ORC poll earlier this year, 50% of Americans said the penalty for murder in general should be death, while 45% said it should be a life sentence. The survey's sampling error made that a statistical tie. Fifty-six percent of men supported the death penalty for murder in general, while 45% of women did.

A Gallup poll last year found 62% of Americans believe the death penalty is morally acceptable, while half as many, 31%, consider it morally wrong.

Critical Thinking

1. Was the execution of Lockett carried out humanely?
2. Does the fact that a majority of Americans believe the death penalty is morally acceptable mean the issue is settled?

Internet References

CNN Justice
http://www.cnn.com/2013/11/15/justice/states-lethal-injection-drugs/
Oklahoma Department of Corrections
http://www.ok.gov/doc/Offenders/Death_Row/

Article   Prepared by: Joanne Naughton

The Archipelago of Pain

DAVID BROOKS

Learning Outcomes

After reading this article, you will be able to:

- Discuss studies done on the effect of isolation on animals.

- Relate what Grassian concluded from his work on the effects of solitary confinement on prisoners.

- Compare prison officials' arguments about the need for solitary confinement with what research shows.

W e don't flog people in our prison system, or put them in thumbscrews or stretch them on the rack. We do, however, lock prisoners away in social isolation for 23 hours a day, often for months, years or decades at a time.

We prohibit the former and permit the latter because we make a distinction between physical and social pain. But, at the level of the brain where pain really resides, this is a distinction without a difference. Matthew Lieberman of the University of California, Los Angeles, compared the brain activities of people suffering physical pain with people suffering from social pain. As he writes in his book, "Social," "Looking at the screens side by side . . . you wouldn't have been able to tell the difference."

The brain processes both kinds of pain in similar ways. Moreover, at the level of human experience, social pain is, if anything, more traumatic, more destabilizing and inflicts more cruel and long-lasting effects than physical pain. What we're doing to prisoners in extreme isolation, in other words, is arguably more inhumane than flogging.

Yet inflicting extreme social pain is more or less standard procedure in America's prisons. Something like 80,000 prisoners are put in solitary confinement every year. Prisoners isolated in supermaximum facilities are often locked away in a 6-by-9-foot or 8-by-10-foot barren room. They may be completely isolated in that room for two days a week. For the remaining five, they may be locked away for 23 hours a day and permitted an hour of solitary exercise in a fenced-in area.

If there is communication with the prison staff, it might take place through an intercom. Communication with the world beyond is minimal. If there are visitors, conversation may be conducted through a video screen. Prisoners may go years without affectionately touching another human being. Their only physical contact will be brushing up against a guard as he puts on shackles for trips to the exercise yard.

In general, mammals do not do well in isolation. In the 1950s, Harry Harlow studied monkeys who had been isolated. The ones who were isolated for longer periods went into emotional shock, rocking back and forth. One in six refused to eat after being reintegrated and died within five days. Most of the rest were permanently withdrawn.

Studies on birds, rats and mice consistently show that isolated animals suffer from impoverished neural growth compared with socially engaged animals, especially in areas where short-term memory and threat perception are processed. Studies on Yugoslav prisoners of war in 1992 found that those who had suffered blunt blows to the head and those who had been socially isolated suffered the greatest damage to brain functioning.

Some prisoners who've been in solitary confinement are scarcely affected by it. But this is not typical. The majority of prisoners in solitary suffer severely—from headaches, an oversensitivity to stimuli, digestion problems, loss of appetite, self-mutilation, chronic dizziness, loss of the ability to concentrate, hallucinations, illusions, or paranoid ideas.

The psychiatrist Stuart Grassian conducted in-depth interviews with more than 200 prisoners in solitary and concluded that about a third developed acute psychosis with hallucinations. Many people just disintegrate. According to rough estimates, as many as half the suicides in prison take place in solitary, even though isolated prisoners make up only about 5 percent of the population.

Prison officials argue that they need isolation to preserve order. That's a view to be taken seriously because these are the people who work in the prisons. But the research on the effectiveness of solitary confinement programs is ambiguous at best. There's a fair bit of evidence to suggest that prison violence is not produced mainly by a few bad individuals who can be removed from the mainstream. Rather, violence is caused by conditions and prison culture. If there's crowding, tension, a culture of violence, and anarchic or arbitrary power, then the context itself is going to create violence no matter how many "bad seeds" are segregated away.

Fortunately, we seem to be at a moment when public opinion is turning. Last month, the executive director of the Colorado prisons, Rick Raemisch, wrote a moving first-person Op-Ed article in *The Times* about his short and voluntary stay in solitary. Colorado will no longer send prisoners with severe mental illnesses into solitary. New York officials recently agreed to new guidelines limiting the time prisoners can spend in isolation. Before long, one suspects, extreme isolation will be considered morally unacceptable.

The larger point is we need to obliterate the assumption that inflicting any amount of social pain is O.K. because it's not real pain.

When you put people in prison, you are imposing pain on them. But that doesn't mean you have to gouge out the nourishment that humans need for health, which is social, emotional and relational.

Critical Thinking

1. Isn't a prison sentence supposed to be harsh?

2. Based on the evidence from animals and people, does solitary confinement help a prisoner become a functioning member of society upon release?

3. Is it more humane to subject prisoners to solitary confinement for rules infractions than to beat them?

Internet References

American Psychological Association
http://www.apa.org/monitor/2012/05/solitary.aspx
The New York Times
http://www.nytimes.com/2014/02/21/opinion/my-night-in-solitary.html

Article   Prepared by: Joanne Naughton

The F.B.I. Deemed Agents Faultless in 150 Shootings

Charlie Savage and Michael Schmidt

Learning Outcomes

After reading this article, you will be able to:

- Discuss the process that takes place whenever an F.B.I. agent fires his weapon.

- Compare the F.B.I.'s internal review of the shooting of Joseph Schultz with independent evaluations.

After contradictory stories emerged about an F.B.I. agent's killing last month of a Chechen man in Orlando, Fla., who was being questioned over ties to the Boston Marathon bombing suspects, the bureau reassured the public that it would clear up the murky episode.

"The F.B.I. takes very seriously any shooting incidents involving our agents, and as such we have an effective, time-tested process for addressing them internally," a bureau spokesman said.

But if such internal investigations are time-tested, their outcomes are also predictable: from 1993 to early 2011, F.B.I. agents fatally shot about 70 "subjects" and wounded about 80 others—and every one of those episodes was deemed justified, according to interviews and internal F.B.I. records obtained by *The New York Times* through a Freedom of Information Act lawsuit.

The last two years have followed the same pattern: an F.B.I. spokesman said that since 2011, there had been no findings of improper intentional shootings.

In most of the shootings, the F.B.I.'s internal investigation was the only official inquiry. In the Orlando case, for example, there have been conflicting accounts about basic facts like whether the Chechen man, Ibragim Todashev, attacked an agent with a knife, was unarmed or was brandishing a metal pole. But Orlando homicide detectives are not independently investigating what happened.

"We had nothing to do with it," said Sgt. Jim Young, an Orlando police spokesman. "It's a federal matter, and we're deferring everything to the F.B.I."

Occasionally, the F.B.I. does discipline an agent. Out of 289 deliberate shootings covered by the documents, many of which left no one wounded, five were deemed to be "bad shoots," in agents' parlance—encounters that did not comply with the bureau's policy, which allows deadly force if agents fear that their lives or those of fellow agents are in danger. A typical punishment involved adding letters of censure to agents' files. But in none of the five cases did a bullet hit anyone.

Critics say the fact that for at least two decades no agent has been disciplined for any instance of deliberately shooting someone raises questions about the credibility of the bureau's internal investigations. Samuel Walker, a professor of criminal justice at the University of Nebraska Omaha who studies internal law enforcement investigations, called the bureau's conclusions about cases of improper shootings "suspiciously low."

Current and former F.B.I. officials defended the bureau's handling of shootings, arguing that the scant findings of improper behavior were attributable to several factors. Agents tend to be older, more experienced and better trained than city police officers. And they generally are involved only in planned operations and tend to go in with "overwhelming presence," minimizing the chaos that can lead to shooting the wrong people, said Tim Murphy, a former deputy director of the F.B.I. who conducted some investigations of shootings over his 23-year career.

The F.B.I.'s shootings range from episodes so obscure that they attract no news media attention to high-profile cases like the 2009 killing of an imam in a Detroit-area warehouse that is the subject of a lawsuit alleging a cover-up, and a 2002 shooting in Maryland in which the bureau paid $1.3 million to a victim and yet, the records show, deemed the shooting to have been justified.

With rare exceptions—like suicides—whenever an agent fires his weapon outside of training, a team of agents from the F.B.I.'s Inspection Division, sometimes with a liaison from the local police, compiles a report reconstructing what happened. This "shooting incident review team" interviews witnesses and studies medical, ballistics and autopsy reports, eventually producing a narrative. Such reports typically do not include whether an agent had been involved in any previous shootings, because they focus only on the episode in question, officials said.

That narrative, along with binders of supporting information, is then submitted to a "shooting incident review group"—a panel of high-level F.B.I. officials in Washington. The panel produces its own narrative as part of a report saying whether the shooting complied with bureau policy—and recommends what discipline to mete out if it did not—along with any broader observations about "lessons learned" to change training or procedures.

F.B.I. officials stressed that their shooting reviews were carried out under the oversight of both the Justice Department's inspector general and the Civil Rights Division, and that local prosecutors have the authority to bring charges.

The 2,200 pages of records obtained by *The Times* include an internal F.B.I. study that compiled shooting episode statistics over a 17-year period, as well as a collection of individual narratives of intentional shootings from 1993 to early 2011. Gunfire was exchanged in 58 such episodes; 9 law enforcement officials died, and 38 were wounded.

The five "bad shoots" included cases in which an agent fired a warning shot after feeling threatened by a group of men, an agent fired at a weapon lying on the ground to disable it during an arrest, and two agents fired their weapons while chasing fugitives but hit no one. In another case, an agent fired at a safe during a demonstration, and ricocheting material caused minor cuts in a crowd of onlookers.

Four of the cases were in the mid-1990s, and the fifth was in 2003.

In many cases, the accuracy of the F.B.I. narrative is difficult to evaluate because no independent alternative report has been produced. As part of the reporting for this article, the F.B.I. voluntarily made available a list of shootings since 2007 that gave rise to lawsuits, but it was rare for any such case to have led to a full report by an independent authority.

Occasionally, however, there were alternative reviews. One, involving a March 2002 episode in which an agent shot an innocent Maryland man in the head after mistaking him for a bank robbery suspect, offers a case study in how the nuances of an F.B.I. official narrative can come under scrutiny.

In that episode, agents thought that the suspect would be riding in a car driven by his sister and wearing a white baseball cap. An innocent man, Joseph Schultz, then 20, happened to cross their path, wearing a white cap and being driven by his girlfriend. Moments after F.B.I. agents carrying rifles pulled their car over and surrounded it, Agent Christopher Braga shot Mr. Schultz in the jaw. He later underwent facial reconstruction surgery, and in 2007 the bureau paid $1.3 million to settle a lawsuit.

The internal review, however, deemed it a good shoot. In the F.B.I.'s narrative, Agent Braga says that he shouted "show me your hands," but that Mr. Schultz instead reached toward his waist, so Agent Braga fired "to eliminate the threat." While one member of the review group said that "after reading the materials provided, he could not visualize the presence of 'imminent danger' to law enforcement officers," the rest of the group voted to find the shooting justified, citing the "totality of

the circumstances surrounding the incident," including that it involved a "high-risk stop."

But an Anne Arundel County police detective prepared an independent report about the episode, and a lawyer for Mr. Schultz, Arnold Weiner, conducted a further investigation for the lawsuit. Both raised several subtle but important differences.

For example, the F.B.I. narrative describes a lengthy chase of Mr. Schultz's car after agents turned on their siren at an intersection, bolstering an impression that it was reasonable for Agent Braga to fear that Mr. Schultz was a dangerous fugitive. The narrative spends a full page describing this moment in great detail, saying that the car "rapidly accelerated" and that one agent shouted for it to stop "over and over again." It cites another agent as estimating that the car stopped "approximately 100 yards" from the intersection.

By contrast, the police report describes this moment in a short, skeptical paragraph. Noting that agents said they had thought the car was fleeing, it points out that the car "was, however, in a merge lane and would need to accelerate to enter traffic." Moreover, a crash reconstruction specialist hired for the lawsuit estimated that the car had reached a maximum speed of 12 miles per hour, and an F.B.I. sketch, obtained in the lawsuit, put broken glass from a car window 142 feet 8 inches from the intersection.

The F.B.I. narrative does not cite Mr. Schultz's statement and omits that a crucial fact was disputed: how Mr. Schultz had moved in the car. In a 2003 sworn statement, Agent Braga said that Mr. Schultz "turned to his left, towards the middle of the car, and reached down." But Mr. Schultz insisted that he had instead reached toward the car door on his right because he had been listening to another agent who was simultaneously shouting "open the door."

A former F.B.I. agent, hired to write a report analyzing the episode for the plaintiffs, concluded that "no reasonable F.B.I. agent in Braga's position would reasonably have believed that deadly force was justified." He also noted pointedly that Agent Braga had been involved in a previous shooting episode in 2000 that he portrayed as questionable, although it had been found to be justified by the F.B.I.'s internal review process.

Asked to comment on the case, a lawyer for Agent Braga, Andrew White, noted last week that a grand jury had declined to indict his client in the shooting.

In some cases, alternative official accounts for several other shootings dovetailed with internal F.B.I. narratives.

One involved the October 2009 death of Luqman Ameen Abdullah, a prayer leader at a Detroit-area mosque who was suspected of conspiring to sell stolen goods and was shot during a raid on a warehouse. The F.B.I. report says that Mr. Abdullah got down on the ground but kept his hands hidden, so a dog was unleashed to pull his arms into view. He then pulled out a gun and shot the dog, the report says, and he was in turn shot by four agents.

The Michigan chapter of the Council on American-Islamic Relations filed a lawsuit against the F.B.I. The group was concerned in part because the handgun had no recoverable fingerprints and because of facial injuries to Mr. Abdullah. It also contends that the dog may have been shot instead by the F.B.I. agents and the gun thrown down in a cover-up.

A report by the Michigan attorney general's office, however, detailed an array of evidence that it says "corroborates the statements of the agents as to the sequence of events," including that bullet fragments in the dog's corpse were consistent with the handgun, not the rifles used by the F.B.I. agents. Such an independent account of an F.B.I. shooting is rare. After the recent killing of Mr. Todashev in Orlando, both the Florida chapter of the same group and his father have called for investigators outside the F.B.I. to scrutinize the episode.

James J. Wedick, who spent 34 years at the bureau, said the F.B.I. should change its procedures for its own good.

"At the least, it is a perception issue, and over the years the bureau has had a deaf ear to it," he said. "But if you have a shooting that has a few more complicated factors and an ethnic issue, the bureau's image goes down the toilet if it doesn't investigate itself properly."

Critical Thinking

1. Do you believe that the F.B.I.'s internal investigation should be the only official inquiry into questionable shootings by F.B.I. personnel?
2. If the F.B.I. deems a shooting to have been justified, is paying $1.3 million to the victim also justified?

Create Central

www.mhhe.com/createcentral

Internet References

Democracy Now
www.democracynow.org/2013/6/21/the_fbis_license_to_kill_agents

Federal Bureau of Investigation (F.B.I.)
www.fbi.gov/news/updates-on-investigation-into-multiple-explosions-in-boston

Gaming the System: How the Political Strategies of Private Prison Companies Promote Ineffective Incarceration Policies by Unknown

149

Article   Prepared by: Joanne Naughton

Gaming the System: How the Political Strategies of Private Prison Companies Promote Ineffective Incarceration Policies

Learning Outcomes

After reading this article, you will be able to:

- Show the effect of drug laws on the high incarceration rates of the United States.

- Explain some of the factors that contribute to the high incarceration rate in the United States.

- Argue that private prisons contribute to the high American incarceration rate.

Introduction

Approximately 129,000 people were held in privately managed correctional facilities in the United States as of December 31, 2009;[1] 16.4 percent of federal and 6.8 percent of state populations were held in private facilities. Since 2000, private prisons have increased their share of the "market" substantially: the number of people held in private federal facilities increased approximately 120 percent, while the number held in private state facilities increased approximately 33 percent. During this same period, the total number of people in prison increased less than 16 percent. Meanwhile, spending on corrections has increased 72 percent since 1997, to $74 billion in 2007.[2] The two largest private prison companies, Corrections Corporation of America (CCA) and GEO Group, combined had over $2.9 billion in revenue in 2010.[3]

As revenues of private prison companies have grown over the past decade, the companies have had more resources with which to build political power, and they have used this power to promote policies that lead to higher rates of incarceration.

The following are some of the main findings in the Justice Policy Institute's June 2011 report, *Gaming the System: How the Political Strategies of Private Prison Companies Promote Ineffective Incarceration Policies.*

The Players

Today, two companies own and/or operate the majority of for-profit private prisons, with a number of smaller companies running facilities across the country.

Corrections Corporation of America

Founded in 1983, the Corrections Corporation of America (CCA) is the first and largest private prison company in the U.S.[4] In 2010, CCA operated 66 correctional and detention facilities, 45 of which they owned with contracts in 19 states, the District of Columbia and with the three federal detention agencies.[5]

In 2010, CCA saw record revenue of $1.67 billion, up $46 million from 2009.[6] The majority of that revenue (50 percent or $838.5 million) came from state contracts, with 13 percent ($214 million) from the state of California;[7] approximately 10,250 people from the state of California are held in prisons run by CCA.[8] The other significant portion of their revenue was from federal contracts, which accounted for 43 percent of revenue in 2010.

The GEO Group (Formerly Wackenhut Corrections Corporation)

Currently, GEO operates 118 correctional, detention, and residential treatment facilities encompassing approximately 80,600 beds around the world.[9] The U.S. Corrections Business Unit is the company's founding operating unit and accounts for over 60 percent of GEO's total annual revenue.[10] Founded in 1984 under the name Wackenhut Corrections Corporation, the company solidified its first contract with the Bureau of Immigration and Custody Enforcement, in 1987.[11]

As of 2010, GEO contracts with 13 states, the Federal Bureau of Prison, the U.S. Marshals Service, and U.S. Immigration and Customs Enforcement.[12] In 2010, 66 percent ($842 million) of GEO's $1.27 billion in revenue was from U.S. corrections contracts.[13] Of the $842 million in revenue, 47 percent came from corrections contracts with 11 states.[14]

On August 12, 2010 the GEO Group acquired Cornell Companies—a for-profit private prison company with revenues of over $400 million in 2009[15]—in a merger estimated at $730 million.[16] With the acquisition of Cornell by GEO, the majority of private prisons are now under the management of either GEO or CCA.

The Stakes

Over the past 15 years, while the incarceration rate in the U.S. has grown, it has been outpaced by the growth in the number of people placed in private prisons. Due to ineffective criminal justice policies that promote incarceration over more effective alternatives, an increasing need for prison beds has resulted in more private prison contracts and subsequently more revenue for private prison companies as states have less money to pay for the construction of their own prison beds.

However, between 2008 and 2009 the number of people in state prisons declined for the first time in 40 years.[17] While the number of people in federal prisons continues to rise, the decline in the state prison population—private prison companies' largest revenue stream—sets the stage for private prison companies to implement an aggressive, multipronged strategy to ensure their growing revenues.

The Strategy: The Triangle of Private Prison Political Influence

Since private prison contracts are written by state and federal policymakers and overseen by state and federal agency administrators, it is in the best interest of private prison companies to build the connections needed to influence policies related to incarceration. For-profit private prison companies primarily use three strategies to influence policy: lobbying, direct campaign contributions, and building relationships, networks, and associations.[18]

Campaign Donations

By maintaining contacts and favorable ties with policymakers, private prison companies can attempt to shape the debate around the privatization of prisons and criminal justice policy. One way to do that is to make direct, monetary contributions to political campaigns for elected officials and specific policies. These updated figures have emerged in the fall of 2011:

- Since 2000, private prison companies have contributed over $7.2 million to state candidates and political parties.[19]
- Between the 2002 and 2012 election cycles, CCA and GEO's Political Action Committees (PACs) have doled out $1,212,889[20] and $1,010,002[21] respectively to federal parties, candidates and committees.

- Since 2000, private prison companies (CCA, GEO and Cornell Corrections) have given $867,010 —to federal candidates alone.[22]

Lobbying

Similar to other industries, private prison companies employ lobbying firms and lobbyists to advocate for their business interests in Congress and state legislatures. Since private prisons make money from putting people behind bars, their lobbying efforts focus on bills that affect incarceration and law enforcement, such as appropriations for corrections and detention.

Over the last decade, CCA, GEO and Cornell Corrections spent, on average, hundreds of thousands of dollars to employ lobbyists to represent their business interests to federal policymakers. Since 2003, CCA has spent upwards of $900,000 annually on federal lobbying.[23]

- Since 2000, private prison companies (CCA, GEO and Cornell Corrections) have spent over $21 million on federal lobbying efforts with the majority,[24] over $17 million being spent by CCA alone.[25]

Relationships and Associations

Organizational theories about relationships and leadership indicate that individual people influence the operations and behavior of an organization through prior relationships, associations, experiences, and networks.[26] In other words, people bring with them the lens of previous affiliations, and a sense of obligation to represent their world view; they may also be subject to pressure from previous professional relations to act in ways that benefit these relations.

Private prison companies have benefited from their relationships with government officials as evidenced by appointments of former employees to key state and federal positions. The pervasiveness of these connections is evidenced with the recent example from the Kasich Administration in Ohio.

After serving 18 years in the U.S. House of Representatives John Kasich retired in 2000 and took a managing director position in Ohio with Lehman Brothers.[27] Lehman Brothers has a long standing history with private prison companies, spending most of the late 1990s and 2000s before their collapse underwriting bonds and managing credit for both CCA and Cornell.[28] After winning the governorship of Ohio in 2010, Kasich laid out his plans for privatizing state prison operations along with appointing a former CCA employee to head the Ohio Department of Rehabilitation and Correction.[29] Rounding out Kasich's connections to CCA is his close friend and former Congressional chief of staff whose lobbying firm was hired to represent CCA in January 2011.[30]

Losing the Game

When private prison companies are successful at the game of political influence, their profits rise, benefitting their stockholders and top management. However, growing evidence shows that many people lose in this political game at the individual and community levels. The policies that private prison companies promote negatively impact communities in terms of costs and public safety. And the increasing use of private prisons due to rising incarceration rates negatively impacts private prison employees. But the biggest losers in this political game are the people who are taken away from their families and communities due to the policies private prison companies promote to increase the number of people going into prisons and the length of time they spend behind bars.

Recommendations

- States and the federal government should look for real solutions to the problem of growing jail and prison populations.
- Invest in front-end treatment and services in the community, whether private or public.
- Additional research is needed to effectively evaluate the cost and recidivism reduction claims of the private prison industry.

Notes

1. Heather C. West, William J. Sabol, and Sarah J. Greenman, *Prisoners in 2009* (Bureau of Justice Statistics, Washington, DC: 2010). http://bjs.ojp.usdoj.gov/content/pub/pdf/p09.pdf.

2. Camille Graham Camp and George M. Camp, *The Corrections Yearbook, 1997* (South Salem, NY: The Criminal Justice Institute, 1997); Tracey Kyckelhahn, *Justice Expenditure and Employment Extracts 2007,* Table 1 (Washington, DC: Bureau of Justice Statistics, 2010).

3. Corrections Corporation of America, *2010 Annual Report,* 2011; The GEO Group, *2010 Annual Report* (Boca Raton, FL: The GEO Group, 2011). www.geogroup.com/AR_2010/images/Geo_Group-AR2010.pdf.

4. Corrections Corporation of America, "About CCA," November 2010. www.cca.com/about.

5. Corrections Corporation of America, *2010 Annual Report,* 2011.

6. Corrections Corporation of America, *2010 Annual Report,* 2011.

7. Corrections Corporation of America, *2010 Annual Report,* 2011.

8. Corrections Corporation of America, *2010 Annual Report,* 2011.

9. The GEO Group, Inc., "Who We Are," December 2010.

10. The GEO Group, Inc., "Who We Are," December 2010; The GEO Group Inc., *2009 Annual Report* (Boca Raton, FL: The GEO Group, 2010). www.geogroup.com/AR_2009_ClientDL/images/GEO_Group-AR2009.pdf.

11. The GEO Group, Inc., "Historic Milestones," December 2010. www.geogroup.com/history.asp.

12. The GEO Group, Inc., "Federal, State, and Local Partnerships," December 2010. www.geogroup.com/federal-state-local.asp.

13. The GEO Group, *2010 Annual Report,* 2011.

14. Alaska, Louisiana, Virginia, Indiana, Texas, Oklahoma, Mississippi, California, Arizona, New Mexico and Florida; The GEO Group, *2010 Annual Report,* 2011.

15. Cornell Companies, Inc., *2009 Annual Report—Form 10-K* (Washington, DC: U.S. Securities and Exchange Commission, 2010). www.sec.gov/Archives/edgar/data/1016152/000110465910010293/a09-36304_110k.htm#Item15_ExhibitsAndFinancialStatem_125526.

16. The GEO Group, Inc., *The GEO Group Completes Transformational Merger with Cornell Companies* (Boca Raton, FL: 2010). www.thegeogroupinc.com/documents/Merger.pdf.

17. Heather C. West and others, *Prisoners in 2009,* 2010.

18. Brigette Sarabi and Edwin Bender, *The Prison Payoff: The Role of Politics and Private Prisons in the Incarceration Boom* (Portland, OR: Western States Center and the Western Prison Project, 2000).

19. National Institute on Money in State Politics, "Correctional facilities construction & management/for-profit Contributions to All Candidates and Committees," accessed September 28, 2011.

20. Center for Responsive Politics, "CCA 2002–2012 Election Cycle PAC Giving — to Parties, Candidates, and Committees," accessed September 28, 2011. www.opensecrets.org/pacs/lookup2.php?cycle=2012&strID=C00366468.

21. Center for Responsive Politics, "The GEO Group 2002–2012 Election Cycle PAC Giving - to Parties, Candidates, and Committees," accessed September 28, 2011. www.opensecrets.org/pacs/lookup2.php?strID=C00382150.

22. Center for Responsive Politics, "Miscellaneous Business: PAC Contributions to Federal Candidates," accessed September 28, 2011. www.opensecrets.org/pacs/industry.php?txt=N12&cycle=2012.

23. Center for Responsive Politics, "Lobbying Corrections Corp of America—Summary 2010," June 2011. www.opensecrets.org/lobby/clientsum.php?lname=Corrections+Corp+of+America&year=2010.

24. Center for Responsive Politics, "Wackenhut Corp 2000–2003 Annual Federal Lobbying," accessed September 28, 2011. www.opensecrets.org/lobby/clientsum.php?id=D000026342&year=2003; Center for Responsive Politics, "The GEO Group 2004–2011 Annual Federal Lobbying," accessed September 28, 2011. www.opensecrets.org/lobby/clientsum.php?id=D000022003&year=2011; Center for Responsive Politics, "CCA 2000–2011 Annual Federal Lobbying," accessed September 28, 2011. www.opensecrets.org/lobby/clientsum.php?id=D000021940&year=2011; Center for Responsive Politics, "Cornell Companies 2000 and 2006–2010 Annual Federal Lobbying," accessed September 28, 2011. www.opensecrets.org/lobby/clientsum.php?id=D000025148&year=2010.

25. Center for Responsive Politics, "CCA 2000–2011 Annual Federal Lobbying," accessed September 28, 2011. www.opensecrets.org/lobby/clientsum.php?id=D000021940&year=2011.

26. Christine Oliver, "Determinants of Interorganizational Relationships: Integration and Future Directions," *The Academy of Management Review* 15, no. 2 (1990): 241–265.

27. *The New York Times,* "Lehman Hires Kasich," January 11, 2001. www.nytimes.com/2001/01/11/business/lehman-hires-kasich.html.

28. Public Services International Research Unit, *Prison Privatization Report International* (London, England: University of Greenwich, 2001). www.psiru.org/justice/ppri44.asp.

29. Mark Niquette, "Private-prison Consultant Chosen to Run ODRC," *Columbus Dispatch,* January 4, 2011. www.dispatch

.com/live/content/local_news/stories/2011/01/04/
private-prison-consultant-chosen-to-run-ODRC.html.

30. Joe Hallett, "Kasich: Ex-advisers Won't Get Lobbying Favors,"
Columbus Dispatch, February 2, 2011. www.dispatchpolitics
.com/live/content/local_news/stories/2011/02/02/copy/
kasich-ex-advisers-wont-get-lobbying-favors.html?adsec=
politics&sid=101.

Critical Thinking

1. What effect has the increased political influence of private
   prison companies had on stockholders top management? On
   communities?

2. Do you believe there are any alternatives to incarcerating
   lawbreakers?

Create Central

www.mhhe.com/createcentral

Internet References

American Civil Liberties Union
www.aclu.org/prisoners-rights/private-prisons
Corrections
www.corrections.com/news/article/34534-unprotected-private-prison-
personnel-and-civil-liability

Article

Prepared by: Joanne Naughton

Study: Pretrial Detention Creates More Crime

ERIKA EICHELBERGER

Learning Outcomes

After reading this article, you will be able to:

- State what is meant by "low-risk" defendants.

- Show that many low-risk defendants who are not released from incarceration to await trial are more likely to commit new crimes later.

- Argue that judges should try to distinguish among low-, moderate-, and high-risk offenders.

D etaining certain defendants before trial makes them more likely to commit a new crime, according to a recent report.

Many pretrial detainees are low risk, meaning that if they are released before trial, they are highly unlikely to commit other crimes and very likely to return to court. When these defendants are held for two to three days before trial, as opposed to just 24 hours, they are nearly 40 percent more likely to commit new crimes before their trial, and 17 percent more likely to commit another crime within 2 years, according to a report released last month by the Laura and John Arnold Foundation, a private foundation that funds criminal justice research.

"The primary goal of the American criminal justice system is to protect the public," the authors of the report say. "But . . . the pretrial phase of the system is actually helping to create new repeat offenders."

The report—based on studies of both state and federal courts—also found that the longer low-risk detainees are held behind bars before trial, the more likely they are to commit another crime. Low-risk defendants who were detained for 31 days or more before they had their day in court offended 74 percent more frequently before trial than those detained for just one day. The study found similar results for moderate-risk defendants, though for these offenders, the rate of increase in new criminal activity is smaller. When it comes to high-risk offenders, the report found no correlation between pretrial detention time and recidivism.

The report noted that recidivism could be curbed if judges made an effort to distinguish between low-, moderate-, and high-risk offenders. "Judges, of course, do their best to sort violent, high-risk defendants from nonviolent, low-risk ones," the report says, "but they have almost no reliable, data-driven risk assessment tools at their disposal to help them make these decisions." Fewer than 10 percent of US jurisdictions do any sort of risk-assessment during the pretrial stage.

Not only does unnecessary pretrial detention create repeat offenders, it costs taxpayers a lot of money. Pretrial detainees represent more than 60 percent of the total inmate population in the country's jails. The cost of incarcerating defendants pretrial is about $9 billion.

Critical Thinking

1. What are the costs of unnecessary pretrial detention?
2. Should risk assessment at the pretrial stage be done as a matter of course in all jurisdictions?

Internet References

Laura and John Arnold Foundation
    http://arnoldfoundation.org/sites/default/files/pdf/LJAF-Pretrial-CJ-Research-brief_FNL.pdf
LLRX.com
    http://www.llrx.com/features/pretrialdetention.htm

Article   Prepared by: Joanne Naughton

War on Drugs Failure Gives Way to Treatment in States, Cities

SAKI KNAFO

Learning Outcomes

After reading this article, you will be able to:

- Discuss some of the new alternative ways of dealing with drug law offenders.

- Describe what has happened in Texas as a result of reforms enacted by lawmakers.

Four years ago, police officers and prosecutors in Seattle decided they'd had enough of the usual ways of fighting the war on drugs.

The police were tired of arresting the same drug users and prostitutes again and again, and the prosecutors had run out of money to keep putting people in jail. So the police department, the prosecutor's office, and the city's elected leaders decided to try something radically different.

With the approval of Seattle prosecutors and politicians, the police began directing repeat drug offenders to social-service workers who offered to help them pay for rent and school and referred them to business owners who were willing to hire people with criminal backgrounds.

The police weren't entirely hopeful that the strategy would pan out. But with a growing number of neighborhood leaders and business owners demanding safer, quieter streets, they had little choice but to try something new.

Today, their doubts are giving way to a growing confidence that they're onto something significant. "People we've dealt with over and over and over again are getting treatment and getting into housing and getting jobs," said Lt. Deanna Nollette, a supervisor in the police department. "It's a pretty big surprise."

"Law Enforcement Assisted Diversion," or LEAD, as the public-safety strategy is known in Seattle, is just one of a fast-growing number of alternatives to the traditional "tough on crime" approach that has defined America's drug war for four decades. Lawmakers throughout the country have increasingly turned to these strategies to deflect the steep costs of incarcerating the soaring population of drug offenders.

Some of these alternatives are more punitive than others, and policy experts and prison-reform advocates disagree on the best way to treat drug offenders. But taken as a whole, these alternatives represent a major shift in America's response to illegal drug use.

"As someone who has been in this now for 25 years, and thought that change was glacial, never mind incremental, what has happened recently is extraordinary," said Howard Josepher, the founder of Exponents, a 25-year-old drug-abuse treatment program in New York City.

In Texas, legislators have sharply increased investments in treatment programs and in drug courts—specialized judicial systems whose judges can order drug offenders to undergo treatment as an alternative to jail. In California, where the prisons are so crowded that the state has been ordered by a federal court to reduce the prison population by thousands of inmates, counties have been granted an expanded role in deciding whether to lock up low-level offenders or connect them with drug counselors. From New York to Arkansas to Florida, states have seen their prison populations decline after years of growth.

The burgeoning availability of these alternatives is largely born out of necessity. Since the mid-1970s, when lawmakers first began enacting tough anti-drug policies that have collectively come to be known as the "war on drugs," the number of people behind bars has increased fivefold, peaking at 2.2 million in 2010. Drug offenses accounted for much of the surge. From 1980 to 2010, the number of those incarcerated on drug charges shot up from 41,000 to more than a half-million.

Criminal justice advocates have long decried the punitive laws behind this trend, stressing the disproportionately heavy toll exacted on racial and ethnic minorities, who make up more than 60 percent of the prison population, despite using drugs and committing crimes at a rate similar to whites.

But only in recent years have lawmakers thrown their weight behind serious reform efforts. And while most of these calls for changes have come from statehouses and county headquarters, federal government officials have begun adding their voices to the chorus of reformers. In recent months, members of Congress from both parties have teamed up to introduce legislation that would reduce penalties for nonviolent drug offenders. And last week, in what has widely been hailed as a historic announcement, Attorney General Eric Holder declared that the Justice Department would do its part to cut down on severe sentences for those convicted of nonviolent drug crimes.

Some of the most striking changes have unfolded in places not always associated with progressive reforms. In Texas, for example, lawmakers have cut billions of dollars from the prison system, while investing hundreds of millions in drug courts and in counseling programs that aim to help people recover from drug addictions and get their lives under control. Proponents point out that the changes haven't reversed the state's decades of declining crime rates:

> From 2007, the first year of the shift, to 2011, the most recent year for which detailed data is available, the number of violent crimes in Texas dropped by nearly 20,000, and property crimes fell by five times as much. The state authorized the closing of one prison in 2011 and two more this year.

In Georgia, meanwhile, where 1 out of every 13 adults are either on probation, parole, or behind bars, lawmakers have passed a reform package that expands the state's treatment programs, drug courts, and the use of electronic monitoring as an substitute for prison time. States that include South Carolina and Kansas have adopted similar measures.

Not everyone is on board with these changes, however. "Probably the biggest obstacle to these reforms is what I would call establishment politicians and officeholders, and this really means on the left or on the right," said Vikrant Reddy, a policy analyst with the conservative Texas Public Policy Foundation in Austin. "I think there are still politicians who haven't broken free of the thinking of the past. They don't seem to understand that there has been a sea change among American voters, who don't always feel that incarceration is the best tack when it comes to what we do about low-level nonviolent crime."

Another obstacle to the universal adoption of these reforms is the continued scarcity of funding for programs that treat addiction. "There aren't a lot of open slots," said Doug McVay, a drug policy expert and the editor of the online book *Drug War Facts.* "And we've chosen to put money into cleaning up the mess, rather than trying to make things better so that there isn't a mess in the first place."

Yet, for those in the growing ranks of reformers—a loose alliance that spans the political spectrum from former House Speaker Newt Gingrich (R) to California Lt. Gov. Gavin Newsom (D)—the debate is no longer over whether to change the country's drug policies, but how. At the center of the conversation is the proliferation of drug courts. While conservatives and many liberals see the expansion of these courts as key to reform, libertarians and some on the left say society's response to drug abuse should take place outside the courthouse altogether.

Seattle's LEAD program, some reformers say, could prove to be a pioneering example of how police departments can help accomplish this goal. Although results from a study of the program aren't finished, cities from San Francisco to New York have already reached out to the program's supervisors for guidance.

Lisa Daugaard, a longtime public defender and one of the program's coordinators, likened LEAD to a drug court "without the stigma and costs of court involvement." Unlike most drug courts, she said, the program doesn't require participants to stay off drugs or even seek treatment. "LEAD is not only for people who are involved in drug activities because of addiction," she noted. "Some are involved for a wage."

About half the program's participants end up accepting some form of treatment, but they do so voluntarily, Daugaard said, without facing any pressure from judges or prosecutors. "It's not that we're indifferent about people moving toward sobriety," she said. "It's that requiring that is not the best way to engage people."

Levi Hoagland, a 34-year-old former high school football star who is preparing to end his year-long stay at a California rehabilitation center, can see the advantages of both the drug court system and the less punitive approach championed by the likes of Daugaard. Several years ago, while suffering from mental breakdown brought on by a methamphetamine binge, he deliberately rammed his car into a parked van and ended up in jail, where he agreed to enter a substance-abuse treatment program under the supervision of a drug court judge.

Some of the more hardened criminals in the jail scoffed at the idea, Hoagland said. But he was ready for a change.

"I couldn't listen to a guy who's got the word 'guilty' tattooed across his back," Hoagland said.

Now, as he gets ready to assimilate back into the outside world, he is wary of the obstacles faced by those who have run afoul of the criminal justice system. Like many other Californians, Hoagland is ineligible for food stamps because of the state's lifetime ban on applicants with past felony convictions, and he's concerned about how his past may look to prospective employers.

Still, it was his brush with the criminal justice system that caused him to seek treatment. And getting sober, he said, has been the "miracle of my life."

"I have two beautiful children and they used to be the most important thing in the world to me, but that's changed," Hoagland said. "The most important thing for me today is to stay clean and sober, and that allows me to be a dad to somebody."

Critical Thinking

1. What has been the experience of Seattle with their new policy?
2. Does incarcerating drug law violators work?

Create Central

www.mhhe.com/createcentral

Internet References

Drug War Facts
   http://drugwarfacts.org/cms/Drug_Courts#sthash.1OivuGaF.dpbs
National Association of Drug Court Professionals
   www.nadcp.org/Drug%20Courts%20Are%20the%20Most%20
   Sensible%20and%20Proven%20Alternative%20to%20Incarceration
National Institute of Justice
   www.crimesolutions.gov/ProgramDetails.aspx?ID=89

Article Prepared by: Joanne Naughton

"The Worst of the Worst" Aren't the Only Ones Who Get Executed

SIMON MCCORMACK

Learning Outcomes

After reading this article, you will be able to:

- Summarize the findings of Smith's study of people who have been executed.

- State some of the criticisms of the study.

- Discuss the Eighth Amendment requirements for the death penalty.

A new study suggests that the people put to death in America are hardly the worst of the worst offenders. The study, published in *Hastings Law Journal,* looked at 100 executions between 2012 and 2013. Some of the most striking results are displayed in the graphic.

Robert Smith, the study's lead researcher and an assistant professor of law at the University of North Carolina, told *The Huffington Post* his research provides evidence that many of the people who are actually put to death are not cold, calculating, remorseless killers.

"A lot of folks even familiar with criminal justice and the death penalty system thought that, by the time you executed somebody, you're really gonna get these people that the court describes as the worst of the worst," Smith said. "It was surprising to us just how many of the people that we found had evidence in their record suggesting that there are real problems with functional deficits that you wouldn't expect to see in people being executed."

One of the people in Smith's study is Daniel Cook. Cook's mom drank and used drugs while she was pregnant with him. His mother and grandparents molested him and his dad abused him by, among other things, burning his genitals with a cigarette.

As Harvard Law Professor Charles J. Ogletree, Jr. documents in the *Washington Post,* Cook was later placed in foster care, where a "foster parent chained him nude to a bed and raped him while other adults watched from the next room through a one-way mirror."

The prosecutor who presented the death penalty case against Cook said he never would have put execution on the table if he had known about the man's brutal past. Nonetheless, Cook was put to death on Aug. 8, 2012.

In various landmark cases, the Supreme Court has found that executing people with an intellectual disability or severe mental illness can be a violation of the Eighth Amendment, which bars cruel and unusual punishment.

The court has also found that severe childhood trauma can be a mitigating factor in a defendant's case, according to a press release accompanying the report.

But Kent Scheidegger, legal director of the Criminal Justice Legal Foundation, said there are serious flaws with the study's methodology. He noted that the authors count someone as intellectually disabled if they score below a 70 on at least one IQ test. However, he said, looking at the lowest score in a series of tests can be misleading.

"How fast can you run a mile? If you run on several different days and have several different times, the speed at which you can do it is your fastest time," Scheidegger said in an email to HuffPost. "Various factors can make you perform less than your best, including simply not trying hard, but nothing can make you perform better than your best. It's the same with IQ scores. The high score is a good indication of performance. The low score means practically nothing."

Scheidegger also said mitigating factors like intellectual disability or a traumatic childhood don't matter nearly as much as the brutality of the crimes that death row inmates have committed.

"Since 1978, defendants have had carte blanche to introduce everything including the kitchen sink in mitigation," Scheidegger said. "The actions of their attorneys in finding and presenting that evidence is scrutinized repeatedly in the years after the trial. What we see in case after case is that even after years of reinvestigation and relitigation, the horrifying facts of the crime remain far more than sufficient to outweigh the minimally relevant evidence in mitigation."

But Smith said the courts have found that, independent of the heinousness of the crime, the prosecution must also show that the defendant is "morally culpable."

"The Eighth Amendment requires that the death penalty be limited in its application to only those offenders who commit the most aggravated homicides *and* who possess the most aggravated moral culpability," Smith said.

"But our research showed that of the last 100 people we executed in America, most of them had severe functional deficits. In many cases, they suffered from several mental illness and years of horrific abuse. And the problem is that there is no standard measurement for these type of functional deficits. For instance, there is no IQ score equivalent for gauging the functional deficits that mark any particular person with a severe mental illness."

Smith also said those who ended up executed did not have adequate representation at the trial level. Juries were often not informed of defendants' intellectual or mental health problems or their family history of extreme abuse.

Smith noted that the reason traumatic childhoods are brought up is not necessarily to make juries feel bad for the person on trial, but because "decades of research" has shown that these types of trauma can trigger the kinds of "functional deficits" that were present in many of the cases examined in the report.

"We're executing people who get the worst lawyers, have the least resources and are the most vulnerable," Smith said.

Sometimes these mitigating factors come out during the appeals process, but by then it may be too late, since judges often give deference to the jury's verdict.

"It's often a tale told too late," Smith said. "How many of these people would have not even come close to dying if they had had good lawyers at trial or pretrial?"

With executions either being outlawed or rarely used in many parts of the country, Smith said the punishment's days may be numbered.

"We're not talking about reform," Smith said. "We're talking about it being on its way out."

Critical Thinking

1. In a death penalty case, should it matter to a jury that a defendant had a traumatic childhood?

2. When asking for the death penalty, isn't it enough for a prosecutor to prove that the defendant committed a heinous crime?

3. Why is it so important in capital cases that the defendant have good legal representation?

Internet References

Slate

http://www.slate.com/articles/news_and_politics/jurisprudence/2014/05 the_death_penalty_is_disappearing_in_america_except_in_the_south.html

The Washington Post

http://www.washingtonpost.com/opinions/charles-ogletree-the-death-penalty-is-incompatible-with-human-dignity/2014/07/18/c0849dea-0e6b-11e4-b8e5-d0de80767fc2_story.html